women's voices
from the margins

women's voices
from the margins
Diaries from Kibera, Kenya

Elizabeth Swart

Toronto | Vancouver

Women's Voices from the Margins: Diaries from Kibera, Kenya
by Elizabeth Swart

First published in 2017 by
Women's Press, an imprint of Canadian Scholars
425 Adelaide Street West, Suite 200
Toronto, Ontario
M5V 3C1

www.womenspress.ca

Library and Archives Canada Cataloguing in Publication

Swart, Elizabeth, author
Women's voices from the margins : diaries from Kibera, Kenya / Elizabeth Swart.

Includes bibliographical references and index.
Issued in print and electronic formats.
ISBN 978-0-88961-588-5 (softcover).--ISBN 978-0-88961-589-2 (PDF).--ISBN 978-0-88961-590-8 (ebook)

1. Women--Kenya--Kibera--Social conditions--21st century. 2. Women--Kenya--Kibera--Diaries. 3. Kibera (Kenya)--Social conditions--21st century. 4. Diaries. 5. Diaries--Authorship. I. Title.

HQ1796.5.Z9N35 2017 305.4096762'5 C2017-900488-3
C2017-900489-1

Cover and Interior design: Susan MacGregor/Digital Zone
Cover photo: © Christian Als/Panos.

17 18 19 20 21 5 4 3 2 1

In memory of June Jordan
Poet, Playwright, and Teacher
who once sent me a poem from Belfast that explained everything.

Table of Contents

Acknowledgements ix

Introduction 1

PART ONE: THE PLACE

Chapter 1: Kenya and Gender 55

Chapter 2: Kibera in the 21st Century 77

Chapter 3: Ethnographic Reflections and Decolonization 95

PART TWO: THE DIARIES

Chapter 4: Working with Diaries as Texts 111

Chapter 5: Hoping God Agrees 119

Chapter 6: Escape.. 135

Chapter 7: Betting against the House.................................. 159

Chapter 8: Gender and Political Violence in Kibera..................... 171

PART THREE: THE IMPLICATIONS

Chapter 9: Learning from the Diary Data 179

Chapter 10: Learning from the Survey Data 189

Chapter 11: Moving Forward..205

Epilogue...213
Appendix 217
Maps.. 225
References.. 231
Index... 242

Acknowledgements

I am grateful to Dr. Jana Jasinski, associate dean of the College of Sciences at the University of Central Florida (UCF); to Drs. Liz Grauerholz, James D. Wright, Elizabeth Mustaine, and David Gay from the sociology department at UCF; and to Dr. Maria Santana from the women's studies program at UCF for their comments and critiques of earlier versions of this book. I also thank Dr. Natalie J. Sokoloff, professor emerita in sociology at John Jay University, College of Criminal Justice, for her ongoing example of how to use and critique intersectionality theory and global feminism.

I am grateful to my colleagues at the University of Southern California's Suzanne Dworak-Peck School of Social Work for their encouragement of this project, especially Dr. Annalisa Enrile, Dr. Carol Ann Peterson, and Dr. June Wiley.

This project could not have been completed without the help of Pat Crowley, whose help with data analysis and research was of unparalleled excellence. I thank her for her invaluable insight and research clarity.

I owe a huge debt of gratitude to the following colleagues and friends for their ongoing conversations about my engagement with whiteness studies and privilege: Martha Bryant-Hall, Mary Daniels, Kimberly Gaubault, Gwenell Hall, Mary Howard, and Fairolyn Livingston.

This book could not have been written without the work and resources provided by Nairobi-based non-profit organizations: AMREF, Carolina for Kibera, FIDA-Kenya, SHOFCO, the Undugu Society, and Women's Hope Kenya.

A heartfelt and ongoing debt of gratitude is owed to my students at the University of Central Florida and at the University of Southern California, especially those in my Global Violence against Women class. They are a constant source of inspiration and hope.

Special thanks to Cynthia Moss and Kathryn Devincenzi for a thousand acts of beauty and kindness that can never be adequately repaid. Thanks to Michael Brennan and Consolee Nishimwe for believing in this project.

The biggest thanks of all goes to the women writers of Kibera. This book is theirs.

Any proceeds from the sale of this book will go to the Kibera writers and to the Kibera School for Girls (SHOFCO).

Introduction

To read this book is to traverse a web of interlocking relationships, theories, and ideas, using as a compass the stories young women have written about their own lives, particularly about intimate partner violence. Through these stories, the reader will make sense of the intersections where global forces create inequalities and how these inequalities are negotiated, managed, undermined, rewritten, and resisted.

This book is about women who live and try to survive in one of the largest slums in sub-Saharan Africa, a place called Kibera (see maps 1, 2, and 3 at the end of the book). The existence of Kibera and other informal settlements like it is illustrative of a major demographic shift on our planet, whereby a majority of its six billion inhabitants now live in cities (UN-HABITAT, 2003; Davis, 2006).

Of this majority, more than one-third live in places like Kibera. According to Davis (2006), "The dynamics of Third World urbanization both recapitulate and confound the precedents of nineteenth- and early-twentieth-century Europe and North America" (p. 11), with some nations, such as China, urbanizing so rapidly that more than 166 Chinese cities have populations over a million. In other nations in the Global South, "urbanization has been radically decoupled from industrialization, even from development per se and, in sub-Saharan Africa, from that supposed sine qua non of urbanization, rising agricultural productivity" (Davis, 2006, p. 13). According to Davis (2006),

> Modern mega-slums like Kibera (Nairobi) or Cite-Soleil (Port au Prince) have achieved densities comparable to cattle feedlots: crowding more residents per acre into low-rise housing than there were in the famous congested tenement districts such as the Lower East Side in the 1900s. (p. 92)

Although Kibera is only about the size of New York's Central Park (see maps 1, 2, and 3), some experts estimate that the population may be as large as seven hundred thousand to a million (Sartori, Nembrini, & Stauffer, 2002; Davis, 2006; UN-HABITAT, 2003), while others more recently estimate that the population is under two hundred thousand (Desgroppes & Taupin, 2012). The fact that no one knows exactly how many people live in Kibera and that there is no reliable census or methodology for obtaining demographic data is illustrative of the ongoing inability of researchers to reliably and routinely know, map, and understand the dynamics of this sprawling informal settlement.

Kibera is divided into 12 villages (see map 4 at the end of the book). Typical families in Kibera live in one-room, mud-walled huts, without secure or regular access to water, sanitation, electricity, or privacy (Davis, 2006). Although referred to as "houses," these single-room dwellings usually serve as kitchen, living room, and bedroom for five or more people. These structures are owned by informal landlords who are recognized by the tenants (who pay \$10–\$20/month) but who have no legal ownership (Mutisya & Yarime, 2011). Overcrowding and poverty are key factors in the production of high rates of violence and crime in Kibera (Davis, 2006). They are also implicated in the high rate of unemployment, which may be as high as 40% of the population (Davis, 2006). Some Kiberans with jobs in the formal sector walk into the main city of Nairobi for work. Others must depend on the informal economy to make a living.

PHOTO 1: The railway track which runs through the Kibera slum. Kibera lacks sanitation, trash removal, drainage, safe drinking water, electricity, roads, and other public services.

Source: Photo by Kibera19, Flickr

Extreme poverty has its greatest impact on the lives of women and children, particularly girls. This is especially true in Kibera, where mothers work hard and take great risks to put food on the table for their children, and where children, if they are girls, enter the cycle of poverty early due to lack of education beyond the primary level. Not unexpectedly, there is a very high rate of gender-based violence in Kibera. And it is on gender-based violence—specifically, *intimate partner violence (IPV)*—that this book will concentrate. Because Kiberan women may experience IPV at more than twice the rate of women in the general population, it is salient and important to understand this experience and how women create strategies for coping with it. Indeed, as this book describes, women have come up with some very creative strategies for coping with intimate partner violence in Kibera. Our understanding of these strategies is derived from two kinds of data. The women whose stories you will read in Part Two of this book have described their strategies in diaries and shared them with us. Other women participated in a quantitative survey on violence against women that serves as a contextual backdrop for the diaries. Using a global feminist lens to interpret these data enables us to see how Kiberan women negotiate dangerous intersections and how they use their local knowledge and personal agency to exercise creative, if limited, choices in their daily lives (Lockhart & Danis, 2010).

The first and most common strategy used by the diarists, what I have called *Hoping God Agrees*, involves how women purportedly conform to social norms while actually defying them daily in order to survive. The second strategy, *Escape*, is the second-most common strategy, but women's attempts at escape are frustrated and prohibited by lack of social services and social capital. Women who attempt escape often end up returning to worse kinds of violence than those they fled. The third strategy, *Betting against the House*, is the least common strategy and involves attempting to beat the odds against women in Kibera by using one male partner against another in order to leverage a way out of poverty on the back of would-be exploiters.

The strategy most successful in keeping women alive is *Hoping God Agrees*, a strategy through which women attempt to minimize violence and maximize safety for themselves and their children. But, when closely scrutinized, all the strategies provide keys to developing contextually specific and woman-centred interventions that may enable women to end violence in their lives *permanently*, not just survive its unrelenting repetition. Each strategy is a clue, a pathway to future action.

Global Inequalities

To understand how these strategies are socially constructed and how they are related not only to global social problems but also to the gritty realities of daily life in Kibera, readers must situate the diaries in a broadly based analysis of global social inequalities and of global violence against women.

We live in an age of globalization, which is often defined as "the expansion and intensification of social relations and consciousness across world-time and world-space" (Steger, 2013, p. 15). Anthony Giddens (1990) has said that globalization links "distant localities in such a way that local happenings are shaped by events occurring many miles away and vice versa" (p. 64). But such linkages are not always positive, especially for the poor. In fact, globalization greatly exacerbates social inequalities, leaving poor, marginalized populations in the crosshairs of its most destructive forces. Joseph Stiglitz (2003) has described the globalization process like this:

> With the continuing decline in transportation and communication costs, and the reduction of man-made barriers to the flow of goods, services and capital (though there remain serious barriers to the free flow of labor), we have a process of globalization analogous to the earlier processes in which national economies were formed. Unfortunately, we have no world government, accountable to the people of every country, to oversee the globalization process in a fashion comparable to the way national governments guided the nationalization process. Instead, we have a system that might be called global governance without global government, one in which a few institutions—the World Bank, the IMF, the WTO—and a few players—the finance, commerce and trade ministries, closely linked to certain financial and commercial interests—dominate the scene but in which many affected by their decisions are left almost voiceless. (p. 21)

The rules of the new globalized economy are made and enforced by three key institutions, mentioned above: the World Bank, the International Monetary Fund (IMF), and the World Trade Organization (WTO). Since the 1970s, these organizations have expanded neo-liberal policies to deregulate global markets and to consolidate structural adjustment policies in the Global South. Under structural adjustment programs, when the IMF and World Bank provide loans to developing nations, the stringent repayment plans often constitute a new form of colonialism. A borrowing/debtor nation is often required to implement the following structural adjustments to qualify for the loan: a reduction on public spending; financial liberalization; competitive exchange rates; foreign direct investment; trade liberalization; privatization of state agencies; and deregulation of the economy (Steger, 2013; Sernau, 2014).

Structural adjustment programs rarely help to "develop" a developing nation. On the contrary, the mandated cuts in public spending result in "fewer social programs, reduced educational opportunities, more environmental pollution, and greater poverty for the vast majority of people" (Steger, 2013, p. 58). The national budget is spent on servicing and repaying debt. In 2005, developing countries paid the equivalent of over $355 billion in debt servicing and received about $80 billion in aid (Steger, 2013).

Market liberalization, for example, was forced on Kenya by the IMF, with negative results. "Financial market liberalization in Kenya," says Stiglitz (2003), "had adverse effects on the countr[y]" (p. 46):

> The IMF had insisted on financial market liberalization, believing that competition among banks would lead to lower interest rates. The results were disastrous: the move was followed by the very rapid growth of local and indigenous banks, at a time when the banking legislation and bank supervision were inadequate, with the predictable results—fourteen banking failures in Kenya in 1993 and 1994 alone. In the end, interest rates increased, not decreased. (Stiglitz, 2003, p. 32)

Indeed, market reforms of the late 1970s through the 1990s have resulted in debtor-nation adversity, as well as, in many nations, increased urbanization. In nations such as China, that urbanization is tied to industrialization, and more than 200 million Chinese have moved from rural villages to smoke-clogged cities where they work in factories and sweatshops that produce Global North goods such as cell phones and iPads (Davis, 2005). In sub-Saharan Africa, on the other hand, urbanization is not about employment—it is about unemployment. In Kenya, for example, urbanization is linked to structural adjustment by-products, such as food importation, the consolidation of small land holdings into large ones, and the competition of local business with the international market. Thus rapid urban growth, in combination with currency devaluation and industrial privatization, has resulted in an increased number of residents in informal settlements like Kibera during the last four decades (Davis, 2006; UN-HABITAT, 1996, p. 239).

Women and Work in a Globalized World

Economically disadvantaged women, like the diarists in Kibera, share many characteristics with other women in the Global South, where historical and unequal power relations result in the exploitation of female labour (Penn & Nardos, 2003) and the relegation of women to the lowest status on the employment ladder, even lower than men of their own race/colour or status. In Kenya specifically, the colour and gender stratification of labour had its origin in colonial hierarchy but, nevertheless, continued after Kenya's independence, which saw European women making more than African men but African men making more than African women. As Ester Boserup has remarked in her groundbreaking study of women's roles in economic development,

> In multi-racial and multi-national countries ... men belonging to the superior [*sic*] group earned more on average than men of the group below in the racial hierarchy. Similarly, women of a superior [*sic*] group earned more than women of the group below, and men in every case earned more than women of their own group.... A labour market organized strictly on race and sex lines is most advantageous to European men and least advantageous to African women who are the least favoured of all the groups. (Boserup, 1970/2011, p. 135, 137)

What is central to this study, though, is women's place in the informal economy, because it is that economy which sustains many women in the Global South, including women in the city of Nairobi in general and in Kibera specifically, who are either at the bottom of the employment hierarchy or completely off the ladder. Mary Njeri Kinyanjui's important study (2014) highlights the agency and resilience of women who create and maintain their own businesses in Nairobi by overcoming exclusionary structural, political, and economic forces. A key example of a trade engaged in by many women is that of a *mama mboga* (vegetable woman) who may, with the help of her cell phone, serve customers across boundaries of class and status and emerge as a real economic agent who actively shapes the nature of the city (Kinyanjui, 2014). Using personal mobility, cell phone technology, self-created social networks, and collective associations, women in the informal economy transform women's social relationships, increase their autonomy, and allow their households to aspire for upward social mobility (Kinyanjui, 2014). Such transformation is apparent in Kibera, too, although women may lack the mobility described by Kinyanjui, or that mobility may be utilized within Kibera exclusively.

Indeed, women's informal economy is everywhere visible in Kibera. Women usually market skills having to do with food preparation, household maintenance, childcare, hair care, or personal grooming, as they extend "the organization of domesticity into the public sphere" (Harrison, 1991, p. 183). All participants in the current study engaged in one or more of the following activities during the course of the diary project: laundry within the slum, laundry for the estates adjacent to the slum, housecleaning, selling cooked food in vending stalls or on the "street," selling cooked food to vendors by walking from stall to stall, styling/plaiting hair, selling charcoal for cooking, selling fresh produce in a vending stall, selling packets of nuts on the highway, or performing childcare for working women.

Of course, these jobs do not always produce enough money for a family's needs and every diarist said she also needed male support in order to survive. Furthermore, the work is extremely arduous and time consuming. For example, if a woman chooses to do laundry, she also must buy and carry the water necessary to wash the clothes. That likely means that she must carry several 20-litre jerry cans of water from a water point, which may be as much as a kilometre away from her residence. The cost of the water must be subtracted from her daily earnings. Similarly, if a woman chooses to sell vegetables at a kiosk in Kibera, she must not only pay rent on the kiosk, she must also travel to a market outside Kibera to purchase fresh items. The cost of the transportation, in money and in time, must be deducted from her resources. A woman's difficulty is increased if she has young children. With childcare virtually non-existent in the slum, either a woman must leave her children with family or neighbours, or the children must accompany her to work.

According to a recent study (Desgroppes & Taupin, 2012), the average income in Kibera is about $39/month, a calculation based on general population per household/per village. It is much less for single women with children (about $22/month), making them the most vulnerable social group in Kibera. They are closely followed by individuals living within a nuclear family, with 68% living below the poverty level established by UN-HABITAT of about $26/month. The United Nations Office of Humanitarian Affairs estimates the daily per capita income in Kibera for women to be about 100 shillings (about $1.22) or less per day (IRIN, 2010).

Considering the monthly income of an average woman in Kibera, she cannot spend the 100 shillings she earns per day solely on food. Spending the full 100 shillings on food would, indeed, produce a healthier and more satisfying meal than spending only part of that sum. And that 100-shilling meal might include vegetables and/or corn meal dumplings (*ugali*), along with a low-cost protein. However, it is not possible to spend the entire daily income on food because rent ($10–20/month) and (if she has children) school fees must also be paid from the accumulated daily wages. Although primary schools have been theoretically free in Kenya since 2002, many Kiberans find that free government schools are too far away from the slum for their children to attend. Therefore, slum residents often find themselves paying for informal private primary schooling in the slum, another way in which the poor pay more for basic services than do people in the general population.

Such expenses lead some Kiberan women into the temptation of such activities as engaging in the brewing of prohibited alcohol, known as *changaa*; selling drugs, such as glue or marijuana; or engaging in prostitution. These activities are often paired for maximum economic gain. A woman or team of women may brew and sell changaa from their place of residence, permitting their customers to drink the brew on the premises, where they may also purchase sexual favours from women residents. It must be noted, however, that there is more than one kind of prostitution in Kibera. There is an active commercial sex industry where some women engage in prostitution in their homes, as described above, in cheap Kibera brothels, or in Nairobi nightclubs, hotels, or discos. Some work independently but most are managed by pimps, especially in the tourist areas of Nairobi. However, there is a second kind of commercial sex, known in Kibera as "survival sex," through which women will agree to sleep with an acquaintance or a neighbour for a fee. The fee is often 100 shillings, just enough to feed the woman's family for a day. Survival sex is largely condoned and sometimes even respected in the slum because it is understood that a woman has no other choice than to exchange her body for enough food to survive. Women, such as the diarists in the current study, make a distinction between prostitution and survival sex. In fact, they often write vehemently in their diaries that they are not prostitutes and that they regret exchanging sex for money. As one diarist writes, "Poorness forces me to do so" (Marya, May 2010).

Indeed, "poorness" forces women in Kibera to make difficult choices about many things as they negotiate daily survival within the bounds of stark slum reality. Thus, everyday interactions—in their homes, in their work, and on the street—determine whether they will succeed or fail: whether they will live or die.

Global Violence against Women

Globalization has not only increased the feminization of poverty around the world. It has also increased global gender-based violence. It has made poor and marginalized women and children more vulnerable to sex slavery, sex trafficking, debt bondage, and prostitution. The United Nations Office on Women (UN Women) states that violence against women cuts across national, ideological, class, race, and ethnic boundaries and reminds us that, although such violence is present in all cultures, the forms it takes are culturally specific (UN Women, 2016; Penn & Nardos, 2003).

Gender-based violence is a personal, social, and political issue for Kenyan women. There are about 20.6 million women in Kenya, comprising about half the total national population of 41 million. The median age for a Kenyan female is 19 years. About 80% of Kenya's women are literate and their life expectancy is about 60 years (CIA, 2015). In Kenya, women live with longstanding and deeply embedded "societal norms of male superiority" (Lawoko, 2008, p. 780). In domestic situations, men are usually undisputed heads of households, making key decisions about everything from finances to family planning. In the macro world, men hold most positions of power relating to government, finance, and law.

Patriarchal standards and attitudes pervade every level of Kenyan society and are especially debilitating for women in the areas of education, employment, access to credit, and property ownership. These factors combine to create a general atmosphere of economic disempowerment for many Kenyan women, making it difficult for them to overcome a network of interconnected constraints that inhibit access to political and economic independence.

In Kibera in particular, gender-based violence (GBV) is a social problem of enormous proportion. In 2012, a survey to determine baseline data on GBV in Kibera (Abebe, Jepkiyeny, & Angaga, 2012) concluded that GBV negatively affected Kiberan women and girls in every aspect of their lives and that community awareness in the area of GBV and the provisions of the Sexual Offences Act (SOA) were urgently needed to address gaps in existing interventions. Similarly, a study in 2013 concluded that

> there is need for increased sensitization and enhanced advocacy on GBV, enhanced awareness education with regard to the provision of [the] Sexual Offences Act, where to seek help and what help is available for the survivors of GBV, strengthening of the legal framework and judicial system, and increasing socio-economic empowerment of girls and women. (Mwereru, 2013, p. 1)

This book deals mainly with intimate partner violence (IPV), a type of gender-based violence that is exerted on a woman by her husband or a sexual partner. Although stranger rape and other types of gender-based violence are rampant in Kibera, the purpose of this study is to explore ways of coping with violence from husbands, boyfriends, and other intimate partners. IPV is common in the mainstream population of Kenya. According to the Kenya Demographic and Health Survey (KDHS, 2014), about 45% of women between the ages of 15 and 49 have experienced physical violence since the age of 15, and the main perpetrator has been "husbands." As we might imagine, though, IPV is exacerbated in Kibera by poverty, stress, unemployment, and substance use. In northeastern Kibera (villages of Laini Saba, Mashimoni, Soweto East, and Lindi), a survey I conducted showed that 84.5% of women had experienced IPV (Swart, 2012).

Although this book concentrates on the problem of intimate partner violence, it also briefly considers the related problem of sexual violence in times of conflict, when normative barriers against certain types of sexual violence may disappear. Several of the diarists experienced the post-election violence of 2007–2008 in Kibera, during which they were kidnapped, raped, and threatened with death. This experience—as well as the knowledge of the similar fates of many other Kiberan women—served as a watershed moment for many diarists about the attitude of entitlement to female bodies that is held by many Kiberan men.

Ethnographic Reflexivity: Whiteness and Privilege in a Research Context

Decolonizing my own vision as a researcher was key to conducting the Kibera diary project. When people from the Global North travel to Kibera, they usually represent some kind of authority from the outside world. Frequently, Westerners in Kibera are representatives of international non-governmental organizations (NGOs), such as UNICEF, CARE, or Amnesty International. Such individuals are viewed with a guarded respect that is akin to confidence but something less than trust. Although the presence of NGOs (both Kenyan and international) in Kibera for decades has done little to mitigate the dire poverty there, such organizations have established schools, clinics, and HIV testing centres and other important social services. Sometimes students visit Kibera from universities around the world—they work as interns or volunteers for local NGOs and often live in estates (housing developments that receive municipal services) adjacent to the slum. Kiberans continue to be hopeful and positive about any help they are offered and, thus, they afford NGOs a somewhat jaded welcome.

Sometimes, too, the Western faces in Kibera belong to journalists, like Mike Davis, who lived in Kibera for several months while writing *Planet of Slums* (Davis, 2006). Moreover, since the filming of *The Constant Gardener* in Kibera in 2005, Kibera residents have also come to understand that Global North people in their midst might be celebrities, like Rachel Weisz and Ralph Fiennes. Indeed, film directors still scout Kibera as a possible movie set, and a residual aura of "slum chic" hovers over the shanties, encouraging some tour operators to include Kibera as part of their larger "safari" itinerary. Other filmmakers have made documentaries that have helped the larger world understand the harsh realities of Kibera; some have collaborated with Kiberans on art projects, such as the play *Kibera Kid*, which became a film but began as street art performed by local actors. Regardless of the reason for their appearance, however, individuals from the Global North are viewed with an enlightened caution in Kibera.

Understandably, then, it was impossible for me (a white, Western woman) to be anonymous in Kibera, as some ethnographic observers choose or desire to be. It was equally impossible not to be seen as a person with power, be it personal or political. The very ability to have traversed the distance between my home and theirs revealed my financial empowerment, regardless of my purpose in Kibera. Luckily, though, because of my history of grassroots advocacy there, I was afforded a cordial reception and, to the extent that it was possible, I was even taken for granted by residents of the particular neighbourhoods in Kibera where I conducted my projects.

I first entered Kibera in 2006, with a Kenyan female friend who was teaching at a Kiberan primary school. She was loved by the students and my association with her provided me with credibility by association. I was also lucky to know (through academic connections and meetings I had attended) the leaders of two local NGOs who worked with young people in Kibera. By 2007, with the help of these two individuals, I had established relationships of trust with a core group of young Kiberan people. At that time, I was teaching sociology and social work classes at a large university in the southeastern United States. I often told my students and departmental colleagues what I saw and learned in Kibera when I visited these friends and observed their work. By the end of my first year of visits, my colleagues and I had initiated some of our own limited and unfunded projects: we assisted Kiberan youth in accomplishing several tasks. Together we established a youth group, a soccer team, a bead-making project for young women, and a scholarship fund to help primary school girls attend secondary school. Each had been a small but successful effort. Thus, a year later, when I first approached Kiberan residents about participating in my research project, I had already established a degree of credibility that served me well. Kiberan residents had seen good results produced by projects my colleagues and I had initiated.

Nevertheless, it was clear from the beginning that my whiteness, my positionality in the Global North, and my resulting privilege would raise important, difficult, and possibly unsettling issues if I attempted to do "research" there—that is, if I attempted to learn more about Kibera residents (particularly women) from their own perspective by using the academic tools that I had learned and brought with me from a white, Western academic world. Would women trust me? Would I be able to put aside—to some degree at least—my white Western privilege? Would I be able to understand data that I collected there and interpret it through the eyes of Kiberian women?

I already had a study design in mind: I wanted to ask women to write—daily, weekly, or as often as they could—accounts (I called them diaries, but that word originated with me) about their lives in Kibera. I also wanted to do a quantitative survey with a larger group of women from the same area of the settlement, asking what it was like to be a woman there. Could I carry out this methodology in a manner that embraced a "partnership ethic" (Cram, 2009)—that is, could I do research "with" them and "for" them, not just "about" them? I thought of the slogan used by my own students of colour in the United States: "Nothing about us without us." Could I learn from the women in Kibera in a way that enabled a larger audience to view their world as they themselves saw it and lived it? Could they be research partners in a way that imbued the study with partnership ethics, as well as partnering methods? And was "partnering" enough to offset privilege? Was partnering alongside privilege even possible?

There were many other fault lines I stumbled over and self-interrogations I wrestled with. First, there was the clear and obvious possibility that the women with whom I might work would want to please me. To the women who might be writing diaries, I represented a connection to the outside world, through which their voices might be heard beyond Kibera. Therefore, it was possible that they might consciously try to write what they thought I wanted to hear. But what was that? Did they think that I partook of a vision of them as victims, prisoners not only of Kibera but also of hegemonic masculinity and male privilege? Did they think I wanted to hear how much they were used, abused, and misunderstood—about how much violence penetrated their lives? Did they think I wanted sensationalism? If they saw me and my purposes that way, they might write all the agency right out of their lives in order to appeal to the Global North idea of what a Global South woman endured as the "eternal victim."

To mitigate this possibility, after the diary project began, I never limited the topics they wrote about. I did not ask them to write about how hard life was or how much prejudice or violence they encountered. They knew that I had degrees in both sociology and social work. They knew I taught classes on violence against women and globalization and wrote about what we bundle together in undergraduate courses as "social problems." And they knew that as a social worker, I was interested in concrete interventions that would create opportunity in places like Kibera where few opportunities existed, especially for women. But there were never any boundaries set on the type of writing they could do, except that, if written in diary form and presented as an account of their daily life, it needed to be true. Some wanted to submit other kinds of writing; I got book reviews and poems and plays, which greatly illuminated the context of those writers' daily lives and inner dialogue.

The main idea was that I wanted to understand their lives—whether social interaction or interior monologue—through their eyes. So, when the diary project began, the only directive I gave was, "Write about what happens to you every day and how you feel about it." That way, I thought, I would get specific stories in the larger context of their daily lives. Throughout the project, then, the women knew that I was interested in the "micro" or interactional-level details of their personal experience from their perspective. This interest produced "thick" description (Geertz, 1973) about how these micro-level details related to the social reality of Kibera and the larger city and country.

As the study began, I continued to be inspired by Cram's (2009) assertion that research should be guided by a "partnership ethic" (p. 308), in which the researcher acknowledges "the need to create meaningful relationships with the people and communities affected by the research" (Cram, 2009, p. 221). This idea was a constant guide for me because my study was one of long duration. I needed guidance about how to create partnerships that were incisive and personal but that still maintained a professional boundary that enabled me to see each diary through the writer's individual lens, as well as the diaries as a whole through the lens of women situated in a postcolonial, globalized world. But ultimately, the partnership ethic was not enough to deconstruct the politics of my own "whiteness" and my historical connection to the colonization that had subjugated Kenya and helped, in its course, to create informal settlements like Kibera. I relied on some important critiques of "whiteness" and "white privilege" (Hunter, 2005; Sullivan, 2006) to admit to myself some of the many prejudices I still (consciously or unconsciously) carried. Looking back now, I can categorize them into three areas: personal image as do-gooder; language/metaphor; and space-taking.

As I mentioned earlier, I was involved in some social work projects in Kibera before I became involved in research. I am a social worker who has for the last 10 years been engaged in both clinical practice and its seeming opposite—macro or policy-oriented work. I keenly understand that empowerment and opportunity are created by asking people what they need and want, not by forcing upon them what I think they *should* want. Following that idea, when I discussed my social work projects in Kibera with my students or colleagues, they never contained "do-gooder" language or intentionality. We were clear in our desire to initiate "opportunity-creating" projects that opened doors to already-existing talents or capacities. For example, we created an opportunity for young men to have a soccer team in Kibera. The kids in Kibera already played soccer very well. My colleagues and I provided some funds to register the team with the city of Nairobi and for uniforms and shoes. Thus, the opportunity was created for Kiberan youth to play soccer in a wider circle of competition.

But when I began conducting a research project, I still made my visits to Kibera and would often fill my suitcase with things that I thought were needed by NGOs working there with Kibera residents. For example, my students collected pharmacy items—toothbrushes, toothpaste, pads for the girls, Band-Aids, aspirin—and I carried these items there and distributed them. And they were appreciated. But looking back, I/we have to ask myself/ourselves if we did not do it in part because it made us feel good/important/superior. Did functioning as a supplier of necessities from the Global North enable us to look at ourselves as "good white people"?

I use that phrase because it came from a student in a Diversity class I once taught as part of a social work curriculum. When trying to define *white privilege* to my (mostly white) students who were drowning in student loans and other economic problems, they (the white students) would often disclaim it. They would tell me that they had overcome it and shed white privilege as a social construction. I would insist that they had not divested themselves of privilege, perhaps never would. There were so many examples of why they had not and could not. For example, they would probably not be stopped on the road and arrested for something as minor as a broken turn signal, as many non-white students were. Nor would they be followed through a shopping mall by security guards, having been profiled as potential shoplifters because of their skin colour. They would, on the other hand, always be taken first in a queue of people lined up for anything, anytime, anyplace. They denied this and said, if it happened, they would reject it. I insisted that they might not even be conscious of it. At this point, at least one of them usually went to the department chair, claiming that I had called them racist and that, far from being racist, they were, in fact, "the good white people."

I was amazed by that phrase, and by their construction of good and bad people within whiteness. The lesson then became, I thought, to teach them that well-intentioned white people could still take their privilege for granted and benefit from it. Some agreed with me by semester's end; some never did. But now, here I was in Kibera handing out little treats and being vociferously thanked. Wasn't I doing and thinking the same thing: I am a good white person, representative of the good white people of the world, coming here and giving you little tokens from the Global North?

The second and perhaps most pervasive way in which whiteness intruded upon and overarched the study was through language and metaphor. All of the writers spoke English and it was easy for me to forget that for them, although they had learned it in school and used it proficiently, English was usually their third language, after Swahili and an ethnic language. Even though the diary project stipulated that they could write in any language they wanted, their frequent and common use of English lulled me into the false belief that this was normal for them. Perhaps, some were accommodating me, being kind, saving me the translation fees. Others probably used English enough to make it normal, especially if they had any reason to liaise with the daily world of the anglicized Nairobi outside Kibera. But I did not remember this often enough and, during meetings or interviews, I spoke to them in English as if that were their norm, as well as mine. As the project continued, I became aware of the privilege I was exerting. I bought Swahili books and tapes and asked for help and learned as much Swahili as I could. But I was never as conversant in their language as they were in mine. Language, then, a residual by-product of a postcolonial society, was always there as a reminder that the Global North had staked a flag into Kenyan soil over a century ago and had only been removed by force when Kenya gained independence in 1964. Over 50 years later, the vestiges of colonization are everywhere and many whites in Kenya still assume and demand privilege, which is not difficult to do given the new colonization of the global market and its infrastructure.

If my arrogant taking-English-for-granted attitude were not bad enough, I also needed a wake-up call about my use of metaphors *within* that language and how they, too, needed to be deconstructed. For example, I more than once referred to the data I was collecting as a "gold mine" of new information. It wasn't until I was reading a 1993 reissue of Adrienne Rich's *Collected Early Poems* that I realized the necessity of seeing into and through my own colonized language. In an appended note to her poem "The Diamond Cutters," Rich wrote,

> I have trouble with the informing metaphor of this poem. I was trying, in my twenties, to write about the craft of poetry. But I was drawing, quite ignorantly, on the long tradition of domination, according to which the precious resource is yielded up into the hands of the dominator as if by a natural event. The enforced and exploited labor of actual Africans in actual diamond mines was invisible to me and, therefore, invisible in the poem, which does not take responsibility for its own metaphor. I note this here because this kind of metaphor is still widely accepted, and I still have to struggle against it in my work.

I had been using the gold mine metaphor in much the same way Rich had used that of the diamond miner—with no awareness of the absent referent, the gold miner herself, the African worker, the writer of these diaries. That my language and, therefore, my frame of reference and intention, were born of exploitation was jolting. It was not difficult to think of other metaphors I used in the same way. I thought of my research as "opening up" new areas of discourse, as though I were an explorer (Mohanty, 2003) travelling to an uncivilized land and coming home with news from a dark continent. I did not actually see Kibera that way—I saw it as a place full of life, and music, and violence, yes, but also vibrancy and determination. How could I express that adequately in my writing, though, if I used metaphors like "opening up" their world to the academic gaze? All of my metaphors had to be reconsidered and deconstructed. To the best of my ability, I have removed offending metaphors from my vocabulary and I point them out when I hear them used by others. If I were to do this study again, though, I would ask the writers to write in their own language only and not at all in English.

The final area where I became aware of my unconscious use and expectation of privilege was in my attitude toward public spaces I thought I was entitled to inhabit in Nairobi and how I used this privilege. In Kibera, certainly, I felt unsure of myself. I was a *mzungu* (a white person) who was out of place and often lost. I was stared at; I was often surrounded by children; and I was patiently corrected when going in the exact opposite direction of where I was aiming. Although I was never really afraid there, I was uncomfortable. That seemed like a good thing, though, and I recalled that a scholar writing on white privilege actually urged white people to "make themselves uncomfortable" (Lugones, 1987).

But outside Kibera, I did not realize how comfortable I felt and how I exercised a taken-for-granted privilege based on whiteness. When not in Kibera, I stayed with a colleague in a suburban, academic neighbourhood in Nairobi. When I met with Kiberan study participants (including the people who administered the survey, the NGO representatives, and sometimes the diarists), we met in cosmopolitan areas of Nairobi at cafes and restaurants akin to the ones I would select for myself in the United States. When I was there, I felt "at home"—I was in my element within areas frequented commonly by white people, although certainly not exclusively so. I ordered from servers—who were usually people of colour—got frustrated if the service was slow, took my time, and spread out my laptop and papers—presuming that my colleagues and I could take up as much space as we needed for as long as we needed it. I behaved as I would in the United States although I was on Kenyan soil. I considered these areas my own space, part of the globalized world to which I was entitled. I never asked myself why I felt this way in Kenya. Would I have been as arrogant in Paris or Rome—did I act entitled here because Kenya had so long been colonized by whiteness? Did I make the Kiberan women or the other Kenyans I met with feel uncomfortable when I brought them to these spaces? If I had to do it over, I would let Kenyans choose where to meet and eat and I would follow their lead.

If the launching of the project seems difficult and fraught with privilege-and-difference issues, analyzing the data at the end of the study created even more potential for falling into the cracks in the world created by global privilege and its consequences. That is, during analysis, I also had always to attend to my own "situated" perspective (Harraway, 1988; Bettie, 2003) as I proceeded to try to say what the data meant through the eyes of the women who had written it. As the analyzer of the women's diaries, for example, I had the power to select and interpret sections of the documents and attach meaning to them. As Julie Bettie (2003) points out, "All perspectives are situated in a place of more or less power" (p. 23). In this case, I had the power to overarch these women's journal entries with my own cultural assumptions about their lives and perspectives. Because it was my earnest desire to present these diaries from the *writers'* point of view, I did everything in my power to "unpack" my "knapsack" of white Western assumptions (McIntosh, 1989) and to make myself "uncomfortable" (Lugones, 1987) so that I would continuously remember I was not reading diaries written by women with my own aims and goals. I had conversations with the diarists along the way and asked them questions to make sure I understood what I was reading in the way they meant it to be understood.

First of all, I wanted to avoid making the assumption that women in Kibera shared my views on gender issues. That is, I did not wish to assume that they wanted to be "liberated" from an unjust patriarchal order or from some portion of that order as it manifests in their individual lives. I also needed to be aware, as Bettie (2003) points out, that the population of "others" (the diarists) was not homogeneous. That is, I needed to avoid "feminist essentialism," through which I might be tempted to view the diarists as "all the same" or as "eternal victims, without agency" (Bettie, 2003, p. 23). To a very large degree, the diaries themselves mitigated that possibility, in that the opinions, lifestyles, and political stances of the authors were extremely diverse, presenting a constant reminder of difference within the population. The women presented different kinds of struggles and strategies for dealing with them, reminding me to focus on the specificity of their unique and individual perspectives and choices.

In addition, I tried to remember, as the study continued, that both the diarists and I were changing in the process of the multi-year study. As Bettie (2003) observes, identity is an "ongoing production, not an accomplished and static fact" (p. 24), and that goes for both the researcher and the research participants. Ultimately, I hope that my work in Kibera led to research that was "for" not "on" the women there and to an understanding that was *situated* in the knowledge base of the participants. I hope I created research that was "sourced from within the community's own values and beliefs" (Cram, 2009, p. 313).

I was also aware of my own temptation to interpret the writers' lives—and their relationship to my own life choices—solely in terms of gender. As Bettie (2003) remarks, it is important to be cognizant of "forces of domination beyond gender" (p. 24), particularly, in the case of the diarists, of structural inequalities that pervade every aspect of their lives. Gender was not the only or most important construction. I needed to remember, for example, that the diarists could not take food or water for granted. Gender was a construction that they used in part to obtain these things—they constructed gender in order to make survival possible. That was a very different use of gender than the concept that was normative in my daily life—gender was a means of exploitation and economic inequality but not on a subsistence level, at least not for myself and my academic peers.

I also had to remember to incorporate age into my understanding of the diaries. These were young women, and their experiences were differently situated—both historically and socio-culturally—than those of their mothers or grandmothers. These women had access to a globalized media culture through music, films, and social media. Most of them owned cell phones, even if they weren't "smart phones." They attended films (in Kibera or in the larger city of Nairobi); they listened to music that included Western rap and rock, as well as Kenyan music and the music of other African countries; they had access to Indian films/music and Nigerian soap operas and to print media from many countries (some of it old, but not too old to reveal to them the latest details in the life of Beyoncé or Kanye or the Obamas). Many of their mothers had not had this sort of global perspective. In fact, many of their mothers, aunts, and grandmothers had come from rural areas of Kenya, where agrarian or small-village lifestyles were still common.

Along with the access to global media, however, came the oppression of a new global racism that exported the goodness and desirability of whiteness (Hunter, 2005). Indeed, I heard of three women diarists during the course of my project who lamented having "dark" skin colour and of one who tried skin bleaching creams. According to Hunter (2005), global racism is described as originating in and being dispensed by the machinery of globalization:

> Globalization, multinational media conglomerates, and the new restructured economy all work together to maintain the US cultural, economic, and political imperialism. Part of this structure of domination is the exportation of cultural images arguably all racial in one way or another. The United States exports images of the good life, of white beauty, white affluence, white heroes, and brown/black entertainers/criminals. As many people in other countries yearn for the good life offered in the United States, they also yearn for the aesthetic of the United States: light skin, blonde hair, and Anglo facial features.... Images associated with white America are highly valued and emulated in the global marketplace. This is part of what makes colorism and racism so hard to battle: The images supporting this system are everywhere and the rewards for whiteness are real. (p. 120)

As Hunter (2005) points out, the establishment of an Afrocentric beauty standard is still being negotiated in relation to colourism, with lightness still associated with greater beauty than darkness. The Kiberan women in the diary project reflected the influence of the global media in regard to colour in the attempt of the one diarist to bleach her skin and in their ongoing remarks about the shade of their skin in relation to Western norms, as in Marya's remark (April 2009), "I wish my skin looked more light like a model's or like Beyonce. I would have an easier life." References to media favourites and idols were named by diarists to be Beyoncé, Rhianna, or Whitney, and were always black not white, albeit of lighter rather than darker skin tone. It will be interesting to see whether an increasing diversity in the voting membership and the nominations of the Academy of Motion Picture Arts and Sciences will result in the export of a darker-skinned beauty standard.

Finally, I needed to remember that, even among Kibera residents, there was privilege. Some of the women were homeless, living with temporary male partners or on the street. Others lived safer lives with families of origin, or with relatives, or with husbands. All of the diarists had attended primary school, but one was privileged enough to have attended secondary school. That meant she had less risk of early pregnancy and/or marriage and greater possibility of obtaining a job.

Fortunately, the theories I employed in my study helped me maintain my perspective.

Theoretical Frameworks

The aim of studying women's diaries was to describe the multi-dimensional daily reality and lived experience of the writers. To that end, I chose an ecological model to provide the study's framework. This model made it possible to describe and analyze how intimate partner violence pervaded various levels of the social environment of the diarists. The version of the ecological model used for the current study was adapted by Heise (1993) from Belsky's study of child abuse (1980) and applied to interpersonal violence. Heise's model (see figures 1 and 2) is based on results from both quantitative and qualitative studies regarding the possible causal factors of gender-based abuse and serves as a framework for understanding the multiple contextual layers within which women experience intimate partner violence. These layers—the micro, mezzo, and macro systems of the ecological model—enabled me

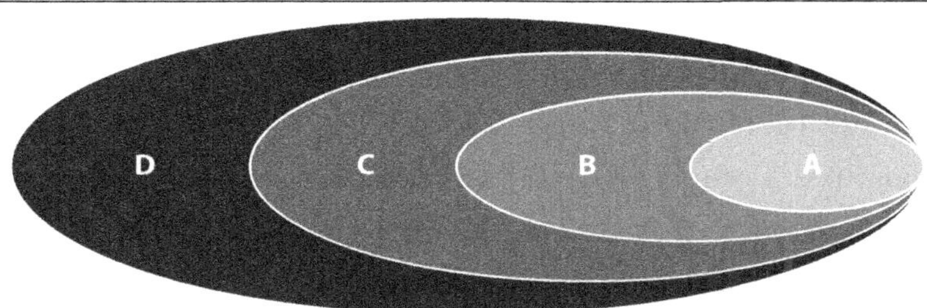

D: Macro System

Gender-based violence as a structural issue; rigid gender roles; institutionalized gender-based violence

C: Mezzo System

Male dominance/abuse in school or work-place; isolation of women from support structures

B: Micro System

Male dominance in the family (father, brother, uncle, husband); male control of economic and psychological environment of the home

A: Personal History

Witnessing domestic violence in family of origin; being abused as a child

FIGURE 1: Ecological Model of Factors Associated with Gender-Based Violence

Source: Heise (1993)

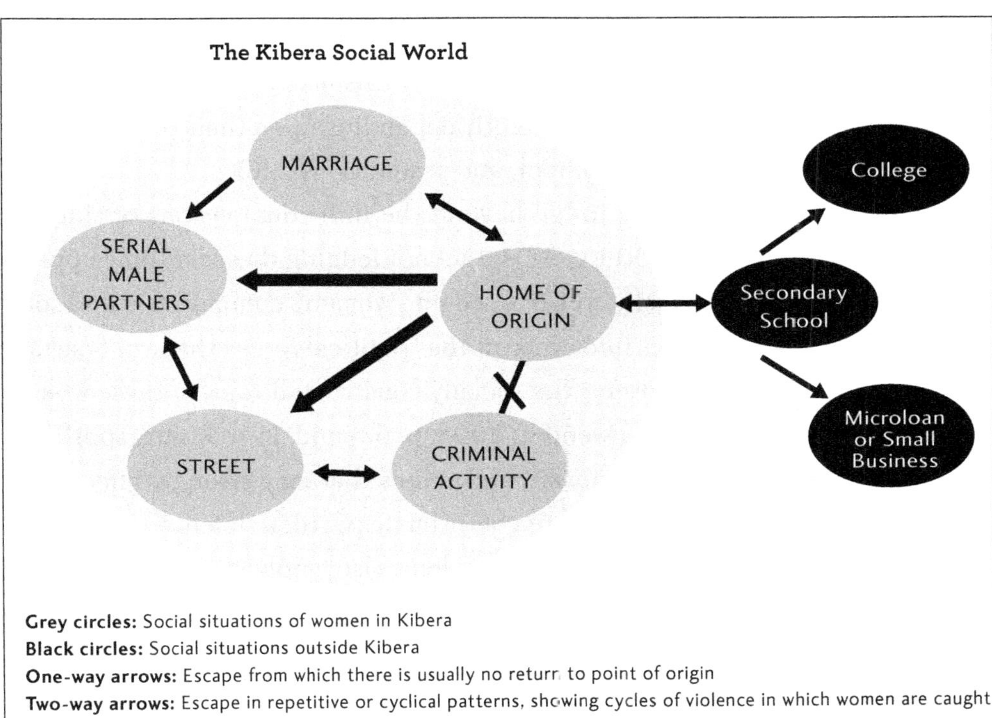

FIGURE 2: Factors Associated with Escape Strategy for Coping with Gender-Based Violence

to analyze women's personal, familial, and societal experiences of abuse and also to understand how these layers of experiences were connected.

Diarists' lives were rooted in intimate partner violence, which was often present in their families of origin and extended through the micro (personal), mezzo (community), and macro (societal) levels of their social environment. The use of the ecological model enabled the analysis of these various levels of violence as they intersected and interacted with one another and as they related to women's identity and agency.

Two particular theories spoke to the overlapping and intersecting of the different spheres within the ecological model and were used in this study to explicate the multi-dimensional aspects of intimate partner violence. Global feminist theory was particularly useful in understanding the macro system that overlay individuals' experiences of intimate partner violence. In particular, this theory provided a "set of analytic premises for thinking about and theorizing gender" (Baca Zinn & Dill, 1996, p. 26). Patricia Hill Collins (2000) has described the wide range of overarching and interlocking inequalities within which women organize their lives as a "matrix of domination" (p. 246), a web through which several fundamental *systems* of inequality work *with* and *through* each other. Baca Zinn and Dill (1996) describe the operation of this matrix: "People experience race, class, gender, and sexuality differently depending upon their social location in the structures of race, class, gender, and sexuality" (p. 26).

Global feminism attempts to "go beyond the individual visions of singular feminist efforts" (Mendez, 2008, p. 37) by acknowledging these multiple oppressions and how they are socially constructed into women's communities and societies (Shohat, 2001). It takes into account the "political forces that exalt certain identities of women and allow for the socially constructed roles of these women to become oppressive forces" (Mendez, 2008, p. 62) and, in so doing, spotlights the overarching social beliefs, norms, and values that may strongly affect both male and female behaviour in the area of intimate partner violence.

Global feminism, with its intersectional lens, also emphasizes the "relational nature" of dominance and subordination, as well as the "interplay of social structure with women's agency" (Baca Zinn & Dill, 1996, p. 27). That is, "within the constraints of race, class, and gender oppression, women create viable lives for themselves, their families, and their communities" (Baca Zinn & Dill, 1996, p.

27) on a daily basis at the interactional level. Such a theoretical approach is particularly applicable to the Kibera study because it can apply within or across cultures (Collins, 2000, p. 248), showing how structural inequalities are mediated through *local* and personal realities: "Regardless of how any given matrix is actually organized either across time or from society to society, the concept of a matrix of domination encapsulates the universality of intersecting oppressions as organized through local realities" (Collins, 2000, p. 246). Global feminist theory helps explicate the relationship between societal and individual realities.

Chandra Mohanty (2003) builds on this relational theory by discussing the importance of understanding *where* that theory is situated and from whose perspective we orient our vision. Mohanty (2003) argues that global feminism must be cognizant of the ways in which knowledge is produced and the ways in which women's knowledge, in particular, is often overshadowed by masculinist discourse. In order to "make effective interventions in the production of knowledge" (Kennedy & Beins, 2005, p. 9), Mohanty maintains that feminists should anchor their "analyses in the poorest of women's communities, arguing that their standpoint helps reveal the totality of power relations" (Kennedy & Beins, 2005, p. 9) in a globalizing world. Mohanty (2003) writes:

> This analysis begins from and is anchored in the place of the most marginalized communities of women—poor women of all colors in affluent and neocolonial nations; women of the Third World/South or the Two-Thirds World. I believe that this experiential and analytic anchor in the lives of marginalized communities of women provides the most inclusive paradigm for thinking about social justice. (p. 231)

She goes on to explain why the situating of perspective among the poor helps explicate systems of interlocking oppression that are often invisible to Western eyes:

> Beginning from the lives and interests of marginalized communities of women, I am able to access and make the workings of power visible—to read up the ladder of privilege. It is more necessary to look upward—colonized peoples must know themselves and the colonizer. This particular marginalized location makes the politics of knowledge and the power investments that go along with it visible so that we can engage in work to

> transform the use and abuse of power. The analysis draws on the notion of epistemic privilege as it is developed by feminist standpoint theorists.... who provide an analysis of experience, identity, and the epistemic effects of social location. (Mohanty, 2003, p. 231)

Like Dorothy Smith (1989, 1991), Sandra Harding (1991), and Patricia Hill Collins (2000), Mohanty (2003) exhorts the need to "study up," that is, to begin with the lives and personal narratives like those of Kiberan women and generate questions and problems from that standpoint.

Mohanty also emphasizes the importance of stories and storytelling in the creation of women's knowledge and pedagogy. It is through sharing stories, she believes, that women can create a new kind of feminist knowledge, "which challenges colonial relations and fosters feminist solidarity across difference" (Kennedy & Beins, 2005, p. 9). Mohanty's theories have clear and profound implications for the current study, which attempts to ground its perspective in that of Kiberan women—some of the poorest of the world's poor—by understanding how they construct the stories about their own *lived* experience of intimate partner violence into narratives of agency and resilience.

I also was keenly aware of the ongoing discourse about "otherness" and "othering" in regard to race and culture (Narayan, 1997, 2000; Sandoval, 2000; Harding, 2006). As Uma Narayan (1997) suggests, "the project of 'understanding Other cultures' is made difficult by the problems one often has in 'seeing' features of one's 'own context ... that might make a difference to the sense of 'similarities and differences' one develops" (p. 96). Narayan (1997), for example, points out that the number of women killed in India by dowry murder is, when seen in proportion to population, roughly equivalent to the number of women killed in gun violence by their intimate partners in the United States (p. 99). That view is vital and makes the point that intimate partner violence is universal and that its American variations may be just as "egregious as those in the Global South, although they are often made invisible by our own social norms." My students who study dowry murder, for example, often react passionately when they read about cultures where dowry murder occurs, calling them "barbaric" (student's word from class discussion, May 2016) without seeing the violence in their own cultures which is similarly horrific. Likewise, in Kibera, I needed to continually challenge myself to look for absences of acknowledgement of violence in my own culture—things I couldn't see which (because of my sightlessness) encouraged a lack of specificity and historicity on my part. I had to continually ask myself, "What kinds of behaviours and violence have been so normalized for me in the United States that I no longer see them as they are?"

The concern with interactions at the level of local realities makes global feminism uniquely compatible with a second theoretical approach—the symbolic interactionist perspective—with its focus on the specific meaning interactions have at the individual level. According to Herbert Blumer (1969), symbolic interactionism is built on three basic premises. First, individuals act toward things based on the *meaning* those things have for the people doing the interacting. Second, meanings are not derived from intrinsic properties of things, nor do they exist as part of the psychological process of specific individuals. Instead, meanings arise through social interaction between individuals and other social actors. Third, although meanings are produced through social interaction, they are constantly modified through an ongoing process of interpretation. Such a theory is especially well suited for understanding gender in the context of the current study because it makes possible the understanding of gender as an ongoing *process*.

West and Zimmerman (1987) coined the phrase "doing gender," creating the theory in which they describe gender as a routine, methodological, and recurring accomplishment that is undertaken by both men and women "whose competence as members of society is hostage to its production" (West & Zimmerman, 1987, p. 126). "Doing" gender is an interactive process:

> To "do" gender is not always to live up to normative conceptions of femininity or masculinity; it is to engage in behavior at the risk of gender assessment. While it is individuals who do gender, the enterprise is fundamentally interactional and institutional in character, for accountability is a feature of social relationships and its idiom is drawn from the institutional arena in which those relationships are enacted. (West & Zimmerman, 1987, pp. 136–137)

Since the "doing gender" idea was introduced in 1987, others have interpreted and interrogated it, extending its use and expanding its base. Thorne (2002), in a groundbreaking study of primary school children, illustrates gender as a dynamic process, varying from situation to situation. She writes, "As individuals, we always display or 'do' gender, but this dichotomous difference ... may be more or less relevant, and relevant in different ways, from one social context to another" (Thorne, 2002, p. 29). Likewise, Connell (2002) describes masculinity and femininity as "projects" that are accomplished differently in different social contexts:

> Gender is, above all, a matter of social relations within which individuals and groups act. Gender relations do include difference and dichotomy, but also include many other patterns.... It is not an expression of biology, nor a fixed dichotomy in human life or character. It is a pattern in our social arrangements, and in the everyday activities or practices which those arrangements govern. (p. 9)

Patricia Yancey Martin (2003) concludes that

> women and men routinely practice gender—as masculinities and femininities—in embodied interactions that are emergent and fluid, grounded in practical knowledge and skills, and informed by liminal awareness and reflexivity.... Only by asking how, when, where, and by what means—both narrative and physical—gender is actively practiced can we gain insights into 'saying and doing' dynamics. To this end, research and theorizing about the twin dynamics of practicing gender and gendering practices are needed. (p. 359)

One of the most important aspects of "doing gender" is the implicit assumption that women have a say in the matter. That is, gender is not handed to women only through a top-down structural process. Instead, women have agency in gender construction and participate on the interactional level in its contextual construction. Connell (2002) remarks that any account of how we "do" gender must "recognize both the contradictions of development, and the fact that the learners are active, not passive. People growing up in a gendered society unavoidably encounter gender relations, and actively participate in them" (p. 79). As Martin (2003) points out, "Some gender scholars imply that people who exercise agency relative to gender consciously intend to practice it and/or are aware of practicing gender when they do. Others suggest that they do so in non-intentional ways or ... unconsciously" (p. 355).

Lucal (1999), for example, discusses agency as a very conscious process when she writes that "if gender is a product of interaction, and if it is produced in a particular context, then it can be changed if we change our performances" (p. 795). Williams (2002), on the other hand, in her study of adolescent girls, sees gender as a "trying on" process, with women exercising their agency in "anticipating, experimenting, retreating, and resisting" (p. 30). Similarly, Silva (2008) discusses how female ROTC cadets negotiate the tension between masculine military culture and traditional femininity. Deutsch (2007) adds to the dialogue by changing the language in which it is couched, reminding us that "we need to reframe the questions to ask how we can *undo* gender" (p. 106). She remarks that:

> If we take a social constructionist position seriously, we must examine resistance to gendered social interactions as a source of change. By examining the effects of subversive action on its audience, we may be able to identify the conditions under which those actions change normative conceptions of gender, and how and when these new conceptions can take advantage of or even drive institutional change. (Deutsch, 2007, p. 120)

Furthermore, Crawley et al. (2008), in one of the most sophisticated and clever analyses of gender construction, describe it as a feedback loop of ongoing performance, surveillance, and resistance. In their words, "It is an interactive, swirling, everyday process of social inputs and body practices that builds humans and societies" (Crawley et al., 2008, p. 243).

Intrinsic to my theoretical perspective is Judith Butler's (1990, 2011) work on gender as a performative category. In Kibera, for example, women might be expected to behave according to a very traditional gender performance expectation—to serve her husband and children; to be a traditional wife whose life revolves around the home, even if it is one room with mud walls. In order to survive in Kibera, though, and to put food on the table, she must often perform a different, hidden gender role: she must sell illegal liquor or sell her body in order that she and her family may survive. Women in this project alternated between the traditional expected gender role (wife, mother)—which they sometimes attended to with a tongue-in-cheek performance—and, the out-of-sight role, through which they might become sellers of sex, purveyors or illegal substances, petty thieves. At no time, though, did they challenge the binary gender construct which is unassailable in Kibera. If any woman in this project openly proposed working a man's job or attaining masculine privilege, she was ridiculed or threatened with punishment, both personal (beating by husband or boyfriend) and societal (rape, beating, or humiliation by the general community).

Kimberle Crenshaw's intersectionality theory was also key in understanding the intersections of gender with ethnicity and class and in helping to explicate the particular kinds of oppression Kiberan women experienced, in interaction with the mainstream culture, as well as within Kibera itself. At the same time that women in Kibera maintained and constructed performances for others (particularly males) in their own community, they intersected with mainstream Nairobi, where they had to assume other performances. A stigma attaches to those who live in Kibera that is akin to a stigma that might attach to someone living in a bad neighbourhood in an American city. Some diarists in this project experienced discrimination when they applied for employment in parts of Nairobi where Kiberans were synonymous with outcasts or criminals—as though Kibera were a homogeneous place where people lacked individuality, agency, and history. So if Kiberan women seek employment, even for a day, in a high-rise adjacent to the slum, they will do their best to look like they come from somewhere else—they will not only wear their "Sunday best" (Catherine, 2009) but they will hold their bodies differently and walk differently. Mary remarked, "If I am at a high-rise looking for work, I meet everyone's eyes and hold up my head as though I am sure of my every step" (Mary, 2010). So, in the course of one day, a Kiberan woman may perform at least three gender roles: that of traditional wife and mother; that of a purveyor of illegal activities; and that of a higher-class potential employee. She will utilize clothing style, verbal language, eye contact, personal space, and body language in these self-conscious performances that enable her to walk between and among the intersections that connect her life. Others conspire with her to accept these performances—or not—and, based on others' finding of these performances as legitimate (or not), a woman's life is made easier or more difficult.

Following Butler and Crenshaw, I was better able to view gender as "the tacit collective agreement" to maintain "discrete and polar genders" (Butler, 1990, p. 179) and to brace myself for the consequences Kiberan women would experience if they chose not to engage in that agreement, either in Kibera or in the larger city of Nairobi. I knew, for example, a woman who decided to try to work on a construction site along with her boyfriend. She was as large and as strong as he was. She was laughed and humiliated out of the idea and threatened with rape. At the same time, there was a tacit agreement *not* to maintain those gender norms, as long as the non-traditional performance was reserved for a non-public space. If a woman sold her body for money for water and food, it was permitted as long as it could be done without a public acknowledgement of this alternative performance and as long as the performative characteristics of that non-traditional role were abandoned as soon as the transaction was accomplished.

The agentic choices women made in relation to their experience of gender-based violence in Kibera helped explain their strategies for coping with violence—strategies that resulted from the interplay of several performances. As Stewart (2003) has remarked, the combination of feminist theory with the symbolic interactionist (doing gender) perspective advances the understanding of gender construction and illuminates "the ongoing interaction between self and society, viewing them as mutually influential" (p. 73). Indeed, many Kiberan women survived solely because they were able to skillfully negotiate this complex interplay of gender performance(s), which they changed according to place and audience. Their level of skill determined their social capital, their social acceptance, and their economic power. For example, performing the expected role of consoling mother and dutiful wife enabled many Kiberan women to maintain alliances with and retain social capital from community organizations (churches, NGOs) while, at the same time, performing a non-conforming role (engaging in survival sex, for example) enabled them to actually earn enough money to survive.

But these performances were also used to cope with intimate partner violence and its consequences. Women changed their performance according to a partner's mood or interests but, more than that, women adapted new performance strategies that played expected norms against one another, enhancing the women's potential agency and mobility. Some women even honed performance strategies so finely that they played one abuser against another in order to escape violence from both. Rarely, though, did women in this project do more than consider stepping outside the binary gender construction. Their range of roles were all within the costume department, so to speak, of women actors, and they were always playing opposite male leads.

An ecological model, then, explicated by two grand theories—global feminism and symbolic interactionism—sheds light on the daily lives of the Kiberan diarists and their strategies for coping with intimate partner violence. Global feminism enables an analysis of the macro system of structural oppression. Symbolic interactionist theory helps understand the micro system of "doing gender" on a daily basis. When women in Kibera "do" gender, they link micro and macro levels of experience through the roles they play in their public lives. By so doing, they negotiate their own survival.

Methodology

The project consisted of two kinds of data and, therefore, two methods and two types of analysis. This mixed method design increased the richness of the project because while it let many voices be heard, it also allowed for individual voices to "solo" in the choir.

Diary Project

The main source of data for this project was in the form of daily and weekly diaries by 20 women residents of Kibera, Kenya. The diaries were begun in March 2007 and continued through April 2014. The project was originally planned to last for three years. It was expanded to five and then to seven because the diarists did not want to abandon the project and the process of decolonizing the project (turning it over to the women) was slow and methodologically complex.

The idea for the "diary project" was originally hatched by me in a meeting with leaders of two NGOs in Kibera. These NGOs are Kenya-based and work on issues of education and girls' health/welfare. I am withholding their names to protect the identities of the participants in this study, who still maintain contact with these NGOs.

We decided to see whether women would be interested in writing accounts of their lives, so we presented the idea to women at group meetings and social events. I was interested in collecting data by women between 18 years of age (the age of consent for an Institutional Review Board application) and 36 years of age. I wanted this age demographic because I was interested in women who were in the process of shaping their lives and making important life decisions about work, marriage, and family. I wanted to see how they exercised agency in regard to these important matters. Some writers who seemingly indicated they were 18 years of age or older at the time of the project's inception later proved to be younger than that age. I do not know if they intentionally hid their youth so that they could participate in the project or if a question on the first demographic data collector confused them. That data collector asked, in addition to name and age, the "age of oldest sibling residing with you." Because the question asking the writer's own age and the question asking the sibling's age were next to one another, it is possible that "age of oldest sibling" was put into the blank where the author's own age should have gone. Either way, the fact that some writers were under the age of 18 when the project began was not discovered until they were, in fact, 18 or over. Therefore, I, in cooperation with my university advisors, decided to let these writers continue without retroactive parental consent, reasoning that obtaining parental consent might reveal the nature of the writings and inadvertently endanger the writers.

I wanted written accounts of daily lives because I thought they would provide more detailed, organic, daily life accounts than would one-to-one interviews, which heretofore I had found answered grand questions and depended on broad generalizations about one's life. I hoped, instead, for intimate details. The NGO leaders were keen on the idea because for them the project would have the ancillary purpose of helping to hone the verbal and vocabulary skills of the participants, since most of the women had only attended primary school. Besides group announcements, recruitment also consisted of posting flyers about the project in Kiberan youth group offices, as well as women's groups and clinics. Thirty women expressed immediate interest in writing for this project. They had an ardent desire to speak to the world, even if that world was at the time limited to myself and a few colleagues at one American university.

After returning to the United States, I created a study design and research protocol through which to analyze the journals. When these documents were approved by the Institutional Review Board (IRB), I returned to Kibera several months later, met with the diarists, and asked their consent to do a study of their journals. After signing consent forms, 26 women shared the contents of their diaries they had written in the last few months that I had been in the United States. Although none of the women refused me access to her journals, I chose only 20 to be part of my ongoing research. There was a wide variety in both the amount of writing submitted and the quality of those submissions. For example, some women presented as few as two entries. Others had written consistently for several months and indicated a desire to write on a regular basis. Diaries selected for inclusion in the study were chosen on the basis of the *consistency of entry*, in that each diarist's work—at the time of the study's inception—represented at least six months of continuous accounts. The other selection criterion was *density of narrative*, in that each selected diary showed a degree of engagement with the work that constituted more than a simple listing of daily activities. So that the study might provide insights into both populations, I made an effort to choose from the journals of both *street* and *housed* women, according to which contributions in each category best met the inclusion criteria. Diarists whose work was selected to be part of the ongoing study continued to write until April 2010, at which time data collection was temporarily terminated for initial review and thematic analysis. After the first analysis, it was clear that the data were rich, complex, diverse, and important. The project was continued through 2014.

Survey Project

In order to provide supplemental and contextual background for diary data, a survey was administered in December 2009 to a group of 200 Kiberan women between the ages of 18 and 36. The survey collected demographic data from respondents, not including the diarists, as well as information about the nature, meaning, and consequences of intimate partner violence that the respondents had experienced. Survey questions pertained to five general areas. The first section collected *demographic* details, including age, birthplace, marital status, living arrangement, and source of income. The second section gathered data on women's *attitudes* toward gender-based violence, including information on whether they ever considered gender-based violence justified and under what circumstances. For example, women were asked if they believed a husband or boyfriend was justified in beating his female partner if she went out without telling him, neglected their children, argued with him, refused to have sex with him, or burned food. The third section presented questions about the *reasons why women may or may not exert control or agency* in relation to their daily lives and, specifically, in relation to partner violence. For example, women were asked to indicate whether they made agentic decisions (to resist or accept violence, for example) based on fear of reprisal from their spouse; on social approval and social norms; or on their own beliefs regarding their partners' behaviours. The fourth section gathered specific and detailed data on the *type and prevalence* of partner violence, presenting women with 11 different kinds of violence and asking whether they had experienced that type of abuse from a partner and, if so, who had perpetrated it and how often. For example, women were asked if their partners had humiliated, threatened, pushed, slapped, punched, or kicked them, as well as whether they had ever been attacked with a weapon or raped by their partner. For every "yes" response, women were asked whether that violence had been perpetrated by a husband or boyfriend. They were also asked how many times such violence had happened—one to five times; six to ten times; or eleven or more times. Finally, the last section asked women about their *coping strategies* in response to gender-based violence and how they felt about the abuse. Women were asked, for example, if they ever talked to anyone about the violence (a minister, family, friends, children, partner, counsellor, or no one). They were asked to indicate what helped most to cope with violence. Among the choices were *having faith in God*; *getting professional counselling*; *getting husband to change*; *becoming a better wife*; or *ending the relationship*. Women were also asked to indicate their subjective response to the violence they experienced—anger, sadness, acceptance, or non-acceptance.

The survey was designed to collect demographic, prevalence, and attitudinal data among 200 women in the same age range as the diarists. It was my hope that the survey would provide rich, contextual detail about the age-group cohort of which the diarists were a part. In this way, following Miller (2008), I hoped to provide "a relatively holistic assessment" of how intimate partner violence among the diarists was "situated in the wider context of youths' neighborhoods and in their peer … relationships" (p. 14). It was also designed to replicate the Domestic Violence Module of the Kenya Demographic and Health Survey (KDHS) so that I might be able to compare results in Kibera with results from the larger population of Kenya.

Ethics and Protection of Human Subjects

Both the qualitative and quantitative components of this study were approved by the Institutional Review Board (IRB). Each diarist participating in the study signed an Informed Consent document confirming that she agreed to allow her journal to be analyzed for the current project. Diaries were turned in to a youth group director every four weeks, at which point they were placed in a sealed envelope and sent to me via Federal Express. As journals were received by me, they were copied to preserve the integrity of the original documents. They were also transcribed into computer files. All dates attached to the diary texts and transcriptions correspond to the dates diaries were *written*, not the date diaries were received by me. Original diaries, copies, and transcriptions were stored in separate, locked filing cabinets in my office. A pseudonym was attached to each diary to protect the identity of its author. No identifiers other than these pseudonyms were attached to any transcribed diary or to any quote lifted from a transcribed diary. I attached pseudonyms that reflected—but not too closely—the diarists' actual first names, which are without exception English names. If there were alternate African names that they used among themselves, I never heard them, although I frequently heard them call one another by their surnames, which was common practice. For example, "Where is Nyambura?" was a frequent question. "She is coming," came the answer.

Survey participants, who had been recruited via flyers and posters distributed through the offices of Kiberan youth and women's organizations, were also asked to sign consent forms before participating, letting them know that they were not required to participate in the study and that they could withdraw from the study at any time. Participants were asked to keep the informed consent document for their records. To ensure the anonymity of participants, no identifiers were attached to questionnaires. The survey was administered by Joyce Ojiema, a Kenyan nurse and women's health advocate employed by the African Medical, Research, and Educational Foundation (AMREF). I recruited her to administer the survey so that she could explain the survey document and answer any questions that might be posed in Swahili instead of English. Ms. Ojiema met with me prior to survey administration to ensure that she was able to answer any questions that might be asked by participants. The survey was administered at the Laini Saba

YWCA in Kibera, a location that was deemed convenient and comfortable for participants. Before survey administration began, informed consent documents were distributed to each participant; when informants had completed the surveys, the questionnaires were deposited into a locked box at the front of the room, which was collected at the end of the session. Thereafter, all questionnaires were stored in a locked filing cabinet in my office.

Participants

Participants in the study, referred to herein by pseudonyms, were all born in Kibera and have lived in Kibera their entire lives. All identified as Christian. They represented three ethnicities—Kikuyu, Luo, and Kamba. Ages given below are women's ages in 2007. During the course of this study:

- Betta (16) lived with her mother, her sisters, and her baby son, who was conceived during Betta's first experience with sex. Her boyfriend disappeared, leaving Betta and her parents with another mouth to feed. Betta was tall and had broad shoulders that made her look older than she was. Consequently, she was sometimes hired to do housework at high-rise apartment buildings near Kibera and she used this work to bring extra money to the household. She also worked with her mother and sisters, making food that they sold on the street. The baby precluded any chance of belated secondary school for Betta, but she loved seeing herself as a mother, hoping she would find marriage eventually with another boy. She smiled rarely in public but she always glowed when she looked at her son. Betta and her parents belonged to the Kamba ethnicity and lived in the Laini Saba village of Kibera.
- Cara (18) lived with and cared for her mother, who had tuberculosis. The disease minimized her mother's ability to work on a regular basis, so the responsibility fell to Cara. In 2006, Cara became pregnant and, since she was not married, she suddenly had the additional responsibility of raising a baby daughter. Her boyfriend who fathered the child fled at the first mention of pregnancy, but Cara embraced the difficult option of motherhood in Kibera with both arms. To support her mother and her baby, Cara did laundry for other women and cooked food, which she

marketed on the street. Cara and her mother were devoutly religious and attended church every Sunday. They belonged to the Kikuyu tribe and lived in the Laini Saba area of Kibera.

- Catherine (19) lived with her family of origin when the project began but was abandoned by them in 2008. After that time, she attempted to support herself and her younger brother and sister through manual labour and survival sex. Her mother eventually came back to the family, although, during the course of this study, her father never returned. As was typical in Kenya, mother and daughters worked and provided school fees so that the boy child could attend school. Even during her mother's absence, Catherine prioritized obtaining those fees, even at the risk of her life and pride. Catherine was eventually given a microloan, with which she purchased a computer and a small space to use as an office. She started a small business, typing and copying documents for a fee. She prospered and, although the office work did not provide enough money to fully sustain her, it greatly decreased the amount of time she had to spend doing manual labour. She always looked to the future and believed she could achieve her dreams. Her resilience and self-esteem were high and her hopefulness was steadfast. She and her family were Kamba and lived in Laini Saba.
- Cathy M. (18) lived in a tense and tenuous household with her brother and sister-in-law. Cathy's parents had nine children younger than Cathy and had great difficulty feeding the family. When Cathy turned 15, her parents negotiated an arrangement whereby she would live in her brother's household (also in Kibera) to lift the financial burden from her family of origin. Cathy worked hard, doing housework at her brother's as well as working at a local kiosk for extra money. However, she was resented by her sister-in-law, who considered the burden of feeding Cathy an unjust and excessive one. Cathy was dependent on boyfriends to obtain small bits of money for underwear, menstrual pads, and shoes. Cathy lived with the ever-present fear of being evicted from her brother's home and becoming homeless. Cathy's family was Kikuyu and lived in Laini Saba.
- Dee (24) lived with her father when she began journaling but was forced by her father to move into her mother's smaller house when she became

pregnant with her third child. She subsequently lived with an uncle, with a sister, and on her own. Dee also lived with boyfriends for limited amounts of time during this project but none of the relationships became permanent. Dee was a quiet girl but, when asked, would gladly talk politics, music, or culture, which she absorbed from radio, videos shown in the slum, and newspapers. She was opinionated and keenly aware of women's plight in Kibera and around the country. Her journals also showed that she was a talented writer with poetic sensibilities. Of all the diarists, Dee was the most reflective and the one who possessed a distinctive voice that was ardent and eloquent for justice, gender equality, and peace. Her journalistic journey came to an abrupt end when in 2010, she disappeared from Kibera. Dee was Kikuyu and lived in Laini Saba, Lindi, and Soweto East during the project.

- Elizabeth (17) lived with her adult sister having left their family of origin because their parents could not support them after their teen years. The two sisters had both been exploited by men who took their virginity with promises of marriage that were never fulfilled. After experiencing more than one fickle and insincere boyfriend, Elizabeth's sadness turned into clear-sighted pragmatism, through which she hoped to extricate herself from Kibera. The two sisters worked hard at several jobs and saved every shilling they could. They talked to each other nightly about their dreams and plans to fulfill them. Elizabeth was determined to turn every choice into a step toward her ultimate goal of rising above poverty. Elizabeth was Luo and lived in Laini Saba.
- Emma (18) briefly attended secondary school outside the slum but failed to make the required grades to remain a student. She returned to Kibera, where she lived with her family of origin. She worked odd jobs doing laundry and housecleaning so that she would have some money to contribute to the household. Increasingly, she became bored with her life and with the small amounts of money gained through her work. She began working in a brothel and, by the end of this project, was living in the brothel full-time. Emma was Luo and lived in Soweto East.
- Gemma (20) lived with her three children. She worked with her mother selling food in a kiosk and made beads to sell on the street to supplement

their income. She often wore the beads she made and walked near places where tourists would see her and admire her beads. With each necklace or bracelet she sold, she bought materials to make more. Finally, she got a $50 microloan with which she bought even more materials. Eventually, she and her mother sustained themselves and the children solely through their beadwork. Gemma and her mother were Luo and lived in both Laini Saba and Soweto East.

- JC (19) lived predominantly with her family of origin but spent some months living with her boyfriend. Her boyfriend was abusive and controlling. JC often considered dropping out of the diary project because she was afraid her boyfriend would punish her for participating. JC loved her boyfriend and had dreams of marrying him and leaving Kibera. But neither of them had secondary education or good employment. Her boyfriend left her in 2010 and JC was devastated. She returned to her family of origin but immediately felt their resentment at the expense her return entailed. She soon found another boyfriend, who bought her personal items and offered some money to her parents. But he was even more abusive than the first. JC confronted the world with hardened pride and resistance. The family was Kikuyu and lived in Laini Saba and Soweto East during the course of this project.
- Jane (16) lived with her family of origin and helped support her parents, as well as three younger siblings. Jane was silently observant of the frequent injustices around her. She was very intelligent but had not been able to attend secondary school. Nevertheless, she keenly evaluated the options available to her and always chose those that benefited the majority of her family, especially the children. She used small change from boyfriends and other male liaisons to buy shoes for the children or milk or water for the household. She saw the world in its rough reality but always sought ways she could make it better. Jane was Luo and lived in Lindi.
- Janet (17) returned to her family of origin after a brief, unsuccessful marriage, which had turned violent almost immediately after vows were taken. Janet was clear and unequivocal about not remaining in a violent marriage and was lucky that her parents welcomed her home. Janet, a serious and deeply religious young woman, retained a cynicism about men through

the rest of this project, although, toward the end of her journaling, she mentioned seeing other men and hoping for a better partnership. Janet did odd jobs to pay her room and board at her home of origin and in 2010, she opened her own kiosk selling produce and household items. Janet was resolute about not experiencing violence again and is a strong example for other women who accept violence as a norm. Janet and her family were Kikuyu and lived in Laini Saba.

- Judy (20) lived with her husband and their baby daughter. According to her journal descriptions, their marriage was romantic and respectful, although Judy recalled previous relationships that were violent. Judy and her husband worked very hard every day. Judy did laundry, often with the baby on her hip or sitting in one of the empty laundry tubs. She also found old cans and planted whatever seeds she could find, successfully growing tomatoes and geraniums in tin cans outside their door. Her husband worked on roads or on construction crews when he could find work. He also scavenged in Kibera's mountains of garbage for things to sell. Both Judy and her husband were Kikuyu and lived in Soweto East.
- Marya (17) lived with her mother and her baby girl. Marya left school when she became pregnant but had hopes of returning and of eventually becoming a teacher. Because her other siblings were all married or on their own, Marya's mother was happy to have her at home to help her pay the rent and manage household affairs. Marya engaged in odd jobs, manual labour, housecleaning, and laundry to obtain money for daily needs. She also maintained boyfriends so that she could get extra cash or loans from them to help with expenses. She spent any extra money she had on picture books and nutritious foods for her baby. Marya was Luo and lived in Soweto East.
- Sally (15) lived with her aunt and brother since the death of her parents when she was a young child. Her aunt, who had a prospering business making the illegal alcoholic brew *changaa*, entertained patrons in her house at night. After customers were drunk, she routinely sold Sally to them and was effectively Sally's pimp. Part of the money from Sally's prostitution went to pay her younger brother's school fees. Sally lived in fear of what man she would have to entertain each night and hated her life. Her aunt reminded her constantly that refusal to have sex with the customers

meant that she would have no shelter and no food. Sally ultimately left her aunt's abode but had great difficulty surviving on her own, using prostitution to supplement other jobs, such as laundry and cleaning. Sally was an excellent, expressive writer and a thoughtful, studious young woman. However, she had great pride and would often not accept offers of help from neighbours or friends. She hoped to get a microloan and to start her own business. Sally was Kikuyu and lived in Laini Saba and Soweto East.

- Sarah (17) lived with her mother and three siblings. Like several other girls in the project, Sarah was resented for remaining in the home after her mid-teens because her parents found it hard to feed and clothe her. She tried to move in with female friends but money problems subverted that arrangement. Sarah went home but kept a regular boyfriend as a way of obtaining extra cash, to supplement what work she could pick up in the area. Sarah refused to be depressed, however. She wore orange or yellow when she could find used clothes in those (her favourite) colours. She wore ankle bracelets that jingled and she walked proudly. Sarah was Luo and lived in Soweto East.
- Susanna (16) lived with her husband and their young son. Although Susanna loved her husband, the relationship was extremely violent, with frequent beatings and lockouts. She believed in her husband for a long time despite his controlling behaviour, violence, and drinking. But after one especially bad beating, she attempted to run away. Her attempt at escape was unsuccessful. At the time of this writing, she was still economically chained to the relationship. But she and a female friend had begun saving small change and were hopeful that they could find a way to leave their abusive partners and support each other through odd jobs and shared childcare. Susanna was Luo and lived in Soweto East.
- Terry (16) lived with her family of origin. She was unhappy there because she thought they unjustly resented the money they paid to support her. She went from boyfriend to boyfriend, and these men provided her with bits of loose change with which to buy personal necessities. In 2009, one of them also got her pregnant. She bore the baby, a boy, alone, and the baby then became an additional burden to Terry's mother and father. Terry hoped to find a man to marry but that was made less likely because

of the need for a new partner to also support the baby. In the meantime, she had boyfriends who helped support her but showed no interest in a permanent relationship. Terry's family was Kamba and had lived in Laini Saba and Soweto East.

- Eliza (22), Ina (19), and Mary (19) lived on the street or with serial male partners. They referred to themselves as "street girls" and did not often work at the odd jobs utilized by the other writers. They used survival sex to gain money for shelter and food and lived day-to-day, according to what money came in. Sometimes they managed to have a house of their own for a month or two, in which case they could see men for sex only if they wanted to. But if they lived with a male partner, sex with him (or with others he brought to them) was often a prerequisite for food, and their boyfriends kept the profits of all sexual exchanges. Eliza was extremely smart and wanted to teach school, but her single mother's alcoholism had forced her out onto the streets early in life, in search of employment or assistance. She never gave up her dream of someday returning to school. Mary left her family of origin because of attempts by her own brother to rape her. She decided to choose her own partners and did so with a talk-back attitude that sometimes resulted in beatings but more often gained her respect from street boys. Ina was devoted to Mary but did not have the confidence to take Mary's risks. More often she submitted to the demands of street boys and became pregnant soon after beginning street life. Her baby boy, born early and tiny, survived and often slept on his mother's breast in a vacant lot, even in the coldest of Nairobi winters. Mary, Ina, and Eliza all sold glue sometimes for extra money and they also sniffed it themselves to ward off the feelings of cold, hunger, and fear that are part of street life.

All of the writers except Catherine and Emma attended *only* primary school. Catherine attended two years of secondary school but was forced to drop out because of her family's lack of school fees. She later returned, completed her exams, and received her certificate. Emma attended secondary school for less than a year.

All of the diarists wrote mostly in English. Although they were also fluent in Swahili and (usually) the language spoken by their familial ethnicity (Kikuyu,

Luo, or Kamba), English is the official first language in Kenya. A rather formal British version of English had been written and spoken by the girls since primary school. Nevertheless, they were given a choice of writing in English or Swahili or their ethnic language. When diary entries came to me in a language other than English, they were translated and back-translated into English so that I could be sure of the validity of the translation.

Analyzing the Diaries

Analyzing qualitative data is a fascinating and challenging process. I relied on two techniques—open coding and axial coding—to analyze the diaries (see tables 1 and 2). I did not use digital data analysis software. To begin, the diaries were transcribed verbatim, from handwritten texts (see figures 3 and 4) to electronic files. Diaries were then analyzed using inductive coding techniques (Strauss & Corbin, 2008), through which they were reviewed and coded to identify patterns and emerging themes, first in regard to the general context of the diarists' lives and later in regard to the specific theme of intimate partner violence, when I realized that violence from partners was, in fact, the diarists' main concern and biggest problem after poverty.

Open coding and microanalysis, through which the diaries as "texts" were examined in a line-by-line fashion, focuses on individual statements, specific words, stylistic technique, and metaphors. This analysis was followed by axial coding, in which categories and subcategories were related to one another "to form more precise and complete explanations about phenomena" (Strauss & Corbin, 2008, p. 124). Finally, selective coding was used to integrate the categories, adding nuance and refinement that enabled theory to be built from the data.

Clearly, open coding is the most tedious process but also reveals the layers of meaning in the diaries. Through this process, I attempted to discover "nuggets" of meaning in diarists' daily accounts (Strauss & Corbin, 2008). I approached the process as a questioning activity, continually asking the same question of chunks of data in a line-by-line fashion: "What is important to this diarist today?" I did not look for closure to that question but, instead, used it to open up lines of inquiry. I wrote key words in the margins of transcribed diary pages and then colour-coded the chunks of text where these key themes appeared. I then went through a period of sorting, in which I sought relationships between key words and concepts, combining them into categories and subcategories.

TUESDAY.

The day came up brightly and here I was still in bed thinking of which step I will follow when I wake up. And definately I made up my mind. This time it was 7:00 am and my brother had left for school without any breakfast because we have been used to since our parents left. We don't know whether people take it or not. That's not our business. Anyway I woke up. Took a cold shower and later started cleaning our dishes which we had used the previous night. later after all that was done I dressed or what I call my Sunday best and went outside our house whereby people are passing by and see if any man will try to talk to me so that we may agree to sleep with him and give me a little money.

I stood there for about thirty minutes and then there is this guy who was passing and it seemed he liked me and started talking to me. within twenty minutes we had agreed he will give me hundred and I rushed to our house ~~and~~ closed the door and I followed him. I timed the time when my brother was coming back from school and made sure I was in the house. At least for him he is lucky because they are been cooked in school, where they take their lunch. By this tyme it was almost 7:00 pm and darkness had already started and it was my duty to know what we had to eat so I prepared our supper and took it later we called it a day.

FIGURE 3: Scanned Copy of a Diary Page by Catherine

08

Problem are following me day by day last
night I did not sleep, my younger son was very sick I
stayed awake the whole night he was crying continuesly
I did all kinds of first-aid but nothing worked at five am
I left the house and I went to Kenyatta hospital at
seven am I was there I went to the reseption I
was asked to pay two hundred shilling for the card
I paid then I was told to wait for my son to
be seen by a senior doctor I waited for half an hour
later my son was treated and I went to the pharmacy
I paid three hundred shilling and I was given the
medication for my son and I left.

When I was coming back I met my former boy
friend who is the father of [crossed out] and [crossed out] when
he saw me he blocked my way I tried to cross
the road to walk away from him becouse I fear
him more than fire, he followed me and he pulled
me, I was afraid becouse I know how he can react,
He asked me where are you from I "answered am
from the hospital" he said "You think am a fool I know
that you want to sell the kid try it and I will kill
you before you enjoy the money".

I was waiting to see if he will walk away
without thrittening me but I was wrong. for the first
time he took [crossed out] and told me to walk away I
pleaded with him to give me child back but I
was beaten strong slaps infront of a big crowed
I still begged but the more I begged the more I
was beaten, This time blood was running down my
nose the onlything I remember is my clothes looking
as if they were dipped in blood.

FIGURE 4: Scanned Copy of a Diary Page by Dee

TABLE 1: Emerging Themes from Open Coding (N=20)

Participant	Themes							
Betta	**Economic Need**	**Gender-Based Violence**	**Work**	Tribal Violence	Family	Spirituality	Mothering	**Hopes/ Dreams**
Cara	**Family**	**Economic Need**	**Work**	**Spirituality**	**Gender-Based Violence**	Tribal Violence	**Female Support**	**Hopes/ Dreams**
Catherine	**Economic Need**	Abortion	**Family**	**Gender-Based Violence**	Duty	**Work**	**Female Support**	**Hopes/ Dreams**
Cathy	**Economic Need**	Despair	**Gender-Based Violence**	Abortion	**Work**	**Family**	**Female Support**	**Schooling**
Dee	**Economic Need**	**Gender-Based Violence**	Fear	Drugs	Schooling	Tribal Violence	**Spirituality**	**Work**
Eliza	**Economic Need**	**Gender-Based Violence**	**Work**	Drugs	Despair	**Hopes/ Dreams**	Abortion	Street Life
Elizabeth	**Economic Need**	**Gender-Based Violence**	**Family**	Men	Anger	**Hopes/ Dreams**	Despair	**Schooling**
Emma	**Economic Need**	**Work**	**Family**	**Gender-Based Violence**	**Spirituality**	**Female Support**	Schooling	**Hopes/ Dreams**
Gemma	**Economic Need**	**Work**	**Family**	**Gender-Based Violence**	**Female Support**	Art work	**Hopes/ Dreams**	**Spirituality**
Ina	**Economic Need**	**Gender-Based Violence**	**Work**	Drugs	**Female Support**	**Hopes/ Dreams**	Fear	Street Life

(continued)

TABLE 1: Emerging Themes from Open Coding (N=20) *(continued)*

Participant	Themes							
JC	**Economic Need**	**Work**	**Gender-Based Violence**	**Family**	**Spirituality**	**Female Support**	Schooling	**Hopes/ Dreams**
Jane	**Economic Need**	**Gender-Based Violence**	**Family**	Schooling	**Work**	**Hopes/ Dreams**	Abortion	Isolation
Janet	**Economic Need**	**Gender-Based Violence**	**Work**	**Family**	Schooling	Abortion	Exhaustion	**Hopes/ Dreams**
Judy	**Economic Need**	**Work**	**Family**	**Spirituality**	**Gender-Based Violence**	**Hopes/ Dreams**	Aesthetics/ Art	**Female Support**
Mary	**Economic Need**	**Work**	**Gender-Based Violence**	**Female Support**	**Family**	Drugs	**Spirituality**	Street Life
Marya	**Economic Need**	**Gender-Based Violence**	**Work**	**Family**	Abortion	Tribal Violence	**Spirituality**	**Hopes/ Dreams**
Sally	**Gender-Based Violence**	**Economic Need**	**Work**	**Family**	Isolation	**Work**	Tribal Violence	Schooling
Sarah	**Economic Need**	**Gender-Based Violence**	**Work**	**Family**	**Female Support**	Drugs	Partner's Drug Use	Schooling
Susanna	**Gender-Based Violence**	**Economic Need**	**Family**	**Duty**	**Despair**	Schooling	**Female Support**	Partner's Alcohol/ Drug Use
Terry	**Economic Need**	**Gender-Based Violence**	**Family**	**Work**	**Hopes/ Dreams**	Schooling	**Tribal Violence**	Drugs

Note: All names are pseudonyms. Common themes in bold.

When I had conducted this process for each diarist's data for the years 2007–2014, I recorded the core themes for each diarist. This process enabled me to understand the setting in which each individual diary was situated and provided a contextual understanding of the physical and social environment in which the diarist wrote.

After I had recorded the primary themes for each participant, I undertook a comparison of those themes, looking for commonalities of occurrence across the diary data. My analysis revealed seven common themes that were present in the diaries of all participants for the years 2007–2014 (see table 1).

This process provided me with an expanded sense of contextual meaning for the group of diaries as a whole. I did not, however, dismiss or "throw out" themes that were not common to all diaries. On the contrary, these themes were very helpful in identifying "negative" and "outlier" cases and were strategic to my later data-analysis process. However, as my initial coding process unfolded, an understanding of themes common to *all* diarists enabled me to understand not only how their contexts overlap but also how and to what extent their main areas of concern—poverty and intimate partner violence—ranked among the other themes that diarists considered important to their daily lives. Common themes emerging among the data of all diarists were economic need, gender-based violence, work, family, spirituality, female support, and hope/dreams.

To better understand the extent to which common themes were stressed in individual diaries, I also created a frequency table (see table 2), which records the number of times per week each diarist mentioned each of the common themes in the diary data. These themes are listed according to the frequency with which they occurred in the data. The theme of economic need was mentioned more than any other theme. The theme of gender-based violence was the second-most frequently mentioned theme, followed by work, family, spirituality, female support, and hopes/dreams.

I used axial coding to discover codes around the single category of gender-based violence. I did not look for common themes but, instead, for all themes, metaphors and images around diarists' descriptions of gender-based violence. That is, I looked for interactions, strategies, and metaphors that related in any way to gender-based violence and that illuminated the context in which that violence was experienced by the writers. Strauss and Corbin (2008) have remarked that

TABLE 2: Frequency Distribution of Common Themes Per Week (N=20)

	Economic Need	GBV	Work	Family	Spirituality	Female Support	Hopes/ Dreams
Betta	5	3	3	3	2	2	2
Cara	2	3	5	5	3	1	1
Catherine	5	4	5	5	4	2	1
Cathy	5	4	4	3	3	1	1
Dee	5	5	5	2	2	1	3
Eliza	5	5	3	1	1	2	1
Elizabeth	5	4	3	1	1	1	2
Emma	5	3	4	2	2	1	1
Gemma	5	3	5	2	1	1	2
Ina	5	5	3	1	1	2	1
JC	5	5	3	3	1	2	1
Jane	5	4	5	2	3	2	1
Janet	5	5	5	2	2	2	1
Judy	5	2	5	5	5	2	1
Mary	5	5	2	3	1	1	2
Marya	5	5	3	4	3	1	1
Sally	5	5	5	5	4	1	2
Sarah	5	3	3	3	3	1	1
Susanna	5	4	3	5	3	2	1
Terry	5	3	5	3	3	2	1

Note: All names are pseudonyms.

axial coding looks for "actions and interactions taken in response to a phenomenon" and "intervening conditions that assist or hinder actions and interactions" (p. 124) as well as the consequences of those interactions. I used axial coding to gain a fuller understanding of the strategies the diarists used to cope with gender-based violence. A case in point was diarist Dee's description of an interaction with a former abusive partner: "I try to find ways that I will not run into him because I fear him more than fire. Luckily, there are many small alleyways in Kibera and many ways that I may become lost and hidden there. If I cannot hide, I pray" (Dee, April 2007).

Through axial coding, I was able to understand the conditions, actions, and interactions Dee used to develop strategies for coping with gender-based violence from this former partner. I proceeded with my analysis by creating two subcategories of the gender-based violence theme for Dee called *Escape* and *Faith*. As I proceeded with this coding process, axial coding enabled me to identify the "links that created a web of meaning" (Strauss & Corbin, 2008) for the diarists as they devised strategies for coping with ongoing gender-based violence.

The survey data were analyzed using SPSS (v 16), which enabled me to understand both the demographics of the survey population, and the relationships between those demographics and participants' experience of gender-based violence. When I was finished, I had 20 individual voices telling stories of their daily lives in which extreme poverty interacted with intimate partner violence, as well as other life experiences and stressors, such as work and family. I also had a context of 200 women of approximately the same age group providing demographic details that would situate the diarists in a larger context of Kiberan women of the same age and geographic location within Kibera. It would, I hoped, be like a snapshot of a large group of women, but one which would allow me to zoom in and out and to focus the lens sharply on the specific lives of 20 individuals.

Organization of the Book

This book is comprised of three sections. Part One describes the place and sets the women's diaries within the context of global policies that impact and interact with Kenyan culture and the urban reality of Kibera. Part Two describes the diaries themselves, as texts created by individually situated authors who are negotiating and defining their personal and cultural subjectivity in one of the world's most challenging places. Part Three describes the implications of this study and investigates how readers, regardless of where they are situated, can help create opportunity in Kibera. To that end, an Appendix contains tools for engagement, including recommended films and websites.

The project lasted for seven years. Today, after learning from these women for almost a decade, I have come to realize that their experiences are more representative of the lives of women around the world than are my own. As Audre Lorde (2000) has reminded us, "Most people in the world are yellow, black, brown, poor, female, non-Christian, and do not speak English" (p. 441). Furthermore, an increasing number of these "yellow, black, brown, poor, female" people live in cities and, of those, many in informal settlements like Kibera.

Indeed, the young women I met while doing this book must be perceived as occupying an important and growing segment of the world's population of women, who live in extreme poverty and with few opportunities. Yet they organize, imagine, eke out, and manifest a daily kind of creative agency, through which they become not passive victims of male and societal violence but actors in their own dramas (Pillay, Rishi, & Kulkarni, 2004). They are on the front line of the struggle against gender-based violence and I, in my privileged place of relative safety, am honoured to tell you their stories.

Part One

The Place

Kenya and Gender 1

According to recent reports (UNICEF 2015a, 2015b), the gender gap in education in Kenya has become smaller during the last decade at both the primary and secondary levels of education. Approximately equal numbers of boys and girls are enrolled in primary-level education in Kenya (84.5% for girls and 83.5% for boys), while 48.4% of girls are enrolled in secondary levels, compared to 51.6% of boys. But the gender gap widens egregiously when it comes to the transition from secondary school to university-level education. While 85% of male secondary school graduates go on to study at a college or university, only 38% of women make that transition (IEA, 2007; AFROL, 2008). This lack of higher education means that women are often locked out of the most highly paying jobs in the Kenyan economy, such as those related to technology, engineering, medicine, and finance.

Women also lag behind men in the area of property ownership. Most property in Kenya is male owned. Even marital wealth that is jointly created by a husband and wife "belongs to the man" (IEA, 2007, p. 44) during the marriage and subsequent to it, should it end in divorce or widowhood. In case of divorce, women are not protected by laws that ensure their post-marital economic sustenance or survival. Many women are left destitute after divorce. Similarly, widows often inherit nothing and their in-laws frequently refuse to allow them to remain in their homes or on their husbands' property even after those husbands have died.

Post-marriage destitution is amplified by women's lack of access to credit in Kenya. Although nearly half of Kenyan women currently have access to some form of "informal savings mechanisms and micro-finance" assistance (IEA, 2007, p. 44), this credit often does not "assist women to vertically expand beyond the micro-level" (IEA, 2007, p. 44), in part because women lack managerial skills as well as contacts that would assist them in expanding local businesses to national and international levels. Consequently, most women's businesses remain small and informal (IEA, 2015), enabling women to survive but not to flourish.

Such a web of interconnected social inequalities means that women have a hard time attaining public or political power in Kenya. For example, it is difficult for a woman to run for political office. Socialized gender norms encourage women to remain in the home. Many men scorn and ridicule women who resist these norms. Attaining education or running a small business may not rock the gender boat enough for women to experience retaliation. But running for political office exposes women to social derision and physical danger. In the 2007 general elections, for example, 269 women gained the nomination ballots necessary to run for political office. Of these, only 15 were elected (IEA, 2007, p. 43). Voting patterns, reflecting traditional patriarchal beliefs, consistently favour male candidates. They also leave female candidates vulnerable to public humiliation, insults, threats, and violent retribution for defying the social norms surrounding womanhood. In 2007, many female candidates running for Parliament were publicly heckled, humiliated, and threatened while campaigning for office. One female candidate was killed by a mob at an election rally (IEA, 2007, p. 43). Attempting to wrest even a vestige of political power away from male leaders is dangerous for women in Kenya. The fact that many of them still do so is a tribute to women's deep-seated dedication to social policy change.

The National Gender and Equality Commission (NGEC) is an independent commission established pursuant to Article 59(4) and (5) of the 2010 Constitution of Kenya. The functions of the NGEC are prescribed by the National Gender and Equality Commission Act of 2011: "to coordinate, audit, monitor, facilitate, and advise as relates to the promotion of gender equality, inclusiveness, and protection from discrimination in accordance with the Constitution" (FIDA-K, 2015). Nevertheless, discrimination and harassment of women candidates has continued, but with fewer incidents overall and a greater number of women elected. According to the Federation of Women Lawyers in Kenya (FIDA-K, 2015):

> In advance of the 2013 elections, the NGEC mounted an advocacy campaign across various parts of the country with the objective of promoting women's leadership, including education of the police force that they have a clear, legal and constitutional duty to ensure the safety and protection of women candidates, voters, and campaigners during the electoral process.... However, the pre-election security environment was compromised, due to police inaction in those places where electoral offences were reported. These offences included the use of violence; intimidation; hate speech; language that is threatening, abusive or insulting; and vote buying/bribery. Women candidates that FIDA Kenya spoke to complained of having been victims to at least one of these offences, yet of not having received any effective assistance from the National Police Service.... Compared to previous elections, though, the 2013 elections were marked by fewer incidents of violence against women and violence in general.... Total women elected to national leadership positions in 2013 were: 16 women elected out of 290 constituency Members of National Assembly; 47 women out of the total 47 County Women Representatives; 82 women out of the total 1,450 County Assembly Ward Representatives; 6 women elected out of 47 Deputy Governors; 0 Governors; and 0 Senators. (p. 6)

Although women running for office still face many barriers, their *right* to stand for election without threat or harassment has become an acknowledged social problem.

As do all women around the world, Kenyan women struggle for gender justice using what means they have available, creating interventions from a patchwork of international conventions, national laws, and ongoing advocacy. This chapter will discuss the importance of one international convention (CEDAW), which has undergirded changes in national policy and social norms. It will also explore the need to follow up national policy change with research that evaluates post-intervention social progress. It is only by understanding how and why interventions are successful that the struggle for gender-based justice can continue and the intersections between poverty and policy in Kibera can be understood.

Convention on the Elimination of All Forms of Discrimination against Women (CEDAW)

Policy and advocacy about gender-based violence in Africa had its impetus in 1979, with the adoption of the United Nations Convention on the Elimination of All Forms of Discrimination against Women (CEDAW) by the UN General Assembly. The convention had immediate worldwide impact because it defined what constitutes discrimination against women and set up "an agenda for national action to end such discrimination" (CEDAW, 1979, p. 2). According to the convention, discrimination against women is

> any distinction, exclusion or restriction made on the basis of sex which has the effect or purpose of impairing or nullifying the recognition, enjoyment or exercise by women, irrespective of their marital status, on a basis of equality of men and women, of human rights and fundamental freedoms in the political, economic, social, civil, or any other field. (CEDAW, 1979, p. 2)

Any country that accepts the convention, through a national ratification process, commits itself to codifying a list of measures to end discrimination against women. Those measures include:

> incorporating the principle of equality of men and women in their legal system, abolishing all discriminatory laws, and adopting appropriate ones prohibiting discrimination against women; establishing tribunals and other public institutions to ensure the effective protection of women against discrimination; and ensuring elimination of all acts of discrimination against women by persons, organizations, or enterprises. (CEDAW, 1979, p. 3)

However, acceding to the convention does not necessarily ensure the implementation of its measures. Although nations accepting the convention are legally bound to move toward putting its applications in place, there are no enforcement procedures associated with the convention. Unfortunately, this situation has resulted in the on-paper acceptance of the convention by many countries that have subsequently refused (or been unable) to pass into law legislation that would domesticate the convention's anti-discrimination principles.

As of 2016, 32 African nations have acceded to the convention, although 14 of those have done so on paper only, having implemented no enabling legislation in their parliaments or legislative bodies. Further, two nations—Ethiopia and Mali—have taken a "reservation," indicating they will not comply with the convention's language on female genital mutilation (FGM). But, although there is no enforcement of CEDAW implementation, there is accountability. Each signatory to the convention must submit a national report no less frequently than every four years to the CEDAW advisory committee of the United Nations. This report must delineate what measures, legislation, or policy enactment has (or has not) taken place to implement the convention and must include local, regional, state, and national measures. Thus, CEDAW provides a means by which to ascertain progress, or lack thereof, in all nations that have become parties to the convention. In Kenya, only one piece of legislation, the Sexual Offences Act (2006), has been passed to implement the convention. While CEDAW is not considered of high importance by the Kenyan Parliament, women's advocates, nevertheless, take CEDAW reporting very seriously. Reports on lack of CEDAW implementation by the Federation of Women Lawyers (FIDA-K) and by the Centre for Legislative Information Concerning Kenya (CLICK) are presented not only to the international CEDAW advisory board but also to the Kenyan Parliament, where they serve as educational and advocacy tools for policy development.

Introduction of the Domestic Violence (Family Protection) Act (2000)

In 2000, women's advocacy organizations in Kenya prioritized the drafting of national legislation that would implement CEDAW policy in the area of domestic violence. These first legislative efforts resulted in the drafting of the Domestic Violence (Family Protection) bill in 2000. Representatives of FIDA-K (2007) wrote:

> Although Kenya has ratified the CEDAW convention, it has not domesticated this convention as required.... The result has been that women in particular have not been able to benefit from the convention; as far as the protocols are concerned, non-ratification has meant that Kenyans cannot access some of the mechanisms for seeking remedies at the international forum. Being dissatisfied by the government's apparent lethargic approach, between the years 2000–2002 [*sic*], the women's civil society organizations started to agitate for and to draft gender-friendly laws such as the Domestic Violence (Family Protection) Bill, that would give effect to the provisions of CEDAW. (p. 16)

However, despite the fact that the Domestic Violence (Family Protection) Act was introduced into Kenya's Parliament in 2000, it has not yet been enacted. In fact, it has, since its inception, been the subject of public and parliamentary scorn and derision (Ndung'u, 2006; FIDA-K, 2008). No parliamentary action was taken on the bill until 2007, when it was allowed to come before the full Parliament as a "motion." After debate, the bill was tabled for "future consideration" (FIDA-K, 2007; Kimuna & Djamba, 2008), an action which implies the relegation of the legislation to what amounts to a parliamentary rubbish bin.

The Sexual Offences Act (2006)

In 2004, the Sexual Offences Act (SOA) was introduced in the Kenyan Parliament by a female parliamentarian, Honourable Njoki Ndung'u. The purpose of the legislation was to "address the rising problem of rape and sexual assaults in Kenya" and to "introduce stiffer penalties for offenders" (Ndung'u, 2006). Until that time, legal allusions to *rape* were spread through the Penal Code, the Criminal Procedure Code, the Criminal Amendment Act, and the Evidence Act. Such diffusion of definition and penalty made rape difficult to assess and punish. The SOA united all rape law under one act and redefined rape as a crime which included not only "forced sexual intercourse" between a male and a female (SOA, 2006) but also "male-on-male rape, child pornography, statutory rape, child trafficking, deliberate infection of HIV/AIDS, gang rape, and drug rape" (Ndung'u, 2006). The final version did not, unfortunately, include the criminalization of either domestic violence or marital rape (FIDA-K, 2006). Although references to both domestic abuse and marital rape had been part of the original bill's language, references to both issues were reluctantly removed in January 2006. The bill was passed into law in July 2006, becoming the first gender-related act ever passed in the Kenyan Parliament.

Ongoing Advocacy

The Kenyan Federation of Women Lawyers (FIDA-K), along with other advocacy organizations, has continued to lobby for the Domestic Violence (Family Protection) Act, as well as to educate women about their rights under the Sexual Offences Act. As of 2016, FIDA-K has conducted dozens of workshops on gender-based violence throughout the country. The organization has also published numerous reports, including a police training manual on *Gender and Human Rights*, which attempts to educate police about gender-based violence, including what acts are criminal under Kenyan law, how to enforce the law, and how to handle survivors of gender-based violence. FIDA-K has also published handbooks on *Gender Mainstreaming in Political Parties, Female Genital Mutilation, Women's Land and Property Rights*, and four critical and extensively researched monographs on women's participation in political parties in Kenya (FIDA-K, 2016).

Relationship among Research, Advocacy, and Policy

Policy advocates cite one reason for the difficulty of implementing gender-related legislation in Kenya. Although Kenya acceded to the CEDAW convention in 1984, no research or data on gender-related issues existed that could be utilized for policy formulation. Frustrated policy advocates began demanding not only policy itself but the data that would make policy possible (FIDA-K, 1998, 1999, 2001). Those data were particularly lacking in regard to informal settlements. In 2002, the African Population and Health Research Center (APHRC) secured funding to conduct a survey to assess the "health and livelihood needs of residents of informal settlements in Nairobi," and, by so doing, quantified for the first time many factors that relate to gender-based violence there. The study discussed poverty and made the link between income level and domestic violence (APHRC, 2002). For example, the authors commented that "slum dwellers contend that the little and unreliable income, and the difficult living conditions limit their access to basic services, thereby exposing them to a variety of problems, such as illnesses, domestic violence and diseases" (APHRC, 2002, p. 9). The report cites one interview with a wife and mother in the slum, who said, "It (domestic violence) is mostly due to the husband not having a job and the result is lack of food in the house and so the wife blames the husband because he is supposed to provide food but he is unable and that is where the fight begins" (APHRC, 2002, p. 9).

In 2003, the Kenya Demographic and Health Survey (KDHS, 2003), a general population census conducted nationally every five years, became the first survey instrument on the continent of Africa to include a module on domestic violence. The survey also streamlined and expanded data collection in other areas vital to women, such as rape, reproduction, nursing, and women's health. The KDHS (2003) made domestic violence and other women's issues visible and measurable for the first time. However, although advocates cited the APHRC (2002) survey as making important contributions to the passage of the first gender-related legislation in Kenyan history and the integration of gender concerns into the machinery of the Kenyan government, the KDHS (2003) domestic violence module seemed to have little positive effect on advocates' ability to lobby for domestic violence or marital rape language in the SOA (2006). The data were not convincing to parliamentarians.

In 2006, the United Nations released the results of a survey entitled *Violence to Women and Girls in the Era of HIV and AIDS: A Situation and Response Analysis in Kenya* (UN-AIDS, 2006), which reported that 49% of Kenyan women experienced intimate partner violence in their lifetime and 83% experienced some form of sexual abuse during childhood (UN-AIDS, 2006). The purpose of the study was to "mainstream" the understanding of gender violence and to make data available for policy makers about the important link between gender-based violence and the spread of HIV/AIDS. The study also paid specific attention to domestic violence, saying:

> In many Kenyan cultures, husbands are deemed justified in beating their wives and marriage is considered blanket consent to intercourse. These

> cultural conditions are so ingrained that two out of three women agree that a husband is justified in beating his wife. Tragically, no law exists on preventing domestic violence in Kenya and abused wives have no viable means of recourse. Wives also have no guarantee of protection from rape by their husbands, as there is no law prohibiting spousal rape. (UN-AIDS, 2006, p. 2)

The results of the UN-AIDS report were released in June 2006. The report appears to have had a significant effect on policy. The Sexual Offences Act was enacted the following month (July 14, 2006), becoming, as discussed above, the first and, so far, the only gender-related law in Kenya.

Research and Policy Enactment

Research, in the form of country-specific surveys and multinational comparisons, is vital for policy implementation in Kenya. Such research externalizes the problem of domestic violence, which is often hidden due to cultural stigma attached to the reporting of domestic abuse (Amnesty International, 2016). Without research, it is impossible to point to the prevalence, extent, or public impact of domestic violence and other forms of gender-based abuse. Kimuna and Djamba (2008) remark:

> There is a lack of information on accurate estimates of the magnitude of physical and sexual violence against women in Kenya due largely to violence being unreported; and in most cases, those reported are not recorded by authorities.... Also because of the stigma attached to sexual abuse in many Kenyan cultures, women blame themselves and fear that they will be ostracized from society if they admit to being sexually abused. Thus, they continue to suffer in silence. (p. 341)

The analysis and interpretation of already-existing data are also imperative. Policy makers are often disinclined to devote staff time to the sifting of particular statistics from masses of data. Nor are they able to apply statistical programs to the interpretation of these data.

Academic researchers using available data sets are, therefore, crucial to providing information for both advocacy and policy-making. For example, Mugisha and Zulu (2004) interpreted statistics from the APHRC (2002) survey on the health and livelihood needs of residents of Nairobi slums. Their study showed the positive correlation between substance use and rape, as well as a connection between gender-based violence and the spread of HIV/AIDS. The paper also heightened the call for more research, which was carried out in 2006 by the United Nation's Commission on AIDS.

Other scholars' analyses of data from the KDHS (2003, 2008, 2014) surveys have likewise been important. For example, Lawoko (2008) used these data to predict attitudes toward intimate partner violence (IPV) in cross-cultural situations. The study recommended the construction of "need adapted interventions tailored to fit" particular cultural contexts (Lawoko, 2008, p. 1056). Kimuna and Djamba (2008) also used the KDHS (2003) survey to interpret the correlates of physical and sexual wife abuse in Kenya. Results of the analysis indicated that 40% of married women had experienced some kind of IPV in their lifetime. Multivariate analyses revealed that income level, religion, alcohol use, and type of employment "significantly increased the wife's risk of physical and sexual abuse" (Kimuna & Djamba, 2008, p. 333).

Post-Implementation Research and Surveys Needed

Baseline research and the secondary interpretation of those data are vital to policy-making activities. But *post-implementation* research is also needed to monitor the mechanics of administration and service provision of the Sexual Offences Act (SOA). Recent journalistic reports have shown that women attempting to report sexual assaults have sometimes suffered from a subsequent sexual assault at the police station itself (FIDA-K, 2008). Others have been required to pay police officers to ensure that their case will be officially reported (Human Rights Watch, 2003). Consequently, a second level of research is necessary, which can analytically evaluate the effect of policy implementation and provide documentation of its failure. FIDA-K, for example, has attempted to assemble statistics on the lack of service provision for women reporting rapes. However, because FIDA-K is a non-governmental organization (NGO) operating on a very small budget, its efforts do not provide national figures in this area. Advocacy organizations have appealed to the World Health Organization (WHO) and the African Population and Health Research Center (APHRC), whose budgets may permit them greater scope to conduct such post-implementation studies.

Poverty Is Sexist

According to the World Bank (2015), extreme or subsistence poverty is defined as living on $1.25/day or less. Most residents in the areas of Kibera where the diarists reside fit this category, which means that each day is a struggle to earn just enough to eat and drink, while saving to pay the monthly rent. It is an arduous life and one that is continually challenged by the vicissitudes of the global market, from which Kiberans suffer but over which they have little control or participatory involvement. But it is more difficult for women than for men. To see why, it is important to look at the whole labour and informal economy in Kibera.

People who live in Kibera, for example, are among the hardest hit by any crisis in the world's food prices, yet they receive far less humanitarian attention than other demographic groups, in part because no municipal agency takes responsibility for informal settlements. Alun McDonald, regional media and communications officer for Oxfam, remarked that

> while there are also very serious food crises elsewhere in Kenya—for example, in the north country, they at least get some attention from governments and donors, whereas the crisis in the cities is often completely forgotten or ignored.... In Kibera, alone, there are over 5,000 children under five years old who are suffering from malnutrition—more than 1,000 of them suffering from severe cases. Severe child malnutrition should not be happening in a modern capital city. (IRIN, 2009)

Food insecurity in Kibera is exacerbated by drought, rising food and non-food prices, and poor harvests. During recent years, and especially during the food crisis of 2008, essential foods such as maize more than doubled in price, while oils and vegetables also became much more expensive than they had ever been. This sudden and dramatic rise in cost of food essentials left residents of Kibera not only surprised but relatively helpless to cope with rising prices with no concomitant rise in income. According to the UN World Food Program (UNWFP), for example, the price of maize rose as much as 130% in Nairobi during 2009. Cooking fuel prices rose between 30 and 50% and the cost of water rose by 90–155% during that same time period (IRIN, 2009). Thus, Kiberan residents experienced a double crisis. Not only was food more expensive but the water needed to wash and cook the food was almost completely unattainable. What water could be afforded had to be used for drinking, with cooking becoming a secondary necessity. Water is often used for more than one purpose, recycled from cooking to bathing to cleaning. Children using dirty water to wash and to drink get sick more easily. Cholera and typhoid are common in the slum. According to McDonald, it is increasingly expensive just to survive in Kibera (IRIN, 2009). Gabrielle Menezes, UNWFP information officer, remarked that fluctuating food prices will continue to affect the Kiberan population and dire crises will continue. Urban slum dwellers, who do not grow their own food, are completely dependent on the market. In 2010, the Kenya Food Security Steering Group called for food price controls, provision of food aid, and the creation of employment opportunities, particularly for those who go without food for extended periods of time. Little improvement, however, has been seen in Kibera.

Living on a Dollar a Day

People living in the Global North have difficulty imagining what life on a dollar a day might be like. We associate that kind of income with begging, with homelessness, or with some personal disorder or difficulty that prevents participation in full-time labour. But that assumption reflects our naivety and privilege. Many people who live on a dollar a day in the Global South are also working all day to produce that dollar. Whether they work in the formal or the informal economy, earning that dollar is difficult and it is more difficult for women than for men.

It is important to distinguish between informal settlements like Kibera (slums that are not recognized or provided services by the municipality in which they are located) and the informal economy. The latter refers to economic activities that are small scale and usually operate without licences or conformity to local business regulations. The informal economy is the economy of the poor. Not surprisingly, most people in Kibera are employed in the informal sector and there is great diversity in type of employment. Informal jobs include selling food on the street, styling hair, washing car windows in traffic, doing errands, and carrying products from one location to another. Many of these jobs are not regular and can only be performed when there is need for the service being provided and when someone is able to pay for that service. Often in Kibera, people are willing to work in the informal sector but there are few buyers able to pay for the services they might provide.

The principal characteristics of the informal economy are (1) there are few barriers to entry, and licensing and skill requirements are low; (2) there is little or no training requirement because most entrepreneurs have learned their skill through a familial or personal connection; (3) few entrepreneurs in this sector have access to formal credit, so capital needs are met through informal loans from family or friends; and (4) few entrepreneurs can afford licences or taxes and operate outside the official rules and business regulations of the city. Informal self-employment is growing in Kibera, as well as in Nairobi itself, at a rate of 40–60% annually (Alder, 1995). At least one-third of all households in Kibera are engaged in the informal labour sector, but that labour is gendered and pays more to men than to women.

The predominately male sub-sector of the informal economy is occupied by what is known as *jua kali*. These jua kali jobs are ones that produce a product or, more typically, render a service. Jua kali jobs are usually occupied by men and are considered inappropriate for women due to the cultural norm that women's work is associated with the household or with occupations where women can stay close to children. Predictably, these efforts pay less than jua kali work, resulting in less money for women who work the same long hours as men. Alder (1995) describes jua kali employment:

> The informal "productive" sub-sector, often known as *jua kali*, plays a significant economic role in the city. It is involved in manufacturing, repair and providing services. Trades include welders, metal workers, mechanics, carpenters, and construction workers. The *jua kali* generate significant value-added and provide goods and services both to residents of informal settlements and to residents of "formal" housing areas. For example, construction workers who began by building housing in informal settlements have graduated to providing construction services to all housing areas. Again, many vehicle owners go to *jua kali* mechanics based in informal settlements. There are, therefore, economic linkages between informal settlements and other areas of Nairobi and between small businesses in informal settlements and formal business and commerce. (p. 101)

Informal retailing, often called hawking, is the woman-dominated part of the informal economy, with about 70% of hawkers in Kibera being women. Hawking includes trade in local goods and services, often in perishable goods or items that are needed daily, like cooking oil, vegetables, fuel, or water. Thus, hawkers who sell food and the means to cook it (oil, charcoal) are assured of a continually returning (although low-paying) clientele.

Alder (1995) describes the informal marketplace in Kibera:

> Most of the participants trade in perishable goods, i.e. vegetables and fruit as well as sweets, cigarettes, charcoal, cooked food, fish, meat and soft drinks. Hawking is largely a response to a harsh urban socio-economic environment. Many of the participants are [female] household heads with no other source of employment, formal or informal. One study found that over half of the hawkers are under 32 years old and another 30 per cent are aged between 33 and 40. Over half are married women. Hawking, therefore, plays a central economic role in a significant number of households.... This sub-sector operates on a subsistence basis. (p. 101)

Most of the diarists worked at hawking at one time or another during the course of this project, many alone but some with mothers, sisters, or friends. It is arduous labour with little return. Cara wrote:

> I made food in the form of *mandazi* [doughnuts] and it took me much time to make them because I took pride in how they were and wanted them to be perfect. I then carried them to an area where there are many kiosks with people selling many kinds of things. I did not have my own kiosk so I asked a lady if I could sit beside her kiosk and she gave me a box to spread my wares. I also gave her some mandazi for herself and to thank her. I sat several hours but had not sold many and so I abandoned my spot and I walked with my food. Everyone who went by I would show and ask if they would like to buy. I was very tired when I came home but I had sold almost all my mandazi. The ones I did not sell is what we ate for our evening meal. (Cara, May 2009)

The gendered division of labour works against women in two ways. First, hawking jobs pay less—sometimes only about $10/month—than jua kali jobs. They also confine women to work that is inside the slum and close to the home.

Men working jua kali, on the other hand, not only get paid more but also have the opportunity to create social capital. They make friends and potential business contacts, who can sometimes help them move from the informal sector to the formal sector, that is, to better-paying jobs that are licensed and provide credentials and the possibility of upward mobility. Alder (1995) remarks:

> Female headed households almost always earn less than their male counterparts. This disparity can be explained by the fact that males have a better chance of obtaining employment as unskilled labourers, construction workers, watchmen, and so forth. Women are also constrained by the fact that they have to take care of young children and are, therefore, confined to income-generating activities that can be carried out close to the home … [such as] petty commodity trade. (p. 102)

What Alder does not discuss is that women are also constrained by social norms, which define what work is suitable for women and what is suitable for men. Diarists who questioned these socially constructed norms were ridiculed or scorned. For example, Marya wrote:

> I envy my brother who works with automobiles. I love cars and I watch videos about cars like *Fast and Furious* and other ones. I tell him I could work with him in a garage because I can learn how to do what he does, fixing cars. I know this is true because one time I watch him for a while as he worked and I saw very many things—motor and carburetor. I have a good liking for this. But he says no and my friends laugh and say, "Are you going to become a man now? Who will you marry?" Then they all laugh so I do not bring up this idea anymore. But inside me, I know it is a good idea and I could become richer than I am now. (Marya, November 2011)

Needless to say, Marya has not become a mechanic (at least not yet). Nevertheless, within the constraints of this gendered division of labour, women use their wits and their agency to eke out a living for themselves and their children, with incredible determination and drive. One widow, Wilbroda Wandera, who lived in Kibera with her 10 children, has remarked:

> I have sold mandazi (donuts) and worked as a cleaner at the Catholic church nearby. One time, I got lucky when the local chief allowed me to build a kiosk near the road; I used the front part as a salon, where I plaited people's hair and lived in the back with my children. However, this was demolished in 2007 to pave way for the Kibera slum upgrading program. Now I live near the river, where I have built a mud structure. We mostly live on one meal a day. This is hard, especially on the children. I have learnt to make meals for the whole family even when I only have 40 shillings (about .49 US). With this, I will buy maize flour for 20 shillings, sugar for five, paraffin for ten, a lemon for two and water for three shillings. This will make a pot of porridge and everyone can get a cup. That takes us to the next day. (IRIN, 2010)

Indeed, for many women in Kibera, working all day provides only short-term gain. It gets them to the next day, when they must again work all day to take one step forward. But women like Cara are always thinking, creating, inventing, and innovating new ways to create strategies to cope with subsistence poverty. They make and carry out, in Cara's words, good plans for themselves and for their children.

An example of the creativity and enterprise shown by many Kibera residents is the fact that many people have gone into business serving the hawkers. Nine of the twenty diarists at one time or another worked as an assistant to a hawker. Others had the bright idea that hawkers, too, get hungry and tired. So they peddled food at lunchtime to the hawkers' stalls, hoping to create an informal business by serving the informal business people. Cara explained:

> My experience with mandazi gave me the idea that ladies at kiosks are hungry. Sometimes they are selling charcoal or oil or plastic utensils, not something they can eat. So I decide to work in my house till lunchtime and then carry my wares to the kiosks and invite them to buy my lovely food for their lunch. This has worked well for me and it has saved me time because I do not sit all day and wait. I offer food at a time when it is wanted and expected. I have made a good plan for myself. (Cara, May 2009)

"Poorness Forces Me to Do So"

But sometimes wit, determination, and pluck are not enough, especially for young women with few friends and no social capital. For these women, there is an area below the informal sector that offers money on an emergency basis and includes engagement in a practice called survival sex. Survival sex is the selling of sex for enough money to provide food, water, or shelter for oneself and one's children. Literally, it is selling sex for the means to survive. All of the diarists but one have written about using survival sex as a form of employment. Women are quick to distinguish survival sex from conventional prostitution, which is usually considered to imply a professionalization of the trade in sex by acquiring a pimp or by working at bars or clubs where prostitution is a routine transaction. Survival sex, on the other hand, refers to selling sex on a one-off basis—resorting to selling one's body only when it is a matter of life or death. Each of the diarists who used survival sex to gain money asserted that she is "not a prostitute" and one remarked that she did not freely choose to sell her body but that "poorness forces me to do so" (Marya, May 2010).

One American visitor to Kibera, shocked to learn how many young girls had to sell sex to survive, wrote:

> With the crowded and desperate circumstances of slum life, women are sometimes forced to exchange sex for shelter, food, or clothing. There is a population of teenage girls in Kibera who are forced into the sex trade just to pay for basic essentials. (Ferraro, 2014)

The essentials to which she refers, in addition to food, water, and shelter, often include things like underwear and sanitary napkins, both of which are difficult to acquire and expensive in Kibera. Survival sex is largely condoned and sometimes even respected in the slum because it is understood that a woman has no other choice than to exchange her body for enough food and water to survive. One diarist wrote:

> My parents cannot pay for me and, although my needs are not great, I must eat and I must drink. Sometimes I beg on the street and get nothing or just a little and so by the end of the day, I am tired and hungry and I look for a boy who may have some money. If I find one who will give me 100 shillings or 150, we have sex and then I go and eat and I drink water and then I rest. Then I make a plan for the next day, to rise early and find some work that will give me money. I would rather find work than find a boy but sometimes God provides only the latter. (Cathy M., May 2012)

Gender and Education

In Kenya and particularly in Kibera, this subsistence poverty in the lives of women is both the cause and the consequence of gender inequality in education. In Kenya as a whole, the gender gap at the primary level has closed, with 84.5% enrollment for girls compared to 83.5% for boys (UNICEF, 2015a). However, the relationship between male and female enrollment widens at the secondary level, where 51.6% of enrolled students are male and 48.4% are female. UNICEF reports that the greatest gender disparity exists among the poorest quintile group of Kenya, with attendance rates being 33.1% and 25% for males and females respectively (UNICEF, 2015a). In Kibera, where exact figures are not known, experts estimate that 43% of school-age girls, as compared to only 29% of boys, are currently not attending school. Of those girls who do attend primary school, about 49% of school-age girls have been held back and have not begun school at an appropriate age so that they can work in the home or assist parents in jobs in the informal sector (Population Council, 2015). This inequality in educational opportunity leads to employment inequality later in life and to lives spent in a subsistence informal economy.

In Kibera, the level of female illiteracy is extremely high in comparison to males and experts estimate that at least 60% more girls are illiterate than are boys in Kibera (UNICEF, 2015a). Because education even at the primary level is expensive—with families footing the bill for tuition, books, and uniforms—parents prioritize sending boys to school. Girls often stay home and work so that their brothers may attend school instead. Girls assist mothers with childcare of younger siblings, with water collection, with cooking, and with labour outside the home. Boys are given educational priority, with families often holding a daughter back from school in order that limited funds may be used to educate male children (Inter-Press Service, 2015).

The anguish this education gap causes many girls is reflected in Ina's journal. She remarked:

> I did not go to primary school enough to learn things I need. My brother he went and I would stay home on days when there was work to be done, like carry and retrieve water or like laundry or to help my mother sell food.

> Never did my brother stay home for these things but only me. I would look at his books when he came back and think I want to see and know. But it was not meant for me to have that learning because boys come first in my family. Even when my brother was beating me or worse, no one would say to him "stop." I was to take his clothes and wash and prepare them for school. I got to go to school myself only if there was not labour for me instead. He went secondary, too, and no one in my house ever imagined that thing for me. It was not a thought in anyone's mind but mine, that grand idea of secondary school. (Ina, November 2008)

Without an education to fall back on, many young women fall back on men for money and are forced into early marriages or relationships that produce children outside of marriage. In either case, they become stuck for the rest of their lives supporting and caring for a family, spending all energy just to obtain food, clothing, and shelter (Inter-Press Service, 2015).

Women in Kibera, as in many other parts of the world, do double duty—caring for their own homes and families, while also hiring themselves out to others. An example of the double duty to supplement male earnings is provided by Judy, who wrote:

> If only I had gotten more school. My husband sometimes finds work on the roadway and sometimes he finds work in building construction. Other times, he goes through refuse piles, looking for things he can sell. Other times, he finds no work at all. Then he is often feeling low and without his head held high. And then he will sometimes go to a bar and drink with a friend or even alone. What happens then is that he comes home at night and has nothing. So we do not eat and maybe just have tea. This means that the next day I must hustle myself and think of something that can be done. So I ask to do laundry for neighbours. Or I wash the shoes and uniforms of a school football [soccer] team. From that money, I buy food for us and then I make sure some is left to sell. We eat a little and I sell the rest on the street. If I could have obtained more school, even secondary, I could help more to create funds or a business. (Judy, November 2009)

Women who do not marry are equally burdened by a lack of formal schooling. Without a husband to provide partial household income, women face a life of hand-to-mouth living in low-earning jobs, mostly in the informal sector. Since many of these jobs do not yield enough to pay monthly rent and cover expenses, unmarried women often depend on maintaining a sexual relationship with a man in order to glean whatever small change and economic help he will give. Betta wrote about the disempowerment of economic inequality and dependence:

> I work hard. I do laundry and I clean houses and sometimes I sell food when I have the time to make it. I work all day and still I am often hungry and, worse than that, I cannot pay the rent. I then must depend on my boyfriend to lend me or give me small change so that I have a roof over my head. For my need, I must do what he says and sometimes he is cruel. Because I am strong in my body I wonder why I cannot drive a taxi or work on the roads like my boyfriend sometimes does. But when I ask about maybe attend driving school everyone laughs. And when I say I will work in the sun like a day labourer, they say this girl is crazy and I think they will do me harm if I try. (Betta, June 2010)

Gender and Politics

Indeed, Kibera is a difficult place for young women who constantly struggle against the weight of extreme poverty. Every day, they make strategic choices that determine whether they will live or die. New projects are needed that will create opportunities for women like Cathy M., who have the strength and determination to put those opportunities into action. And changes must be made on the macro level that ensure women's input into Kenya's policy decisions for the future. With the passage of a new constitution in 2010, the hope for change took a step toward realization. The Constitution of Kenya (2010) aims to include women in macro-level policy-making by implementing a rule that "not more than two-thirds of the members of elective or appointive bodies shall be of the same gender" (Constitution of Kenya, 2010). Opponents raised objections that implementation of this idea was unrealistic for several reasons, one of which was that it was too expensive because it would increase the size of Parliament by reserving seats for women. In a comprehensive and far-reaching report, the Institute for

Economic Affairs (IEA) published a report that rebutted the economic argument and sought to

> promote informed discussion and debate on one of the most important gender issues of our time and among the most significant of the Uhuru Kenyatta administration, as the first government elected under the Constitution of Kenya 2010. Kenya has an ambitious vision that is contained in the national development blue print Vision 2030 [see Appendix]. This guiding document seeks to create a globally competitive and prosperous nation with a high quality of life by 2030. It is impossible to realize this laudable national vision without fully including the majority of the population in representation and public leadership and decision making positions. Gender equality is not just a Constitutional requirement, it is an economic imperative for any country seeking to compete globally. As part of the broader constitutionally mandated changes to the governance framework, it is also a prerequisite to the realization of Vision 2030....
>
> There are changes that are by their nature incremental, progressive if you will, but even incremental change has a tipping point. At a time when it can be said "this is who we were" and "this is who we are," Kenya is faced [with] just such a decision....
>
> This is an historic time and we are privileged to be a part of it. Kenyans will witness the audacity of visionary leaders who will dare to urge us forward and who understand that the present and future of successful nations demand adherence to certain basic principles, fidelity to the Constitution, integrity, equality and the rule of law. (IEA, 2015, p. ii)

The report concludes that reserving seats for women would be neither expensive nor without precedent and would cost Kenyan taxpayers only a few shillings per year:

> Reserved seats are an effective way to increase the meaningful participation of women in national legislatures, politics and decision-making. The experiences of Uganda, Rwanda and Denmark demonstrate a clear process of which the extremes are quite distinct. In Uganda, the reservation of seats for women ensures their participation in high numbers through

> affirmative action. The same is true in Rwanda, where a longer period and more deliberate action toward inclusion of women in politics has influenced women's participation outside of reserved seats. Women parliamentarians elected to seats that are also open to men now outnumber those in affirmative action seats reserved for women alone. In Denmark, efforts to correct the historical marginalization of women in politics are now decades old and affirmative action in the form of reserved seats is no longer necessary. That is the journey that Kenya must begin. (IEA, 2015, p. 34)

Nevertheless, the journey has not begun promptly. As the Institute for Education in Democracy (IED) reported,

> The Supreme Court of Kenya on 11th December, 2012 held that gender equity as an affirmative action right for women is progressive in nature and not an immediate realization. The Court gave Parliament up to August 27, 2015 to come up with legislation on how the one-third gender rule will be met in the 2017 General Election. While this decision helped avoid a constitutional crisis, it removed the pressure from political parties to search for and nominate female candidates. The decision of the Supreme Court effectively postponed the implementation of the gender quota, as well as the failure of the outgoing Parliament to pass appropriate legislation before elections. (IED, 2015)

While public and political debate continues on women's role in macro policy in Kenya, women in Kibera like Judy and Cathy M. use their individual agency to take for themselves the power that the Kenyan Parliament will not easily cede. Said Judy, "I am determined that my daughter will have a life different from my own" (Judy, February 2014). With or without the cooperation of Parliament, I believe Judy's child will thrive.

2
Kibera in the 21st Century

A large and growing proportion of Kenya's population is concentrated in the province and city of Nairobi, in which more than two million people currently reside. Nairobi contains 16 major slums within its city limits. Others are part of the city's urban sprawl but are *not* considered part of the city proper. Kibera is one of the former, a burgeoning informal settlement close to the city centre.

This chapter will first look at the growth of the "postmodern slum" globally in order to understand the situation in Kibera. It will then move to a discussion of the history and geography of Kibera to give context to the diary project. After an examination of the dangers of life in Kibera for women and girls, in particular rape and intimate partner violence, the chapter will look at some of the recent innovative projects that are occurring in Kibera that have the potential to improve safety, quality of living, and education for women and girls in Kibera.

The Growth of the "Postmodern Slum"

Mike Davis (2006) has described the rapid and voracious urbanization of the planet:

> The earth has urbanized even faster than originally predicted by the Club of Rome in its notoriously Malthusian 1972 report *Limits of Growth.* In 1950, there were 86 cities in the world with a population of more than one million; today there are 400, and by 2015 there will be at least 550. Cities, indeed, have absorbed nearly two-thirds of the global population explosion since 1950, and are currently growing by a million babies and migrants each week. The global countryside, meanwhile, has reached its maximum population and will begin to shrink after 2020. As a result, cities will account for virtually *all* future world population growth, which is expected to peak at about 10 billion in 2050. Ninety-five percent of this final build-out of humanity will occur in the urban areas of developing countries. (pp. 1–2)

Such burgeoning urban growth has given rise to the term *mega-city.* Mexico City tops the list of mega-cities in the developing world, with a population of 22.1 million, closely followed by Sao Paulo, Mumbai, and Delhi. But a city doesn't have to be a mega-city to have a mega-slum in it or attached to it. In fact, slum growth everywhere in the Global South has outpaced urbanization per se. Davis (2006) explains that

> in the Amazon, one of the world's fastest-growing urban frontiers, 80 percent of city growth has been in the shantytowns largely unserved by established utilities and municipal transport, thus making "urbanization" and "favelization" synonymous.... The African situation, of course, is even more extreme. Africa's slums are growing at twice the speed of the continent's exploding cities. Indeed, an incredible 85% of Kenya's population growth between 1989 and 1999 was absorbed into the fetid, densely packed slums of Nairobi and Mombasa. (pp. 17–18)

Kibera is a mega-slum, whose booming population can be attributed not only to a high birth rate but also to such factors as rural droughts, climate change, ethnic conflict, and wars in bordering countries that create refugee populations. Whatever the cause of migration, though, settlers often find there is no going "back." In fact, informants participating in the current study have written that they or their families have tried to go "home" to rural areas, only to find the land being overtaken by large farms or other concerns, newly built dams have dried up rivers, or the weather is no longer favourable to farming and cultivation. Such families are forced back to Kibera, seeking sustenance in urban squalor. Unfortunately, Kibera is illustrative of what Davis (2006) describes as the urban trend for the next millennium:

> Thus, the cities of the future, rather than being made out of glass and steel as envisioned by earlier generations of urbanists, are instead largely constructed out of crude brick, straw, recycled plastic, cement blocks, and scrap wood. Instead of cities of light soaring toward heaven, much of the twenty-first century urban world squats in squalor, surrounded by pollution, excrement, and decay. (pp. 18–19)

History

Kibera has a fascinating and complex history. Although it is located only about four miles from the city-centre of Nairobi, it stands in stark historical and demographic contrast to the city itself. This shanty-city-within-a-city is bordered by the Royal Golf Course on the northeast and the Ngong Forest on the southwest, with the Nairobi River forming a meandering southern border. Although those borders are porous, crossing them means crossing a complex historical intersection of colonialism and corruption. Indeed, the founding of Kibera has its very roots in colonialism and the complexities of domination. When Kenya was still a British colony, British officials gave the land that is now Kibera to former Nubian soldiers (name deriving from the Nubian word *kibra*, meaning "forest"), who had served the Crown in World War I. At that time, it was a forested area outside the city proper and was informal "unclaimed" land. The Nubian soldiers were not native Kenyans and, therefore, could not be settled into the "Native

Reserves" of the early 20th century, and Kibera was deemed an appropriate award for their services. Nearly 300 Sudanese were the original settlers in Kibera, receiving residency permits there as an unofficial pension for 12 years of service in the King's African Rifles (KAR). The British soon regretted this decision, as living conditions decreased and crime increased in Kibera, and one official wrote that the area was "too valuable and too near European settlement to be left to Africans" (Parsons, 1997, p. 91). In 1919, a brief but unworkable plan to relocate Kiberans was scrapped due to the huge expense the undertaking would be. The KAR announced that no more residency permits would be given. At the same time, they washed their hands of the area and in 1928 they handed over authority to the civil administration (Parsons, 1997), which tried to ensure that new settlers were related to original permit holders, but that proved difficult as settlers continued to pour in.

Meanwhile, the former KAR soldiers began using their land permits as unofficial permission to rent the land to even more settlers (Parsons, 1997). By the 1930s, the British were bent on demolishing Kibera but every plan they came up with was either logistically impossible or too expensive (Wangui & Darkoh, 1992; Parsons, 1997). The situation was further complicated by the fact that British officials were loyal to the old Nubian soldiers but had no such similar feelings for the new residents, about whom they remarked, "The second generation of hybrids arising from mixed unions are degenerate" (van Zwanenberg, 1972, p. 190). Thus, the colonial administration fell back on two plans, one short term and one long term and neither benign.

The first plan was what one recent writer has called "malicious neglect," through which the British government refused to provide services, saying that to do so would only encourage more settlers. They hoped that living conditions would become so unlivable that Kibera residents would voluntarily resettle. The back-up plan, as the British saw it, was that the original KAR soldiers would eventually die, at which time the British colonial administration would reclaim the land. But both of these plans took a back burner by the 1950s, as the British turned their attention to the looming possibility of Kenyan independence (Parsons, 1997). And as independence became more and more a reality, many new migrants, particularly from Western Kenya, came to Kibera, while the original Sudanese made a desperate final-inning bid for permanent land rights and failed. On the eve of independence, the colonial government declared the land comprising Kibera to be "state property," thereby passing the problems of its future onto the nascent Kenyan government (Clark, 1972).

After independence in 1964, Nairobi's population exploded. The new Kenyan leaders regarded Kibera in roughly the same way the British had done, vacillating between attempts to demolish it while, simultaneously, hoping that the withholding of municipal services would force people to go elsewhere (K'Akumu & Olima, 2007; Syagga & Kiamba, 1992). These failures at policy had no more success for the newly independent Kenyans than they had had for the British, and the number of Kibera residents increased from about 3,000 in 1960 to an estimated 17,000 by 1968 (Amis, 1988; Temple, 1974). With such overwhelming numbers of settlers flooding into Kibera, the government abandoned hopes to clear or demolish it. Furthermore, settlers in Kibera could no longer officially be considered squatters because they were paying rent for the structures in which they lived to Sudanese or (an increasing number of) Kikuyu landlords, even though the housing was considered "temporary." The government's next plan probably laid the groundwork for a no-holds-barred population increase in Kibera: the government announced it would offer permits to build in Kibera, thinking that this would allow the government to demolish any non-permitted structures. But this new possibility of a rental economy burgeoned (with most permits going to Kikuyus, but with Sudanese also participating in this potential for income dividends). As a result, Kibera "filled up very fast" (de Smedt, 2009, p. 218).

This potential "real estate bonanza" (Amis, 1984) resulted in permit-holding landlords constructing low-cost, one-room homes with cheap, temporary materials—wood, sheet metal, and mud. Poor Kenyans from rural areas streamed into Kibera, especially during the 1960s and 1970s. This encouraged landlords to rent smaller and smaller dwellings at higher and higher prices and to use cheaper and cheaper materials. After all, no one wanted to invest in housing that might in the future be threatened by government demolition. Consequently, the slum has become progressively degraded with hundreds of thousands of cheap one-room houses lying virtually one on top of the other. And it has never had municipal services—no electricity, running water, garbage removal, or sanitation. Today, the population continues to rise and most social services (clinics, schools) are supplied by national and international NGOs (Mutisya & Yarime, 2011).

Today, Kibera is really a city of its own within the boundaries of Nairobi but with mountain-high piles of garbage, streams of open sewage, and other egregious consequences of the long-term denial of municipal services. The overwhelming aura of Kibera, though, is one of a bustling informal economy within an overarching situation of extreme poverty. Unpaved paths upon which it is difficult to keep one's footing wind through Kibera, revealing discos and barbershops and churches and mosques and women selling food on nighttime streets. There are chickens and children and an overwhelming crush of shoulder-to-shoulder people everywhere. In Kibera, noise, chaos, music, colour, fear, and hope exist all at once and in a swirl of disorder and drive where families live in subsistence poverty, on less than a dollar a day.

Geography

Kibera is located along the southwestern edge of Nairobi and its southern border is bounded by the Nairobi River, which flows into the Nairobi Dam (see map 2). On the north, it is bounded by the Mbgathi Highway and by the upscale Royal Nairobi Golf Course. The Uganda Railroad runs through the centre of the slum, adding to the pollution and noise of the settlement. Because residents' shacks are built up to and almost touching the railroad track, train accidents and car derailments are disastrous, with derailed train cars sometimes crushing Kibera residents in their shacks (*Daily Nation*, 2009). Because of the slum's river-basin location, it is frequently flooded, especially during the rainy season. Being in a valley also means that paths and alleys through the slum are often on steep inclines, causing mudslides and making paths treacherous for pedestrians. In fact, water pours right into and through Kiberan "houses" when it rains. One resident has remarked, "When it rains, no one sleeps in Kibera. Everyone must stand up for the night, leaning against the wall with his possessions, especially his mattress, beside him" (Simon L., personal communication, December 2009).

The borders of Kibera's villages are indistinct and permeable. The 12 villages include (from west to east) Kianda, Soweto West, Raila, Gatwekera, Kisumi Ndogo, Makina, Kamdi Muru, Mashimoni, Laini Saba, Lindi, Silanga, and Soweto East (see map 4). Ethnicity in Kibera is not tied to villages and, in fact, the population of

Kibera is extremely diverse. Although some ethnic enclaves do exist in Kibera—Mashimoni holds the largest Muslim and Nubian populations, for example, and Laini Saba is almost exclusively Kikuyu—the population of the slum is not for the most part ethnically stratified. Instead, it is remarkably fluid in terms of ethnicity and religion. Because Kibera experienced ethnic violence in 2007–2008, however, some of the current study's informants have reported that residents are intentionally moving to areas of the slum where their particular ethnicity is dominant. Luos, the other most prevalent tribe in Kibera, are situating themselves in Luo-dominated areas. Such intentional relocation within the slum may produce a degree of ethnic and tribal stratification that has not heretofore existed in Kibera.

Kibera also "shows surprising heterogeneity" from village to village in terms of population density, belying some experts' allegations of the homogeneous "cattle feedlot" crowding from one end of Kibera to another (Davis, 2006). One study (Desgroppes & Taupin, 2012), for example, conducted through a combination of geographic information systems (GIS) and ground survey, concluded that

> Kambi Muru and Laini Saba have a density of 48,000 inhabitants per sq/km while Soweto West and Kianda are highly dense with 129,000 inhabitants per sq/km. Soweto West and Kianda have the highest rates of children, while Kambi Muru and Laini Saba have the highest rates of single and business people. The average density is around 87,500 inhabitants per sq/km. (Desgroppes & Taupin, 2012, p. 26)

Indeed, Kibera resists homogeneous metaphors and descriptions. What Kibera is depends on where you are in the slum, and descriptions reflect an ever-changing reality.

There is currently no reliable map of Kibera and the layout of the slum changes constantly, partly because there are no paved streets, only mud paths and alleyways. One expert has called Kibera "a jumble of garbage-strewn streets and alleys, the exact lay-out changing from week to week. Finding a path through the shantytown presents a constant challenge even to locals" (Underhill, 2010). However, with the advent of GIS technology and sophisticated cell phone apps, this situation is quickly changing.

Environmental Degradation

Not only does Kibera have problems with overcrowding and with the existence of other negative stimuli, such as noise, but it is also heavily polluted by garbage, human and animal waste, smoke, and soot. Because there is no municipal garbage removal in the slum, huge mountains of garbage surround Kibera, through which many people sift for food and saleable items. It is not uncommon to see children standing on a mountain of refuse, picking through rotten fruit for bites to eat. It is also normal for the garbage dump to become a person's "place of business," since scavenging through these mountains of trash provides a subsistence-level income for many who retrieve wire, paper, and plastic for resale.

Furthermore, there is no public sanitation or sewage system in Kibera. Public latrines ooze human waste into the groundwater, and open sewage runs along alleys and paths throughout the slum. Some water is piped into Kibera at ground level through a spaghetti-like maze of easily cracked plastic and PVC pipes, resulting in the contamination of piped drinking water by groundwater. Diseases such as cholera and typhoid are common. Although NGOs and private companies have built a few sporadic cement-block-and-concrete toilets throughout the slum, there is usually a fee for using them. Furthermore, toilets are dangerous places to go at night, especially for women, who risk rape if they attempt to visit a toilet facility (Pflanz, 2010). Hence, people eliminate waste into plastic bags, tie them, and throw them into a garbage dump or into the street. Davis (2006) has remarked that

> in Nairobi, the Laini Saba area of Kibera in 1998 had exactly ten working pit latrine toilets for 40,000 people, while in Mathare there were two public toilets for 28,000 people. As a result, slum residents rely on "flying toilets" or "scud missiles," as they are called. They put the waste in a polythene bag and throw it on to the nearest roof or pathway. (p. 139)

Indeed, Kibera is littered with fetid and smelly plastic bags, which, once the waste has seeped out or dried, linger on the ground and crunch underfoot like ominous dry autumn leaves.

Dangers to Women and Girls

Environmental degradation contributes to, but is certainly not the only cause of, dangers to women and girls in Kibera. In fact, Kibera has been called one of the most dangerous places in the world to be a woman. A 2010 report by Amnesty International remarked that

> for many women living in informal settlements, poverty is both a consequence and a cause of violence. Many women who suffer physical, sexual or psychological violence lose income as a result and their productive capacity is impaired. Violence against women also impoverishes their families, communities and societies. For women in abusive relationships, poverty makes it harder to find avenues for an escape. While economic independence does not shield women from violence, access to economic resources can enhance women's capacity to make meaningful choices. The violence women face helps keep them poor in part because their poverty inhibits their ability to find solutions. (Amnesty International, 2010, p. 12)

Rape and intimate partner violence are rampant in Kibera. But few women report the violence they experience. The reason is twofold. First, they fear being stigmatized by their family and community. And, perhaps more alarmingly, they do not believe there will be any punishment for a perpetrator. According to focus groups conducted by Amnesty International:

> Most of the women interviewed did not believe that female victims of violence could get any justice, as the system barely functioned. They felt that there was little or no police presence in the slums and settlements and that they had to overcome a number of obstacles before they could even report such violence to the police. Many women refrain from reporting the violence they suffer because they are afraid of reprisal attacks by perpetrators.
>
> Other women will not report cases of violence, particularly rape, because they are afraid of being stigmatized. A lack of knowledge of the law and how the justice system works also stops women from reporting

> violence. Violence against women in Nairobi's slums and informal settlements takes different forms, and is exacerbated by the environment within which these women live. The violence is inextricably linked to their daily lives and routines. Inadequate access to essential services, particularly the lack of access to health care, sanitation and public security, significantly increases women's vulnerability to violence. (Amnesty International, 2010, p. 14)

The lack of accessible and affordable health clinics in Kibera means that there is no readily available treatment for injuries, beatings, rapes, or STDs. The city of Nairobi provides no health services to the slum and what clinics exist are run by NGOs. Even these have long lines and sometimes fees for services. Consequently, many Kiberan women go without health care, even when pregnant. The time (standing in line) and cost of a clinic also means that women frequently forgo family planning assistance they need in the form of birth control pills, IUDs, injectable birth control, or condoms. Clinic inaccessibility results not only in unwanted pregnancies but also in the danger of HIV/AIDS infection. Due to the gendered power imbalance in marriages and intimate partnerships, many men refuse to wear condoms, or at least refuse to buy them. Judy wrote: "If I have one, he may wear it but if I don't, I am sure he does not take the time or thought to obtain one" (Judy, 2013). And she is not alone in her experience. In a survey conducted in 2007 among young sexually active residents of Kibera, 40% of girls surveyed said that they were not able to say no to their partner when he wanted to have sex. Only about 37% said they were able to insist on condom use during sex (Erulkar & Matheka, 2007).

Susanna also wrote about her powerlessness to have safe sex within the confines of her marriage. She wrote:

> I intend to go to the clinic but I always say tomorrow. Last night when Sam said to have sex, I did not have a condom. He is my husband but I have no trust and think he sees other girls. So now have I put myself in danger of infection. I did not have condom and he would never have one. He says it is not his business to protect me. It is his business to have sex. (Susanna, January 2012)

Betta also described this powerlessness in relation to condom use:

> I always ask my boyfriend to use condom. He is my only boyfriend now and he says that it is not necessary and that he has not got HIV. But I do believe he has other girls. And I know he has not been tested for his [HIV] status for long time. So I think he is too sure of himself and he only thinks condom will limit his pleasure. He disrespects me when he says he will not use one and I am left thinking all this time, do I have HIV or do I not? I feel like getting tested every day. I am afraid but I have no control over his decisions since I depend on him for my support. (Betta, March 2013)

In Kibera, women are also exposed to danger because of lack of private and accessible sanitation facilities. Kibera is notorious for its lack of sanitation, with one public toilet per 150 people in some parts (Amnesty International, 2010; Davis, 2006). The lack of accessible toilets contributes to sexual violence. A 2010 Amnesty International report found that women were targeted when walking long distances to reach a latrine at night, increasing the incidence of rape and gang rape:

> The majority of slum residents, including most of the women interviewed by Amnesty International, use shared pit latrines, if these are available and mostly only during the day. Most women interviewed in all the settlements visited by Amnesty International pointed out that the available pit latrines are usually few and far between. They testified that on average one pit latrine would be shared by up to 50 people living in different households. Previous research by other organizations has put the average number of people using a given pit latrine at an even higher figure. One study pointed out that 150 people shared one latrine facility on average in Kibera settlement. More than half of the 130 women interviewed by Amnesty International stated that they used shared pit latrines, usually not situated within the plot in which their houses or structures were situated, and that they had to walk for some minutes to access the facility. Most women have to walk more than 300 metres from their homes to use the available latrines. Access to the latrines is especially unsafe for women

> and particularly at night. The common use of "flying toilets" (human waste disposed of in plastic bags thrown into the open) in settlements is a result of the inaccessibility of toilet facilities. (Amnesty International, 2010, p. 15)

Susanna described the dilemma well:

> The toilet is a far distance from my plot. If it is night or even twilight, that can be a dangerous walk. I know a girl who was raped while coming back home from the toilet. She cried and cried and is now fearful to ever leave her house. I was chased one night on my way back from the toilet. It was only about 9 pm but three boys gave chase to me and tell me they will take me down if they catch me. I am a fast runner and I got home and locked the door tight and said a prayer. But I do not go out to the latrine after dark any more. I use plastic bag or sometimes bucket which I empty outside the house. (Susanna, July 2011)

Police and security personnel in Kibera also constitute a threat to women and girls. Diarists recorded experiences of being attacked or raped by security forces during the post-election violence of 2007–2008. But according to Amnesty International, violence by police is not just relegated to times of political emergency:

> Nairobi's slums and informal settlements are inadequately policed and residents have complained that they lack sufficient government security services. However in some instances when the police and other government security personnel have intervened or carried out security operations, they have reportedly committed human rights violations. These have included cases of sexual and other forms of gender-based violence committed by the police. (Amnesty International, 2010, p. 14)

Jane wrote a short entry in her diary that sums up the situation very well: "I have heard that when women get brave and report violence like rape and they go to the police station, they are raped again while there. That does not surprise me. We are on our own here" (Jane, 2011).

Map Kibera Project

But things are beginning to change in Kibera and there may soon come a day when women are not on their own to sink or swim, live or die. For example, in 2009, an innovative project was initiated which attempts to "map" Kibera and create a user-friendly depiction of the slum's layout. As envisioned, the map will contain "all the information that the inhabitants—rather than the authorities—need for survival" (Underhill, 2010, p. 3). Indeed, very early in the project, its creators effectively marked dangerous places for women, including places where recent rapes and attacks on women had taken place. The map is useful to women on multiple levels. It shows

> the location of a range of landmarks and facilities from water pumps, latrines, schools and health clinics to shops, churches, and mosques. But the map is intended for much more than navigation. Its backers see the project as part of a wider drive to empower slum residents, providing the data they need to deal with the authorities and take control of their own future. (Underhill, 2010, p. 3)

The Map Kibera project received initial funding from the US-based organization Jumpstart International and partnered with several Kenyan-based NGOs. Project leaders then trained a team of cartographers armed with basic GPS devices to "pinpoint the sites they considered important, then upload the data onto the computer" (Underhill, 2010, p. 3). The benefits to the Kiberan community are twofold. First, the map provides a continuously updated understanding of Kibera's geography and social services, and it helps "NGOs to fill the gaps in basic services—whether it's sanitation or electricity—that the community badly needs" because it makes these gaps visible (Underhill, 2010, p. 3). Furthermore, the project is utilizing Kiberan students and residents (some of them women and girls) to help create the map, thereby providing jobs and expertise, as well as "spreading technological know-how" (Underhill, 2010, p. 3) among residents of the slum.

Since its inception, the Map Kibera project has also incorporated a blogging component called Voice of Kibera, through which participants can blog with

Wordpress and Ushahidi software to report on issues that affect the Kiberan community.

> A team of reporters works ... editing the sites and writing articles and reports as well as illustrating [them] with photographs. The teams report about anything and everything that is of relevance to the community, including breaking news, critical issues, and lesser known local efforts and talents. [Reporters] use SMS integration with the Ushahidi sites so that residents and reporters can text in news for the editorial team and post to the sites. (Map Kibera, 2016)

The project has also added a Video Team, whose purpose is to "visually represent the kinds of important stories that happen in the slums and other communities" (Map Kibera, 2016). Project coordinators wanted to reach a wider audience and so, with the help of Flip handheld video cameras and other camera styles, they create videos that are mounted on Youtube, as well as through in-house Voice Kibera platforms. Reporters are youth from the slum; they shoot, edit, narrate, and "conceptualize" stories so that the views presented are the views of the residents, not those of outside media sources. Videos include interviews with residents, as well as the many untold stories not covered in mainstream media. The project has also initiated a Humans of Kibera feature, modelled on the popular Humans of New York project. By featuring portraits of individual Kiberan residents, along with a first-person paragraph narration of their story, the site (which can be followed around the world on Facebook or Tumblr) gives readers a glimpse into the diversity, social problems, and incredible heterogeneity of Kibera.

Kenya Slum Upgrading Programme (KENSUP)

There have been, and continue to be, attempts by national and international organizations to improve the quality of housing in Kibera. In the 1990s, the National Housing Corporation constructed the Kibera Highrise "in order to provide quality housing for slum residents" (Ekdale, 2010). However, the government changed its intention for the building and, once completed, it sold or granted these units to middle-class Kenyans instead of to slum dwellers (Huchzermeyer, 2008). In 2007, the Kenyan government, in conjunction with the United Nations

(UN-HABITAT) and other non-governmental agencies, began the Kenya Slum Upgrading Programme (KENSUP) in Kibera. The program hoped to "facelift the housing and sanitary conditions" (*Standard*, 2008) of the slum. When plans were originally laid out, it was thought that the upgrade would take approximately nine years to complete and would re-house all Kibera residents in new housing on or adjacent to the site of the current slum. As envisioned by its planners, the new community would include schools, markets, and playgrounds. On September 16, 2009, the first group of 1,500 Kibera residents were moved from their mud shacks into 300 newly constructed apartments in what looked like a very successful beginning to the new enterprise.

However, problems soon began to arise. First of all, poor families who moved from the slum into the new high-rise apartments were soon found to be subletting the new places to middle-class families and moving back to Kibera. Further, it soon became clear that three other significant factors would delay—if not defeat—the planners' vision. First, building materials could not be left unattended on-site without a substantial portion of them being stolen. Second, the lack of proper building foundations made new construction unstable and dangerous. Because much of the ground upon which Kibera sits is literally garbage, many new structures collapsed when the slum experienced flooding. Finally, the overcrowded and cramped conditions of the slum made construction extremely difficult. Because there are no paved roads, there was no easy access for construction equipment, such as bulldozers. And much of Kibera is on a steep incline, which further impeded construction, even if a temporary road was made by demolishing standing structures.

Lawsuits were also filed that attempted to stop the upgrade. The most prominent litigation has come from a group of 80 landlords (descendants of the original Nubian landlords) who claim that the land Kibera is built on is theirs and, therefore, the government cannot demolish existing shacks and construct new buildings. In July 2010, the Kenyan High Court announced yet another delay in upgrade construction and relocation, saying that the project could not move forward until a high court ruling was obtained (*East African*, 2010). As problems and impediments continued to multiply, one expert remarked that, at its current rate of progress, the Kibera upgrade will take 1,178 years to complete (*The Standard*, 2009). Indeed, as one expert has pointed out, "instead of improving the lives of slum dwellers by enabling access to adequate housing, poorly targeted slum upgrading improves the lives of the *better-off* and displaces the original residents into expanding slums or newly forming slums" in other parts of the city (Huchzermeyer, 2008, p. 25).

Normalization of Education for Girls

An important change in Kibera that may build a future of more opportunity for women is the normalization of the idea that girls should be educated. Although all the diarists in this study had completed primary school, many had not completed it at an appropriate age because they had been held back so that their families could educate male children first. Kenya's Population Council estimates that about 61% of boys but only 49% of girls in Kibera start school at the appropriate age (Population Council, 2015). Many girls had also missed much of their primary education because they stayed home on days when water had to be collected or when other household chores were deemed more important than school. They also stayed home when they had their periods. But now an organization called Shining Hope for Communities (SHOFCO), founded by Kibera resident Kennedy Odede (and being operated with his wife, Jessica Posner—see Appendix) is popularizing the idea of educating girls by placing free schools for girls in the centre of community programs of holistic services (SHOFCO, 2015). SHOFCO's first free girls' school was opened in Kibera in 2009, with transformative effects on community attitudes and opportunities. The Shining Hope School offers not only education but also daily meals, health care, psychosocial support, and after-school programs. The school is free; there is no charge for uniforms or supplies. Journalists Nicholas Kristof and Sheryl WuDunn (2014) describe the Shining Hope School:

> School was free, but the parents had to commit to working five weeks during the year in lieu of tuition. The parents also had to commit to attend[ing] monthly meetings. Admissions officers looked for two qualities in prospective students: the poorest kids and the brightest ones. The competition was excruciating, with almost 500 children competing for twenty slots in each new pre-kindergarten class. Word spread about the school and foreigners dropped by—and left behind large checks.... The

> classrooms in Kibera School for Girls are warm and inviting, very much like the best suburban schools in America, with student artwork on the walls and eager students frantically waving their hands to be called on. Elsewhere in Kibera, the student-teacher ratio is about 80–1; in these classrooms, it is 8–1, and class is in session fifty weeks a year. In a writing class we watched, the girls were coached to write "juicy sentences": they practiced taking drab, formulaic sentences and recasting them with scenes, emotions, and active verbs. In Kibera School for Girls, laughter echoes down the hallways, and the girls are boisterous, self-confident, and excited to see visitors. They call out in English, the language of instruction. Even though English is the third language for most girls, the latest assessment showed 86% exceeding the United States standards for their grade level. (pp. 137–138)

The idea that a girls' school can become a "portal for large scale social change" transforming urban poverty and creating women community leaders is essential for long-term policy change on the micro and macro levels. It is also key to ending gender-based and intimate partner violence. Odede, whose two sisters had both been raped by the time they were 16, thought that one way to stop rape would be to start a girls' school so that everyone would respect them and that the school could, in time, become the centre for a broader outreach program on women's issues. And it has. Shining Hope's reputation is burgeoning and its model is being replicated and expanded to other centres of urban poverty. A Shining Hope School has now opened in Mathare, another Nairobi slum. As girls' education progresses, young women are taking their place as leaders in community, political, and artistic action in Kibera. Soon the old idea that girls should not be educated will seem as naïve as it was impractical.

3 Ethnographic Reflections and Decolonization

The time I spent working in or writing about Kibera made me more conscious than ever of my white Western privilege. Harding (1991) has described insiders who adopt a critically reflective stance toward privilege as "becoming marginal" (p. 277). But I do not believe that any amount of reflection and reflexivity can make me marginal, if that word is understood to connote a standpoint, a place I can occupy in the same way a person from the Global South occupies it.

However, Alison Bailey has adapted that idea and introduced the concept of privilege as performative, as a series of ongoing choices that can be accepted or rejected. That is, those of us who are critically reflective of our privilege can reject the script that history has written for us, and we can make this ongoing script-rejection into a conscious political act. As Bailey puts it, we can learn to think and act from a privilege-cognizant script that we choose with the help of social theories generated by emancipatory movements (Bailey, 2000). We can choose to act in ways that do not reinforce the systems of domination around the globe and act instead in ways that generate liberatory knowledge.

Being in Kibera helped me do this and to reject privilege in a more honest and powerful way than I had heretofore attempted. Although I had always performed the expected acts of small daily social justice (refusing my place at the head of the line, literally and figuratively), Kibera taught me how resistance might be made more honest and more real. I was keenly aware that the lifestyle I enjoyed in the United States was not the global norm. Bailey (2000) has remarked that privilege-cognizant individuals "must try to get out of those locations and texts in which they feel at home ... and put our privileged identities at risk" by developing new habits and by resisting the temptation to retreat to our own worlds where we feel safe (p. 293). If we expose ourselves to discomfort, says Bailey (2000), "our identities fall apart, our privilege-evasive scripts no longer work, and the luxury of retreating to a safe space is temporarily removed" (p. 297). When we are not in our Western-privileged contexts, our privilege-evasive scripts become visible and "we get a glimpse of how we are seen through the eyes of those whom we have been taught to perceive arrogantly" (Bailey, 2000, p. 295). Being in Kibera, indeed, helped me put aside my script and to imagine what life would be like if I had been born in Kibera. What opportunities would have been available? What would I have done with these opportunities? Would I have survived, and how would I have survived? I asked myself these questions often. They scared me.

After several years of travelling to Kibera, though, I became used to feeling different. It was good for me, of course, but eventually, my feelings of difference started to feel normal, perhaps even self-congratulatory. Thankfully, I could always count on the diarists to wake me up with the verbal equivalent of a bucket of cold water in the face. They never hesitated to remind me that my Western taken-for-granted reality was not reality in Kibera. They called me on my own contradictions and foibles, acting as a constant check-and-balance when I took privilege for granted. When I asked silly or insulting questions, they told me those questions were insulting and why. "Does it help you," I once asked, "to write about your hardships in a journal?" "No," Catherine tersely replied. "If you don't have food, you don't have food. It doesn't help to write it down."

Another example occurred when the 16-year-old sister of one of the diarists was having a birthday. I decided to give her a pretty pair of earrings that I had bought at an airport kiosk. They were brightly coloured and they sparkled. My thought was that she would have something frivolous and pretty, something that contrasted with the drabness of Kibera. She took the gift but looked disappointed. I did not understand but I could see she felt saddened and perhaps offended by the gift. I pressed her for a reason and she finally said, "I don't have clothes, I don't have shoes, I don't have food. If I don't have those, what good are earrings to me?" I realized then that the t-shirt she was wearing was the same one I always saw her wear. Later I learned it was her only shirt. Her shoes were the cheapest rubber flip-flops and even those had holes in the soles. It must have hurt to walk around the rock-strewn hard mud of Kibera in those shoes. And it must have hurt even more to be hungry. How could I not have seen this without being told? Virtually all the young women I was meeting and working with were in the same position. And yet I had the privileged idea that a hungry, shoeless young girl would want sparkly earrings. I felt instantly ashamed.

Indeed, daily survival was the issue here. Food and water and clothing could not be taken for granted. These women had to find food and water each day, for themselves, their children, their relatives. If they did not get up with that idea in mind and if they were not motivated and strong and lucky, they would not eat or drink. My gift to the birthday girl showed that I still lived in a world where food and water were taken for granted and the day's decisions were about what to buy when the necessities were already there. Suddenly, I saw myself as they saw me—I was still unconscious. Although I was well intentioned, I was thoughtless and cruel. I felt very uncomfortable that day and for many days thereafter. I never again forgot that nothing—not even a drink of water—is taken for granted in Kibera.

But I was not the only one growing and changing. I realized by the end of the project that the diarists, too, were, to use Bailey's metaphor, making themselves uncomfortable. Intimate partner violence is mainly a private matter in Kibera. When the project began, even diarists who knew one another did not openly speak about intimate partner violence or sexual experiences. In my opinion, which may be Eurocentric, this silence limited their ability to vent, to share, to voice objections to the treatment they received at the hands of men. The taboo around speaking out about intimate partner violence also meant there were no support groups, even in the form of groups of women informally assembled to talk about shared experience. But writing about their experiences in diaries may have changed that. Diarists who did not speak to or look at one another in 2007 were in 2014 sharing experiences and discussing strategies to alleviate violence. Such discussions were not pervasive and they did not appear to be easy. But they were happening and they represented change in the way women used their voices, communicated their concerns, and interpreted social norms. It was becoming normal among this group to talk about violence from husbands and boyfriends. These women were taking control of their own knowledge and the rules that surrounded its making and dissemination. They were challenging and changing social rules and experiencing the social discomfort that came with changing societal scripts.

For my part, after this study was complete, I decided that I needed to continue this challenge in my own life. Why wait for trips to places like Kibera to experience feelings of cultural unease? Maria Lugones (1987) has used the term *"world" travelling* to describe the effort to put oneself in social and cultural situations where one feels ill at ease or off-centre, whether those settings are in a place like Kibera or in among different cultural groups in one's own city. Going to a mosque if one is non-Muslim or to a Spanish-speaking hair salon if one is Caucasian might be enough to get the anxiety flowing and to experience instant unease. I now practise uncomfortable cultural immersions in my city and state and encourage my students to do the same. "World" travel, as Lugones (1987) describes it, can begin in your own neighbourhood.

It was a good and productive task to continually self-question and to reflect repeatedly on my own positionality and theoretical framework in relation to the women in Kibera, and for them to reflect on their relationship to me and to one another. It helped ensure that the project was done through a partnership ethic (Cram, 2009), with a reflexive consciousness, and with reference to the ongoing discourses on critical whiteness studies.

But what about the future? The purpose of the study was exploratory—to understand (from the participants' point of view) what coping strategies women in Kibera used to survive intimate partner violence. But, as the study ended, the next questions became, How might these coping strategies be enhanced? How might indigenous interventions be created? How might this project become an indigenous research project, guided by the community of women participants? Could this project increase self-determination and economic empowerment, heal the wounds of violence rooted in colonialism and patriarchy, and pursue social justice agendas for socially excluded women in Kibera? Could this project become an indigenous research project and would the participants choose to go forward?

Sandra Harding (1991) has distinguished between methodology and method by saying that "a research methodology is a theory and analysis of how research does or should proceed," while a method "is a technique for or a way of proceeding in gathering evidence" (pp. 2–3). Linda Tuhiwai Smith (2012), speaking of research in an indigenous context, has elaborated, saying that

> within an indigenous framework, methodological debates are ones concerned with the broader politics and strategic goals of indigenous research. It is at this level that researchers have to clarify and justify their intentions. Methods become the means and procedures through which the central problems of the research are addressed. Indigenous methodologies are often a mix of existing methodological approaches and indigenous practices. The mix reflects the training of indigenous researchers, which continues to be within the academy, and the parameters and common sense understandings of research, which govern how indigenous communities and researchers define their activities. (p. 144)

Under Indigenous Eyes

Smith (2012) has defined the overarching imperatives of indigenous research to be the struggle for self-determination and the need to take back control of indigenous destinies, through acts of reframing, reclaiming, and reconstituting indigenous languages and cultures. In Kibera, these same priorities are present because residents of the slum suffer not only from the history of colonialism that applies to all of Kenya but also from an ongoing process of social exclusion by other Kenyans. The social exclusion and stigmatization of people who live in slum communities is tantamount to a second colonization, rooted in neo-liberal capitalism and globalization.

Because of rampant urbanization, slum dwellers face an ongoing and contemporary loss of ethnic tradition and community. Many ethnicities have pushed and shoved their way into Kibera and live in a mix of almost a million people without a common geographical ancestral home. Although within its 12 villages one ethnicity may be demographically dominant, and although the 2007–2008 post-election riots may have increased village-based homogeneity, it is still a place where residents of different ethnicities and tribal languages often live side by side. Although this may be a good thing in that Kenyan governmental officials hope to discourage tribalism in favour of one unifying Kenyan identity, it is also true that Kibera residents have lost "the village," the smaller intrinsic community that previously provided cohesion, history, and support in their lives. Reacting to the fragmentation of ethnic cultural traditions, Kiberan youth frequently embrace a world culture of rap music and reggae style. Ethnic myths and stories, although still present to some degree, are fading. As Mary remarked in her journal, "I want to sing my child the lullaby my mother sang to me. But I don't remember it and my grandmother is now passed" (Mary, 2012).

Smith (2012) has described 25 indigenous projects that are currently being pursued by indigenous communities around the globe. Although it is recommended that readers partake of Smith's more elaborate descriptions of these projects, what follows below is a paraphrase constructed for the confines of this book:

- *Claiming* means rewriting histories and identities and reclaiming lands, rights, and knowledge from colonizers;
- *Testimonies* include the presentation of oral or written evidence, as if presenting truth to power, in a formal manner to set the historical record straight. Testimonies often position the speaker as a witness, telling the truth of their experience to an unschooled or colonial audience;
- *Storytelling* is about gathering individual stories and oral histories that become part of a collective story of a people whose voice has been denied legitimacy in the colonial culture;
- *Celebrating Survival* includes documenting and celebrating ways in which indigenous cultures have survived despite overwhelming odds. Gerald Vizenor has called this combination of survival and resistance "survivance," and focuses on stories, events, and artistic endeavours that emphasize resistance and overcoming domination;
- *Remembering* means bringing a community together through shared remembrance of pain and trauma. Sometimes it involves naming the

silences that have been too painful to express but that, when communicated collectively, can create a path of empowerment;

- *Indigenizing and Indigenist Processes* attempt to re-centre a politics of indigenous identity and indigenous cultural activity that grounds itself in alternative world views and different value systems than those of the colonizer;
- *Intervening* refers to the process of being and becoming a proactive worker for change, particularly cultural and structural change;
- *Revitalizing and Regenerating* refers to the intentional bringing back to life of indigenous language, art, and culture but also to educating, broadcasting, and creating community-based programs to further these efforts;
- *Connecting*, according to Smith (2012), "positions individuals in sets of relationships with other people and with the environment" (p. 149);
- *Reading* involves the critical rereading of Western-based colonizer-centred history. The rereading of imperialist history by postcolonial and cultural studies scholars not only provides a critical approach to history but also makes visible indigenous narrative and perspective;
- *Writing and Theory Making* refers to the growing literature of indigenous people around the world in the form of fiction, drama, poetry, literary criticism, biography, film, and scholarship. Not only does this project enable a centring of indigenous perspective, it also enables a critique of colonialism and engages a new indigenous audience in dialectical conversation;
- *Representing* includes both projects aimed at increasing political representation as well as those which frame indigenous voices as legitimate and centred parts of global conversations;
- *Gendering* refers both to gendering debates and political dialogues within the indigenous community as well as insisting on an indigenous voice in representations of international feminism;
- *Envisioning* asks indigenous people to imagine a future in which they can rise above colonial histories and dream a new dream to set their own goals;
- *Reframing* involves taking greater control over the ways in which indigenous issues and social problems are discussed and handled. For example, issues are seen as community problems, not as indigenous problems.

Furthermore, the relationships of forms of oppression to one another are stressed. Indigenous women point out the futility of critiquing patriarchy without simultaneously addressing imperialism and racism;

- *Restoring* refers to restoring well-being on physical, emotional, material, and spiritual levels;
- *Returning* seeks the return of lands, rivers, mountains, as well as artifacts to their original owners;
- *Democratizing and Indigenist Governance* is a process of extending participation outwards by reinstating indigenous principles of collectivity to governance;
- *Networking* refers to stimulating the flow of information, educating people, and creating international conversations about indigenous issues;
- *Naming* refers to renaming the world using the original indigenous names. It also includes the important idea that by naming the world, people name their realities and, therefore, make them visible;
- *Protecting* refers to protecting not only communities, languages, art, and ideas but also sacred sites, customs, and traditional ways of life;
- *Creating* is not only asserting imaginative, artistic, and spiritual creativity but also embracing the idea that indigenous communities have much to offer toward solving contemporary world problems;
- *Negotiating* refers to thinking and acting strategically, with long-term goals in mind;
- *Discovering the Beauty of Our Knowledge* involves making indigenous knowledges and value systems work for indigenous development;
- *Sharing* is about the important project of sharing indigenous knowledge between and among indigenous communities across the globe.

Decolonization: An Intersectional Process

With these projects as guide and inspiration, on a sunny day in December 2014, the diarists met for what we hoped would be a critique of our seven-year project and a discussion of what it would look like to apply some of the knowledge we had gained to improve their lives and futures. Twelve of the twenty diarists were present for the meeting, which lasted for five hours and included lunch. Most women brought their children, transforming the day into a lively mix of discussion and play. We rented a primary school classroom that was not being used that day. We set up a wobbly easel, mounted tear-off butcher block paper, and armed ourselves with pens and markers.

We began with a discussion of whether the diarists would like the project to go forward, taking control of it themselves and setting their own research goals. The consensus was decidedly "yes," with only one participant saying that she did not see how she would have time to go forward with this endeavour. I told them that I had learned that they used many effective strategies to cope with intimate partner violence. We discussed reasons why this violence was not their fault but the fault of structural poverty and socialized gender norms. We then discussed what structural poverty and socialized gender norms meant in the everyday ways they experienced them: gender discrimination, denial of schooling, early marriage, and violent partnerships that were taken for granted in the general culture.

They were happy to hear their coping activities described as "strategies," a word that implied that their efforts were thoughtful, smart, and self-chosen (rather than imposed). Marya said, "It was as I wrote in my journal that I thought about how men have all the good things and women get the rest. I began to see that I had always been smart and found ways to survive and that made me proud of myself." Susanna echoed that thought, saying, "I never questioned that women were born to serve men until I married and experienced abuse. It was then that I said, 'No, it cannot be that God meant women to be hurt so much. These marriage rules are men's rules, not God's rules.' And that is when I started to change and decide I have a right to make things different." Other diarists concurred with specific examples from their own lives, but several still felt that their experience of violence was private and not an acceptable topic for group conversation. Seven of the twelve women participated, sharing stories about the social acceptance of violence to women. I was surprised and pleased that self-disclosures were followed by supportive words and gestures from the group. I was also pleased that the women who chose to speak appeared comfortable and empowered in having their voices heard.

After an hour's fruitful conversation, we turned to the pertinent topic of the meeting: How might this writing project be redesigned and configured in order to benefit the writers? How might it create change or empowerment? Cathy M., who remarked in a tongue-in-cheek fashion that the best thing that could happen is that the pages would turn to gold and provide money, knew of a community organization that had been seeking poems from young women. Another diarist knew of an NGO that had encouraged young people, both male and female, to document their lives through donated cameras. It was generally agreed, though, that neither of these projects was long term or lucrative. Cara brought up the idea of seeking a partnership with the local university or perhaps receiving a grant from a community-based organization to continue writing. This idea was considered to be one worth pursuing, but several diarists admitted that they felt intimidated by university faculty and thought they might not be comfortable working with them. Judy then remarked that she would only be interested in working with such a project if they let her write or think about what she wanted to write and think about. When I asked what that was, she said, "Mostly it is ways that I can go forward. How can I—how can all of us—improve our life in a practical way—a business opportunity, that is what I am set on."

I grabbed the strategic word *opportunity* and brought it to the centre of the conversation. How might we create a project that helps create opportunity—either for the writers as individuals or for women as a group in Kibera? How might writing lead to or enable social change in women's lives? We structured our conversation around the list of 25 indigenous projects articulated by Linda Tuhiwai Smith and described above. I talked about Smith and her research to the diarists and passed around one of her books. I also spread out a map of the world so that the diarists could see where Smith was writing from (New Zealand) and explained in very (unfortunately) general terms the history of the Maori people in relation to the dominant culture. Although the diarists were not surprised by the geography of the Pacific rim, having apparently received a better education in primary-school level geography than many American students, they were surprised to hear of a tribe of people with black skin who were experiencing many of the difficulties native Africans had for centuries experienced under colonial rule. They beamed when they heard of Maori efforts to empower and resist colonialism and were excited by the fact that many Maori activists and academic researchers are women.

I wrote each of the 25 project titles on the easel paper and, as we discussed each one according to Smith's definition, let the diarists find footing for the ideas in their own terms and in their own words. Cara, for example, commented on the project (#9) called Connecting. She said,

> We wrote by ourselves and for ourselves. And it has connected us to the outside world because of the people at the American university who read what we write. This project has been a connecting project because now some people in America know our thoughts and our lives.

Cathy M. agreed and added that

> it has also connected us here in Kibera. Each of us writers now knows at least some of the other writers. And we have come to consider ourselves friends. Before the project, we had no knowledge or sharing with one another. Now we share and connect and can almost know each other's true struggles.

Susanna said that she saw comparisons between the diary project and both Testimonies and Storytelling projects. She said,

> I never knew the word *testimony* as she [Smith] has used it. I think of that word as used in court. But I do believe that in some ways, my diaries have been my testimony to the world and I have said my strongest beliefs on some of [their] pages. I have also told the story of my life so far and seen my life as a long thing with a beginning and an end. And I have conveyed that story and shown how it unfolds.

The two indigenous projects that received most interest from the diarists, though, were Intervening and Naming, of which the idea of intervening spoke the loudest to them. They wanted the leaders of their families or the law or the police or some representative of legal or societal authority to intervene on their behalf to stop the intimate partner violence they endured. However, as Cathy M. remarked, "My family head is a male, the police are mostly male, the judges are male, and the Parliament are male. Who is going to say that I, a woman, should not be hurt?" Marya suggested taking self-defence classes, which are offered by more than one women's organization in Nairobi, one of which regularly provides free self-defence instruction for slum-dwelling women. They agreed, however, that it was not enough. Self-defence might help in a one-to-one encounter but the majority of males in authority could outnumber, through social norms and policy decisions, any one physically empowered woman. Susanna said, however, "It would still make me happy to prevent any other man from inflicting the kind of pain my husband gave to me. I want self-defence." Finally, though, Cara had the idea to let writing act as a stepping stone to an intervention that would be organized on their behalf by an NGO. She said,

> I say we write our stories of injustice at the hands of men. We all know there is now a law. We have been to seminars. I say we write our stories as crisply and perfectly as possible and give them to the FIDA [Federation of Women Lawyers in Kenya].

Others agreed and they set their first goal: to write descriptions of incidents of intimate partner violence, complete with as much pragmatic data as possible (time, date, place, extent of injury) and, once these data were collected, submit them to FIDA-K and ask for a meeting in which they might be advised of a direction forward.

The second indigenous project that was compelling to the diarists was Naming. They understood the concept of Naming to mean that activities, attitudes, and norms in the slum were different for men and for women. They understood it to mean that women's activities or perspectives were often not acknowledged or named. Susanna gave the example of being locked out of a house by a landlord when the rent is not paid on time. She pointed out that this process is harder on women than on men because women who are locked out are in danger of being raped on the street or of having to sell themselves to men for money. The also may lose their livelihood through the lockout. She explained:

> My mother sold food on the street. Sometimes she would be locked out of the house for not paying rent and inside the house there are all her utensils for making money. How can she work and pay the rent when everything she needs to work—her pans, her food supplies—[is] in the house? She cannot do it. She is completely without anything and with no way to make money to pay the rent. Then sometimes the landlord will sell everything and she has to start over again from scratch, with completely nothing in hand.

She pointed out that men could, if locked out, simply hire themselves out for day labour and earn money to restore access to the house. A woman's work was in the house and, therefore, not accessible. Other diarists agreed that being locked out for late payment was for women a potentially devastating and life-changing event.

They pointed out several other activities that had an unacknowledged gender component that made those activities different for women than for men. They mentioned going to the latrine at night (dangerous for women but not for men). They discussed missing school on days when they had their periods. These were lost learning days for girls but not for boys. They also talked about the way they saw their environment and that they often saw it differently than men did.

Marya said, for example, that she classified mud into different kinds, depending on the danger it posed to her children. There was harmless mud that children played in; there was dirty mud that was so full of silt that it stained clothes so that they would never come clean; and there was dangerous mud that was contaminated with waste overflow from latrines and could spread cholera or other diseases. She said, "You see, to men, mud is mud. To me, I see good mud, dirty mud, and dangerous mud." She laughed but the point was well taken and caused an intriguing silence to take hold of the room. It was as if the women had discovered that they had never fully named their world and that naming was power. Paolo Freire remarked, "Name the word, name the world" (in Smith, 2012, p. 158), and the diarists had just struck a note that resonated with Freire's concept. They had seen that their vision was unique, important, and, once named, held a power that both illustrated and legitimized their creativity. Their second decision, therefore, was to use their writing to identify things seen through women's eyes that had not been named—and then to name those things. Cara remarked that she would like to share this Naming idea with female relatives. Marya brought up the idea of collecting stories from mothers and grandmothers, saying, "They might have named things and not told. Now they can tell and share those names." Sarah said she would like to write down her mother's recipes as well as her stories, and that sometimes the recipe was a story. Clearly, their ideas were expanding and expansive, and they were delineating a women's history project that was, for this afternoon at least, bigger than any of us could comprehend. Cathy M. closed by saying, "Yes, we think big and maybe too big. But you don't get very far if you don't dream."

As the afternoon ended, the women decided to call themselves the Kibera Women Writers Project and to reach out to FIDA-K for assistance, advice, and support. The afternoon had brought lofty goals and much excitement. I wondered if they would be able to maintain their excitement and their goals in a world where earning enough to eat always had to be the first challenge of every day.

Part Two

The Diaries

4 Working with Diaries as Texts

The history of narrative data collection and analysis in the United States can be traced to the Chicago School of sociologists. Thomas and Znaniecki's *The Polish Peasant* (1918/1927) is commonly cited as the "first significant sociological use of life history" for sociological analysis (Chase, 2005, p. 653). However, it was the second wave of the feminist movement in the 1970s and 1980s that popularized the use of personal narratives, diaries, and autobiographies as "essential primary documents" for research (Personal Narratives Group, 1989, p. 4). Such autobiographical and diary data allowed researchers to access "previously silenced voices" and to "challenge knowledge about society, culture, and history" (Chase, 2005, p. 654). Issues of race, class, gender, sexual orientation, and nationality were given prominence as "central aspects of women's lives" (Chase, 2005, p. 654) and studies of women's diaries and autobiographies gained academic prominence in the 1970s and 1980s (Ruddick & Daniels, 1977; Jacobs, 1979; Babb & Taylor, 1981; Hunt & Winegarten, 1983). These works contradicted the previous use of narrative data as being "primarily useful for gaining knowledge about historical events" (Chase, 2005, p. 654). Instead, feminist scholars were "interested in women as social actors in their own right and in the subjective meanings women assigned to events and conditions in their lives" (Chase, 2005, p. 654). Stimulated by this burgeoning feminist research in the social sciences, literary analyses of women's diaries also began to appear, exploring the relationship between women's inner selves and their public roles. Schiwy (1994) posited that women may use diaries to advance unconventional thought (Schiwy, 1994; Swart, 2008), and Culley (1986) explored ways in which diaries may provide emotional and psychological support to their writers (Culley, 1986; Swart, 2008). Currently, women's blogs constitute a new kind of narrative data, one which is alive and produced in situational contexts—in *relationships* between writers and readers (Riverbend, 2005). Clearly, the field of narrative data analysis is expanding to include new territory and unconventional definitions of what constitutes "narrative." The current study is indebted to previous narrative scholarship and has found in this body of work a home base from which to launch new explorations.

Working with handwritten texts presented unique concerns but also fascinating opportunities. The diaries were typed and stored on computer files once I had them here in the United States. But I always looked first and for a long time at the original pages—the handwriting style, the doodles in the margins, the thin layer of red Kibera dust that still clung to the pages—all of these things instantly brought Kibera into my office and immediately made me aware that these pages represented women's dramas unfolding in front of me. Sometimes it was frustrating, though, just to have a written page. I often wondered how my project might have been different had I been conducting interviews with the writers, instead of reading their diaries. There were times when I would have liked to ask the writers to elaborate on something, or simply to go into more detail about a certain subject. Working with written data, however, did not afford me such possibilities. But, although analyzing these texts was not an interaction between two people conversing across a table, it was, nevertheless, a "mutually accomplished story" (Fontana & Frey, 2005, p. 714). And, despite the fact that I was not able to query the writers for clarification or ask them follow-up questions, my narrative analysis was still a partnership—a story that could only be created by the writer in collaboration with me, the reader. Like face-to-face interviewing, analyzing these texts was a dialogue, a relationship between reader and page that took place in a particular situational setting. I found that I had to understand not only what a text *said* but also the *context* in which it was written—the situation in which meaning was made by the author. Indeed, understanding context was crucial to understanding and interpreting these narrative texts from the writer's point of view.

As I analyzed diary data for themes, I became increasingly aware that I needed to be cognizant of the situational reality of individual entries and of the fact that the diary entries were living artifacts existing in both physical and cognitive space. The written words on diary pages were not just flat denotations of past activities; they were living, breathing "speech acts" (Searle, 1969) that could be read as situated dramas.

Paradigm Moments: Text as Drama

Such an understanding of narrative text as drama was particularly important to my research for three reasons. First, understanding context enabled me to anchor my reading in the *writer's* point of view, not my own. That is, it helped me to truly *read* the diaries, without reading *into* them. Second, because the diaries were received by me as they were being written—not all at once at the end of the study—I began the project with little information about the writers. When data collection was complete and I began the formal thematic analysis, I had the chronological context of the project itself on which to rely for perspective. But, as I read the early diaries of each study participant, every cue I could pick up from the texts as documents was important in helping me situate the writer within her own psycho-social space. Finally, understanding unwritten cues within the texts was important because diarists' contexts frequently changed and there were sometimes unexplained or discontinuous gaps in narratives. For example, a diarist might write from one place of residence, not write for a month, then pick up writing again from another place without explaining the transition. Such blank spaces in narratives were jarring and, at times, confusing. Reading for unwritten cues often helped me pick up the trail of circumstance that the diarist had not explained.

As I worked with the diaries, I developed a technique that I called "interviewing the text." I would literally think of each diary entry as a piece of a larger, ongoing drama. I would then "ask" each narrative, "What am I missing because your writer is not present today? How can I understand her diary as a dialogue between her 'self' and her social context? Talk to me."

Ethnographic interviewing techniques—particularly those aimed at interpreting *non-verbal* communication in an interview situation—proved particularly helpful to me in analyzing the diary data because they alerted me to unwritten cues within the narratives. For example, such techniques helped reveal the relationship between the physical act of writing and the cognitive space the writer inhabited. Furthermore, they helped me identify and understand silences. Finally, because the diaries were handwritten, the techniques helped me understand indicators in script such as writing style and diary decoration, which provided important clues to personality, strategy, meaning, and meaning-making.

Fontana and Frey (2005) remind us that "nonverbal techniques are important in interviewing" and that the interviewer should "carefully note and record respondents' use of these modes" (p. 713). As I proceeded with analysis, I realized that it was also important to be aware of the unwritten communication of a text and that it was helpful to consider the diaries as "dialogic characters" (Saukko, 2000, p. 303). By so doing, I acknowledged that the narratives were communicating artifacts, from which, if asked the right questions, a complex understanding of the four major forms of non-verbal communication might be elicited. This type of non-narrative textual analysis, when used in conjunction with traditional thematic coding, enabled me to uncover hidden clues and cues that would otherwise have gone unnoticed.

Timing Is Everything

Ethnographers have defined *proxemic* communication as "the use of interpersonal space to communicate attitudes" (Fontana & Frey, 2005, p. 713). Instead of understanding this to mean only a speaker's use of physical space during an interview, I expanded the definition to include the diarist's spatial relationship with her actual diary and with her writing as an activity. My analysis of diary data included a consideration, for example, of *when* and *where* a diarist wrote. Considering these variables was helpful to me in understanding how a diarist's narrative (her cognitive space) fit into her physical space and time. That is, did she write in the daytime or at night? Did she write when she was alone or did she compose, instead, in the company of others? Did she write at home or in a public space? Were the place and time always the same or did they vary? A diarist's choice of writing-time and writing-place revealed much about the relationship of her writing to her perceived safety, her privacy, and her available leisure time. It also revealed how her writing was viewed by others, as well as how she prioritized her writing in relation to her daily activities. This was an easy narrative detail to analyze because many diarists described when and where they wrote. Dee, for example, almost consistently composed at home and at night, after her children were asleep. Occasionally, she varied from this chosen time and wrote in the morning. I learned to be alert for such changes and to examine them. In Dee's case, an analysis of changes in the timing of her diary entries provided a minor revelation. I reread her diaries to see if there was any particular reason for her to switch to a morning writing-time. And, indeed, I found my answer. She wrote in the morning instead of at night when finances were particularly stretched because at such times there was no money for the light—spliced-in electricity—needed for nighttime journaling. This "proxemic" cue had spoken to me and helped me understand that nighttime writing was a luxury, indicating more available funds and less financial stress in Dee's life.

Ethnographers also describe a type of communication they call *chronemic*, which is "the use of pacing in speech and length of silence in conversation" (Fontana & Frey, 2005, p. 713). I expanded this definition and applied it to diary analysis by examining the pacing and length of diary entries, as well as their silences and gaps. For example, I was careful to see if diary entries were short or long. Some diarists wrote long entries that comprised several pages at one sitting and then did not write again for a few days. Others composed entries on a consistent basis—short, daily entries. I took note of the pacing of their writing because it alerted me to periods of safety and non-safety in their lives, periods of privacy and non-privacy in their daily experience. Those who composed at length and then took a "break," for example, may have been facing at-home circumstances that prevented them from writing except in gushes. I examined back copies of the diaries of JC (May 2008) and found corroboration for this hypothesis. JC had a boyfriend she sometimes lived with who disliked her participation in any non-traditional female activities. For example, she was not allowed to attend a weekly youth support group in Kibera. As I looked at her diaries, I conjectured that the timing of her writing "spurts" might be alerting me to days when the boyfriend was away or out of the home for long periods of time. On the other hand, I became alert to the fact that diarists who composed regularly but only in short entries might have safety to write but limited leisure for such an activity. I looked at the diaries of Cara, whose work fit the short-but-regular entry description. Indeed, Cara had safety to write but, because she cared for both her baby and her mother, she had little free time.

Clearly, my consideration of chronemic non-written communication helped me to understand more about the diarists' lifestyles—leisure time, male-delimited time, safe time—than what they had written directly on the page.

Silence and Imagery

It is important to note the "length of silence" in conversation or face-to-face interview (Fontana & Frey, 2005, p. 713). When analyzing written data, too, it is important to note the gaps or *silences* in diary entries. I learned to be highly alert for what diarists omitted from their accounts. I especially looked for silences that surrounded major or ever-present situations in a diarist's life. For example, Cara lived with her mother, who was suffering from tuberculosis. However, there was never any mention in her diary of the details of the disease or the care that must be administered. Such care was one of Cara's main jobs, since there was no other adult living with the family. The disease, as it progressed, likely had a fearful and distasteful appearance. Yet for five years until her mother's death, Cara said nothing except a simple declarative statement in an early journal that her mother had tuberculosis. Qualitative experts indicate that silence often surrounds a subject that is disempowering, hated, or feared (Charmaz, 2003). That was not the case for writers in the current study, who were quite frank about subjects such as hunger, humiliation, and physical and sexual abuse. However, they *were* often silent about taken-for-granted realities of slum life that would appall Western readers. For example, the reality of Cara's caring for her mother is actually the taken-for-granted centre of the diarist's life—a huge and gaping reality, all the more onerous for its being treated completely casually by the author. There were similar silences about the lack of toilet facilities in the slum or the frequent contracting of diseases such as malaria or syphilis. Silences around these subjects appeared to indicate that they were so normal and taken for granted that they were usually not noted in diaries.

It is also important to consider *kinesic* communication, which includes "body movements and posture" (Fontana & Frey, 2005, p. 713). This may seem like an impossible form of communication to seek from a written text. But actually, the "body language" and "posture" of the writing itself proved to be extremely important. For example, Catherine's writing was tight and tense and became more so as she descended lower and lower into the intricacies of poverty. Cara's writing style was similar and might have been a reflection of the daily, unabated tension she experienced, even in her own home. Dee's style was big and cursive, especially when she lived with family members and experienced less stress than other diarists and more social support. I also learned to consider writing-style changes from entry to entry. If a writer's handwriting changed from its usual style to a different one, such a change would cue me to be alert for changes in her physical and emotional context. For example, Dee's writing, while always large and flowing, sometimes degenerated into a messy scrawl, indicating, perhaps, periods of greater stress and instability. Judy's consistently pretty writing paralleled her discussion of such things as putting plants outside her door or magazine photographs on her dried-mud walls. When her writing became scribbled and scrawled, I was alert for signs of familial or financial trouble. The analysis of writing style and spatial positioning of words on a page revealed much information about a writer's mood, her physical and emotional safety, her mental attitude toward her work, and simply her available time frame for writing.

Finally, *paralinguistic* communication "includes all the variations in volume, pitch, and quality of voice" that can be heard in an interview (Fontana and Frey, 2005, p. 713). It was also helpful to analyze this type of communication in written texts. Underlines, exclamation points, and other means of indicating emphasis were incredibly important in my analysis. For example, Catherine's repeated underlining of the word *my*, in such sentences as "It is my duty to do all the household chores because I am the only lady in the house," implied perhaps sarcasm or cynicism or rebellion. Although I was unable to ascertain her exact intent, I noted that there was definitely an added importance to the meaning she was trying to convey. I realized that such underlines were, in fact, flags that should cause me to pause and consider meaning in each case in which they were discovered. Indeed, any underscoring or other emphatic punctuation in any journal was flagged by me and questioned in an effort to extract the author's meaning. Furthermore, I was aware of other indications of emotive writing, such as drawings in the margins of texts. One diarist, Emma, would occasionally draw a sun at the top of a diary page. Was this a rising sun or a setting sun? Was it an indication of optimism or pessimism or simply a doodle? Another diarist, Ina, sometimes drew cartoon-like caricatures of individuals in her margins. Were these people in her life or did they represent her own changing persona? Certainly, they indicated that she liked to draw and had the talent to do so.

Indeed, "interviewing" the texts and understanding them as daily situated dramas helped me understand the changing relationship between the writers' physical and mental space; the importance of silence or omission; and the importance of writing style, syntax, and emphasis.

Moreover, these techniques kept me grounded and focused in the writers' reality—seeing the stories unfold from their perspective, not my own. It was as close as I could get to nullifying my Western perspective and "decolonizing" the data. The application of interviewing techniques to these texts reminded me that I could do more than simply read a diary. I could also "interview" its pages and let them "speak" to me in their own language.

In the following chapters, I'll be looking in greater detail at the experience of working with written texts instead of with oral interviews. With oral interviews, one sees the subject; one can modify questions; one can observe facial expressions and body language. But with written texts, none of that is possible. The oral interview is replaced by a static, written page. As I read and reread the diaries, though, I realized that they were still living dramas, oral expressions situated in an important time and place. I created new means through which I enabled the diaries to speak to me.

5 Hoping God Agrees

As Julie Bettie (2003) has remarked, "forces of domination beyond gender" (p. 24) stack the deck against women in many parts of the world, particularly in places like Kibera. It might be argued, for example, that the coping strategies discussed in this book are, in fact, *dual* strategies, created to cope with both gender-based violence and the poverty that propels women into violent relationships with men in the first place. For the purposes of this book, then, poverty and economic deprivation are understood as pervasive and overarching daily motivations for women in Kibera, where the rigid patriarchal system forces women to seek solutions to hunger/thirst/shelter in relationships with men. The current analysis of strategies for coping with gender-based violence, then, assumed that structural inequalities—manifested in extreme poverty and the ever-present possibility of starvation—both intensified and magnified gender-based violence (APHRC, 2002). Men, even unemployed slum dwellers, had greater economic power than did women, who had to engage in some kind of relationship with men simply to survive. This created a secondary level of difficulty for women in Kibera, who had to be skillful enough to survive their chosen means of survival.

The most commonly mentioned strategy among diarists for coping with gender-based violence was the strategy of *Hoping God Agrees*, which I define as survival by any means necessary, even means that went against the norms for women's accepted behaviour. These women are "doing gender" (West & Zimmerman, 2005) in ways which not only illustrate the social construction of the concept but also show how the active performing of gender can be a survival strategy. The phrase "hoping God agrees" became my operative definition for these pragmatic and gritty strategies, in which women "perform" gender in order to survive while, at the same time, eliciting God's help and support for unapologetically stepping outside accepted moral boundaries.

Interestingly, this strategy was often accompanied by an abundance of prayer and recourse to faith, perhaps because some of the survival techniques were not things that one would normally think of as pious—for example, engaging in survival sex or enduring, for the sake of survival, acts of exploitation by men that the diarists thought were undeserved, degrading, or immoral. The strategy was used by 12 of the 20 writers. Prayer was both palliative and cathartic. In fact, many women assumed the stance of simply informing their god of what they had done that day to survive. They asked for help but not forgiveness; they didn't apologize. One woman wrote that she confessed to God that, when she engaged in prostitution, she believed she was doing the right thing. She wrote, "And I hope, dear Lord, that you agree" (Sally, May 2013).

The large number of women engaging in survival strategies was not surprising. In a 2007 report on gender-based violence in Kenya, Amnesty International (AI, 2007) remarked:

> Violence against women is widespread in Kenya. Every day, women are physically and sexually abused. Rape occurs in all social and ethnic groups. It is a crime that traumatizes the victim and reflects the acceptance of

> discrimination against women in Kenyan society. Yet it is largely suffered in silence. (p. 1)

The report also described some of the social norms that disempowered women in the face of gender-based violence and limited their options in response to it:

> Kenya is a patriarchal society, where the husband is the head of the household and women often have little influence in decisions affecting their lives. This extends to sexual relations, where women are frequently unable to refuse to have sex with their husbands. In Kenya, customarily, women do not own property or the land that they work, which causes them economic hardship and places them in positions of dependence.... consequently, AI is concerned that some forms of violence have become entrenched. For example, wife inheritance, bride price (in which a man's family pays the wife's family thereby giving men the idea they own their wives), forced marriage, and female genital mutilation are institutionalized through culture. The state does not ensure that women are protected against the acts of violence that these practices either embody or support. (Amnesty International, 2007, p. 1)

Similarly, a qualitative study specifically on attitudes in Kibera found that tolerance of gender-based violence (GBV) was especially prevalent in the slum. The study examined "the attitudes, beliefs, and perceptions of violence in the context of the social, economic, religious, and cultural setting in the Kibera community" by conducting 15 in-depth interviews and six focus groups (Community Structures, 2008, p. 1). The study sought to

> understand perceptions of domestic violence among the Kibera community, identify relationship formation patterns in this population, and examine how the experiencing of GBV varies across types of relationships in this cultural context. A secondary aim was to conduct a community needs assessment in an attempt to identify innovative strategies to reduce the levels of GBV in Kibera. (Community Structures, 2008. p. 2)

The study found that "women in the [Kibera] community express hopelessness and many feel that continuing a violent relationship is better than the alternative of having no source of income if they leave their partner" (Community Structures, 2008, p. 3). Second, the study showed that

> there are no awareness campaigns in Kibera that educate the community about sexual violence being a crime in Kenya with the advent of the new Sexual Offenses [*sic*] Act that was recently passed in 2006. The Sexual Offenses [*sic*] Act is a landmark in Kenya regarding its stance against GBV. However, it will have little impact unless the communities suffering from GBV are aware of their protected rights under this new act. (Community Structures, 2008, p. 3)

Finally, the study suggested that there needs to be "a strong focus in Kibera on changing the perception that violence is not only culturally accepted, it is a normal part of any relationship between a man and a woman" (Community Structures, 2008, p. 3).

At the same time, Kenyan custom and socialization do legitimize participation in and reliance on religion in times of trouble. Kenya is predominantly a Christian country, with approximately 78% of the population identifying with that religious faith (45% Protestant; 33% Catholic), while the rest belong to either Islamic (10%), Hindu (10%), or indigenous (2%) faiths (CIA, 2009/2011). Furthermore, religion is extremely important to Kenyans. A 2009 Gallup Poll, conducted on religiosity in 146 countries around the world, asked simply, "Is religion an important part of your daily life?" In Kenya, a staggering 94% of respondents said "yes," as compared to 26.5% in the United Kingdom and 65% in the United States (Gallup, 2009). It was not surprising, therefore, that when women in the current study were confronted with culturally accepted gender-based violence, they found solace or catharsis through culturally accepted religious expression, even when the means of coping were not sanctioned by any institutionalized church.

For example, this *Hoping God Agrees* strategy was described by Catherine, who wrote about the violence she experienced and her recourse to prayer. Catherine was abandoned by her parents in Kibera and found that she must support herself and her younger brother. Catherine wrote:

> My life has become so miserable. My parents left to go to rural areas and left me and my younger brother. They decided to leave because they had

> so many debts whereby every day somebody [would] come to our house claiming their money which my mum had borrowed.... So what I will do ... is to practice prostitution with the men who are around whereby at the end of it they give me a hundred [shillings] and then I am able to buy food ... and call it a day and wait for another day to come.... I have lost hope in life and I ask myself why are we poor?
>
> If I had gone to college I could have gotten a nice job and our life could change but I hope one day God will hear my prayers. (Catherine, April 2008)

Despite her entreaty to God, Catherine did, indeed, enter into a period of using survival sex to keep herself and her brother alive. She described the first time she made an arrangement to exchange sex for money:

> My brother had left for school without any breakfast because we had not been used to [breakfast] since our parents left.... I dressed in what I call my Sunday best and went outside our house whereby people are passing by and see if any man will take to me so that I may agree to sleep with him and he will give me a little money. I stood there for about thirty minutes and then there is this guy who was passing and it seemed he liked me and started talking to me. Within twenty minutes, we had agreed he will give me a hundred and I rushed home and closed the door and I followed him. I timed the time when my brother was coming back from school and made sure I was back in the house. (Catherine, April 2008)

Catherine bought food with the hundred shillings and prepared supper for herself and her brother. However, she did not go immediately back to selling sex because the first experience had been painful and traumatizing. The next day she wrote, "This day I am very tired and I didn't want any business with any man because the previous man had did me very tough, claiming that it's his money but what could I say" (Catherine, April 2008). She had endured the rough treatment and did not look forward to another similar experience. She decided, instead, to go with other Kiberan women to wait outside a nearby housing estate to see if any of the tenants would offer work. Such a strategy was a gamble because it involved waiting—and possibly wasting precious time—for an outcome that was not guaranteed.

Catherine was lucky, however, and was offered a job cleaning house and washing clothes, for which she received two hundred shillings. She budgeted this money to last for several days but by the end of the week, it was gone. She wrote:

> So here we are again not having anything to eat and no money. In fact, money is the root of all this problem because if we had money I could not be hustling like this. So this time my brother noticed that there was no sign of anything to be eaten so he left to play with friends and here I was left alone. I [didn't] know where to start or end. We had completely nothing ... I made up my mind and decided to go to one of our neighbour[s] whom I talked with and I agreed with him to have sex in exchange for money. He gave me two hundred and I was happy to know that I had something at the end of the day. So after the act, I returned to the house. No one noticed and I was happy for that. (Catherine, April 2008)

Catherine continued to experiment with other strategies for survival—ones that did not involve exposing herself to gender-based violence. She washed clothes, for example, and she borrowed small amounts of money from female neighbours. But her delicate balance of resources was easily tipped. When faced with mounting financial trauma, she inevitably resorted to survival sex again, since it was the one source of income that was virtually guaranteed and was relatively quick to accomplish, despite its concomitant risks. One day, when she had just spent several hours doing back-breaking laundry at a nearby housing estate, she returned home to another crisis:

> The lady gave me a hundred and I departed back home only to find my brother had been sent home from school because he didn't have some of his books ... he was hungry since he had not had his [school] lunch. Problem always comes with another problem.
>
> Now here I had only a hundred bob. What do I do? In fact, I am very stressed. So I decide to divide it in half and give him half for school and then spend the rest for our supper because I was also hungry since I had not eaten anything throughout the day.... I cooked our supper ... the darkness had already started ... I thanked the almighty father for the day and went to bed. (Catherine, April 2008)

The problem was there the next morning, though:

> Where to get food and pay rent since it is almost the end of the month? I didn't know but everything I left to my God.... I stayed in the house thinking what step I should take. So I decided I will wait for darkness to come and then I will move outside where people are passing by and try to see whether I will get any man who is in need of me just to see whatever he will give me... (Catherine, April 2008)

Thus, prostitution became a part of her survival strategy. Although she survived, Catherine was now at the mercy of her customers, who, although they did not *always* inflict direct physical violence, always represented the risk of HIV infection, as well as the possibility of pregnancy (Zulu, Dodoo, & Ezeh, 2002; Mugisha & Zulu, 2004; UN-AIDS, 2006). Catherine would ultimately abandon the *Hoping God Agrees* strategy in favour of alternate methods of coping.

Another example of *Hoping God Agrees* as a strategy was illustrated by the diary of Marya, when she discussed her relationship with her intimate partner:

> I feel that sometimes we have to accept that life is like that expesily when your family can't afford your daily needs and other things.... So I have to run to get a boyfriend who can give me some money to buy clothes and other needs.... because I can't afford, I have to obey and do anything to be on top like other girls my age. So I always do what my boyfriend ask me to do. (Marya, March 2010)

She recognized that his jealousy was one thing she must endure. She wrote that "sometimes he even beats me when I walk with the girls. He doesn't want me to talk to them" (Marya, March 2010). She also recognized that she had to put up with his infidelity: "Yesterday I went to my boyfriend and I found him with another girl on the bed but I didn't do anything. I just went back home" (Marya, March 2010). She felt that she has no option but "to continue the relationship with him" and "to stay with him until I get another guy" (Marya, March 2010). Even when Marya became pregnant with her boyfriend's child, she had no leverage over him or his affections. In fact, the pregnancy became another excuse for beating her. She wrote, "Last year, when I told my boyfriend I have [gotten] pregnant, he rejected me and say I have a lot of guys and I am a prostitute and he beat me" (Marya, March 2010). Marya found her only solace in her religious beliefs: "We live through hardships in life here ... all we have is God and Jesus who died for us on the cross. I hope God understands my cross to bear ... God bless us all" (Marya, March 2010).

Yet another example of *Hoping God Agrees* was illustrated in the journal of Terry. She also found that having a boyfriend was an economic necessity because her family could not fully support her. She wrote:

> When he is drunk, he even beats me when I refuse to have sex with him. He takes advantage because he knows that my parents can't afford even the needs of the family.... I can't say having a boyfriend is good. But we have to have the thing. Sometimes they treat me well, sometimes bad.... any way, here in Kibera, life is very hard. You can't even get a good boyfriend. Most of them smoke *bangi*, drink *chagua*, and even some are thieves and use guns. It's very hard.... [My boyfriend] sometimes forces me to have sex with him even when I am in my period. And even things that I can't explain in writing ... I don't agree with everything he does to me in bed but nothing I can do about the situation. (Terry, April 2010)

Like Marya, Terry found refuge from her ordeals in her faith. She wrote that "life is not always just the way we want it to be but we thank God that we *have* a life ... and every day we wake up and pray to our living God to help us continue to make our way in this world" (Terry, April 2010).

A further example of *Hoping God Agrees* in the face of gender-based violence appeared in the journal of Betta:

> Daily we cook maize and we go around the village to sell ... with my child and also my sisters and my mother also. It's a hard business.... It's hard because some guys want to take advantage.... Truth is that I can't watch my child suffering and no money to pay medicine.... I went and sleep with a guy and [he] gave me 100 shillings and he promised [if I do it again] he will give me 200 shillings. But all I buy [is] some medicine and a maize flour and I went and started to cook and we ate. But I am not happy to

> do this ... life forces me to do so. Hope tomorrow things can change for the better. (Betta, February 2010)

Betta's journal showed that her pattern of prostitution continued. The next day, she wrote:

> Then about 6 o'clock, I went to see this guy and we did it again.... [He] gave me 150 shillings and then I went to buy food and we ate.... When you read this, don't think I am a prostitute. Only if it was you, what would you do, getting a child, no money, no father, no money for yourself or somebody to support you. Already you love your child so much—may be she or he can become a person to help the family in future [or] ... a leader of the country. (Betta, February 2010)

Betta, too, found comfort and hope for the future in prayer: "I pray the Lord will help and see my child going to school and also my sisters. May God keep my wits sharp. May bless this family" (Betta, February 2010).

Similarly, Jane described her own situation, as well as that of other young women in Kibera. "A lot of girls suffer because of their boyfriend. They beat them ... others are raped by boys" (Jane, March 2010). She saw men as being universally exploitive of women but considered that a normal part of life. She wrote, "But men is just men. They can't even let you grow to be at least a woman with 18 years. They just want to sleep with you now" (Jane, March 2010). She described her current relationship as an improvement on a previous relationship:

> This is the second boyfriend I have right now. There are some who help and some who take advantage of the situation. The first didn't even help me or even buy me pads when I am in my period ... he even beat me when he smoke bangi. It was very bad days for me.... Now I have [a new boyfriend] but he don't beat me. He try to help me [and] even my family, like buying unga and milk.... So help me God to keep being smart till I see he is stable and marries me. (Jane, March 2010)

Yet another diarist echoed the same sentiments about a similar situation. Cathy M. wrote:

> Sometimes I have to face hardship with men because in our family, we are so many. I am in a family of ten kids.... The only person working is my father who is the breadwinner and we have to depend [for] everything on him.... I have to find some small coins of my own in order to buy my personal items ... and since I am jobless, I have to seek these in men and to attain this, go [through] so many hardships.... There are those who misuse me. They demand sex every day and I have to serve them because it is my way of life. Sometimes I blame myself for being born into a poor family whereby we have to struggle with life.... In these relationships I go through, I.... also get pregnant and if I tell the man he says he is not responsible and I have to go with other men and raise some money. Sometimes I stop this habit but [then] I stay so broke [that] I have no other option and I turn back again [to prostitution] because when I look at my family, my young [siblings] who can't say when they ever had new clothes or a pair of shoes and I say if I can raise a little, I could buy them ... God knows I have to do this and I pray to be able to continue. God help us now and forever. (Cathy M., February 2010)

Another very cryptic and sad comment came from Jane, who lived with her mother and siblings. They were all dependent on the bits of extra cash that Jane obtained from her various boyfriends. She wrote:

> I work so hard all morning in the house and then my mother and I do laundry for other ladies so that we can each get about 100 shillings. When it is time for rent to be paid, if we don't have enough, I go quietly and find a boy who likes me or a man on the street and I go with him. When I come back, I have another hundred shillings, sometimes two. So we can pay rent. I pray to god above that he will continue to make men like me and give me what we need to live. God, if you are listening, it is almost time for rent and I need you to send me a man. I know I am not married, some say God does not approve. I say he approves. He wants me to live and be strong. (Jane, December 2012)

Diarist Emma echoed the same feelings, when she described how it was to wake up in the morning with no food and to feel responsible for finding provisions for younger brothers and sisters. Emma wrote:

> Well, it begins again. I face the morning with my mother drunk and my children asking for food, which we do not have. I go quietly into a corner by myself and I decide. Will I be a good girl or will I be a good provider? I am hungry, too, just like them and I decide to be a good provider. I will sleep with a man today for money and tomorrow, when I attend church, I will hold my head high and know I did my duty to my family, as I have been taught and believe. (Emma, March 2013)

Emma is not the only writer who names and calls out the complicated performance of gender that comes with being a woman in Kibera. Marya also discusses the way she sometimes has to construct and perform two selves that are separate and require different performances:

> Why must there always be two me's? It seems like there must be the me who acts the way everyone wants me to act and the me that makes her way to surviving and living this daily life. In daytime, I work on laundry and I go to church and I do things to care for others, as my mother taught me. But there is the other me that has to get some money to live and so that me does what it has to do, sometimes sell glue or sell my body. There are those men who are ok when you ask for help and those who hit you. Most often I have met the ones with the fists. But that me who gets the beating for the money earned does not admit it to the other me, who is good and pure. Only hoping that god likes both of me because someday when I die I will have to account for this. But I guess god made me here in Kibera so he wants me to live here the best I can. (Marya, February 2014)

Yet another diarist commented on her different gender performances when she wrote that she was "doing my jobs and they require very much attention so that I can be one minute mummy and the next minute selling *changaa* [illegal alcohol]. But I hope that heaven knows I do not want to do latter but it lets me do former" (Gemma, March 2013). She continued:

> When I am home alone or when children are sleeping I am very quiet and I get on my knees and I pray about many things I have in my life as problems. I pray that there is food tomorrow and I pray that I have courage tomorrow and I pray that someday I find a good job or a way to live that I am not always day by day. But when morning comes and there is no food I do what I must do to get it. Life is life and must be lived. Yesterday I and another girl got a tube of glue from some street boys and we sold it little bits at a time and made more than we spent. So now I pray that I do not do that again because the ones who bought will now be not better off but worse off because of me. But I took that money and get tea and sugar [in] very small [amounts] and vegetables and maize to cook. See, god, I have been once again a good mother and put food on our table. (Gemma, March 2013)

It was not until the project was reaching its conclusion that I read any diary accounts in which women described leveraging two roles in the interest of a longer-term goal. It may have been a function of her age or her by-now adroitness at assuming two contradictory roles, but in 2014, Judy describes a bigger plan. She aims to take control of her household:

> My husband is very strict and I see that he does not like if I am not all day at home with our daughter. I do all my work and also take care of her very well but there is not much to be made from laundry and home tasks. I have daily by daily expanded my thoughts for our future. I am set on having business for myself. So that I may begin that, I take my child to a neighbour and there she stays. I cook *mandazi* [doughnuts] and other food after my husband leaves for his work. I hurry and go to where I share a kiosk with a lady who doesn't mind sharing and for her, I pay with food. I then sell for several hours and make sometimes 500 or 600 shillings, much more than I would make staying home with laundry buckets. When finishing, I buy ingredients for tomorrow and I also pay my neighbour some small bit when I get my child. I am home when my husband comes

> back and he does not yet know I am having success because I hide the money and shall not tell until I have all I need to have my own kiosk. Otherwise he might drink with the money. When I have my business he will not fight me or threaten me. But for now if he does not know then it is safer. (Judy, February 2014)

Analysis of *Hoping God Agrees* Strategy

Micro Level

The *Hoping God Agrees* strategy functioned in various spheres of the writers' lives, not only connecting the spheres but also enabling the women to navigate between/among them. For example, on the micro or personal level, the strategy provided a subsistence-level survival on a day-to-day basis, enabling women not only to buy food for themselves and their families but also to purchase daily necessities, such as water or sanitary napkins. However, micro-level activities associated with this strategy reflected macro-level institutionalized values of sexism and violence. Because the strategy consisted of having an ongoing relationship with at least one male partner, it also involved regular sexual activity, which in turn incurred considerable risk. That is, short-term survival came at the cost of beatings and other violence by the male partner and/or the possibility of pregnancy or HIV infection (Mugisha & Zulu, 2004; Kimuna & Djamba, 2008).

Although this strategy might ensure that the victim went on living from day to day in the *short* term, it made no such promise for the long-term future. However, as the project came to a close in 2014, two women had honed their survival strategies and combined them with long-term goals—both intended to establish their own businesses. Their examples show that the *Hoping God Agrees* strategy may be transformed into a pattern for the achievement of a long-term goal.

Mezzo Level

At the mezzo level, this strategy formed a bridge between private needs and public activities. Because very limited job opportunities exist for women in Kibera, this strategy both supplemented and became a substitute for a regular job (Van Putten, 2011; Muchomba, 2014). Indeed, many diarists referred to the process of having a "boyfriend" almost as though it were a job, reflecting their dissatisfaction with the inevitability of the relationship but agreeing that—like a job—"you've got to have one" (Terry, March 2010). Among the negative attributes associated with this strategy was its tendency to reinforce complacency in the face of gender-based violence. Informants in the current study commented on their lack of choice in sexual interactions, saying that they saw no way of protecting themselves from HIV/AIDS or pregnancy. Although some expressed anguish about their plight, they also expressed a feeling of acceptance based on lack of choice. One writer remarked, for example, "I take whoever comes and can satisfy my needs. And in this way, life goes on" (Jane, April 2010).

The strategy could backfire, however, leading women to become permanently entrapped in such a lifestyle, with prostitution as the only source of employment. Because women had little or no say in how sexual relationships were conducted—particularly if sex occurred in exchange for money—they could not usually force men to use condoms during intercourse. In a study of adolescents, young women in Kibera reported that they had no ability to force their partners to have protected sex, even if the woman knew her partner was HIV positive (APHRC, 2002).

Consequently, many young women became pregnant without being married and ultimately had more than one child with different fathers. Once a woman was in this situation, she was virtually trapped for life. The more children she had, the more difficult it was for her to find legitimate work. There were few jobs to which a woman could take her children, and day-care facilities were scarce or non-existent. Unless she had social support to provide childcare (a mother, sister, or friend), there was little left for her but to engage in prostitution to feed her family. Once she reached this point, it was unlikely that any man would marry her because he would decline to support the children of other men. The woman, on the other hand, would be more dependent on men than *ever* because she had more mouths to feed. Continued and increased prostitution was often her only possibility of survival, carrying with it increased risk of more pregnancies that, in turn, entrenched her further into dependency on men. The circle was, indeed, a vicious one.

Macro Level

At the macro level, the *Hoping God Agrees* strategy was the avenue through which the informants conformed to the social norms that pertained both in Kibera itself and in mainstream Kenyan society. They accepted—in some cases *expected*—intimate partner violence to be a normal part of their relationships with male partners. Indeed, experiencing such violence was part of being a woman. Through this strategy, they acted out the institutionalized oppression of Kiberan women. Although the diarists had little access to television or newspapers and most had not attended school since age 10, they, nevertheless, observed mainstream norms as they were manifested in the cumulative fabric of daily life. Men had power. Women did not. Few if any residents of Kibera overtly questioned this main, overarching assumption that characterized relationships between males and females.

It must also be noted, however, that there was an essential irony at the heart of the *Hoping God Agrees* strategy. Although the women who embraced this strategy did it in part because they had been socialized to accept gender-based violence, the actual situations in which they experienced gender-based violence represented rebellions from social norms. For example, it was not a mainstream social norm for a young, unmarried woman to have sex with more than one male partner on a regular basis. It was not a social norm for women to engage in survival sex or other forms of commercial sexual activity in which money was exchanged for intercourse. It was not a social norm for women in Kibera to work or aspire to work independently or in traditionally male occupations. Ironically, the women who relied on the *Hoping God Agrees* coping strategy rebelled against social norms and created non-normative relationships with male partners or activities to secure their own survival. However, once engaged in these partnerships and activities, the women fell back on acceptance of the accompanying routine violence. They continued to rebel in prayer—asking God's acceptance and help with their dangerous choices—but there the strategy stopped. Due to economic and other structural constraints, only two saw a path through which to rebel any further. So they asked God to help them continue with the dangerous choices of their daily lives. Through cunning, endurance, stubbornness, grit, and brazen determination, they survived.

The next chapter, though, will tell the dangerous stories of those who *did* seek and find paths of further rebellion, where the stakes were much higher and the rate of survival much lower.

6

Escape

Another strategy for coping with gender-based violence in Kibera was the *Escape* strategy. This strategy was defined as a quick, usually unplanned, exodus from a current living or employment situation. Such escapes might happen early—for example, from a woman's home of origin. Or they might occur later, once a woman had already embarked upon a married or partnered life, which became untenable. Escape strategies were often unsuccessful because, although they propelled the escapee to a different setting, the gender-based violence she experienced there was often similar to—or worse than—that which she escaped. Sometimes there was a way back to the previous (although unsatisfactory) situation. Often there was not, leaving the victim in a worse situation—one from which she must organize yet another escape.

Thus, the strategy usually offered no true relief from gender-based violence but only a circular or repetitive movement from one kind of abuse to another.

For Mary, the violence began within her home of origin, propelling her onto the street, where she faced a different kind of violence. After an attempted rape by her brother in her home of origin, her father accused her of causing the incident. Threatened with punishment from her father and ongoing sexual attacks from her brother, Mary had little choice but to escape into the street, where she lived with a series of male partners. Eventually, she felt she had no choice but to engage in prostitution. Ironically, being wrongly accused of *being* a prostitute by her male relatives led her to actually becoming one:

> It was because my brother wanted to rape me, and when I refused, he came and told my father that I have started sleeping with men. And it was lies. But father threw me out, and he told me never to go to his house again ... and because I didn't have food, I started street life. Until now, I am continuing with this life. (Mary, November 2007)

Other women embarked on early marriages only to find themselves in violent relationships. The lucky ones were able to return to their parents. Janet was one of those, reporting that

> I got married once for about a month but I returned back home because this man was mistreating me and he started seeing other girls and he was demanding sex every day and even when it came to [providing] food, he could not satisfy me. So I decided to turn back home. (Janet, March 2010)

Susanna also experienced a violent marriage from which she sought escape. But Susanna already had a young child and could not return to her family, who could not bear the additional expense. Susanna experienced a cycle of violence within her marriage, describing a "war in our house" (Susanna, January 2010). Susanna's cycle was comprised of violence, escape, reconciliation, and resumption/escalation of violence. Although she regretted not making good on her escapes, she was passionately in love with her abuser and wanted to believe that he would change. However, aborted escapes only worsened the violence once she returned home.

A typical cycle was reported by Susanna in the following passages. After a good day of sharing laughter and visiting a sick friend, she wrote that "in the evening, we had the same silly usual fights. I had to sleep outside again. What kind of life is this" (Susanna, January 2010). She described waking up in the street because her husband had locked her out for the night. She made an emotional decision to bolt from the relationship:

> My son's voice woke me up … I was shivering with cold. I had slept out. I was sick and tired of always waiting for a man who will never change and neither shows love and affection toward his wife. I took John [her son] and run off. I didn't know whether to go right or left—all I knew [was] I had to run away from that home. We had a long way to go. We didn't even know where we were going.… As I was crying like a baby, a very good friend of mine happened to be passing by. She promised to take both of us to her house. She even promised to look for a job for me. I followed her as we had so much to talk about along the way. (Susanna, January 2010)

Her friend, Lia, provided Susanna with food and shelter for the night. Furthermore, the next day, Lia returned from her job with news of a possible job for Susanna:

> She came home with some vegetables which we used to cook a delicious meal. She surprised me by telling me she had find a job for me in one of the offices in town as a messenger. I felt relieved because I knew all my problems were solved. I was amused by how she got a job fast for me and I have to thank her for showering my problems away. We later headed to sleep. I slept like I would never sleep again. (Susanna, January 2010)

The next day began hopefully, but the hope didn't last long:

> The sun's rays were shining brightly like broken pieces of mirror exposed to light.… At least now, all I have ever dreamt of was to [come true]. Not even one single day [did I] dream of depending on a man for survival. I have always dreamt of catering for myself and for my child.… At around 4 pm in the evening we went for a walk around town. What sort of thing

> ruined my day? I run into John's father but he didn't see us at all. As soon as I saw him, what came to my mind was guilt. I thought a coward runs away from problems instead of being a very brave woman who stands firm. (Susanna, January 2010)

Her guilt made Susanna susceptible to the sudden reappearance of her husband a few days later at her friend's home:

> Just as we were about to leave gess who barged in. Who else rather than Sam [her husband]. He was on his begging knees pleading with me to forgive him. I had no time for such nonsense.... He all of a sudden started crying like a crying baby. I felt pity for him. I didn't know that I was about to engage myself to another mistake. If only I knew I would have never listened to him.... He told me not even to go to work anymore since all my needs he would take care of them. I thanked Lia for all the facilities and love she had shown me for the few days we had stayed in her home. I don't know whether Sam has charm that makes me go mad as soon as he talks.... You know that I threw [away] again my dreams just like that all because in the name of love. I gess he has manipulated my mind and heart which makes me [go] mad as soon as I see him. [The next day] I found myself in my home. I woke up as a good wife is supposed to do, meaning take care of my husband and child. Exactly that is what I did. I can't imagine I lost my job ... what was I thinking? Those were the kind of questions I was always asking myself as my husband set off to work. (Susanna, January 2010)

The next day went well, although there was an uneasy silence around the evening meal. Susanna wrote, "In the evening I started and prepared a nice delicious meal. That night we eat as a happy family except Sam did not share his laughter with us. We were all quiet ... I wish if all our days could be like today" (Susanna, January 2010).

But the violence began again the following morning. She wrote:

> Oh, no, another fight again. This time he claimed that why is his breakfast not on the table. I tried to explain that I had not yet set his table because he hadn't finished dressing. He really makes little conflicts to turn up

> and seem big. It came to the point that he even left without having taken breakfast. I kept telling myself that it was nothing I could be blamed for. (Susanna, January 2010)

But despite her best intentions, Sam didn't come home for supper that night. Later Susanna found a note he had pinned to the door "saying that he would never come home again until I leave to go to my parents. Tears cascaded down my visage. I could not help myself" (Susanna, January 2010). Things got worse when she realized the following day that her small son was ill and, without Sam's financial presence in the home, she lacked the funds to take the child for hospital treatment:

> Another tragedy. Why is all this happening to me? John is very sick. How could I take him to the hospital while I had no money. I did not care I just rushed him without caring how or when I will get the money. As John was being treated, I rushed to Sam's place of work. He saw me first and I didn't see him so [he] told one of his friends to tell me that he was not in. He was sent somewhere. I sat down and just cried. I wish the whole world would swallow me alive. The doctors were saying that he [John] was in critical condition and he needed urgent attention, if only I had ... the money. I tried calling all my friends but they all had some sort of reasons. Luckily Sam came and paid the bills. Later he sped off. He was nowhere to be found. (Susanna, January 2010)

Susanna spent the next night without her husband and the following day in the marketplace, securing food for the evening meal. Little did she know that her husband would accuse her of obtaining the food through suspicious or dishonourable means:

> I prepared some food. Just as the food was ready my husband arrived. He looked angry. He was not happy that I was cooking food and he had [provided] none. He started insulting me and calling me all cruel words in the whole world. As he was about to kick the food [into] the fire I [pleaded] with him not to as tears cascaded down my visage. I know he felt guilty that's why he left. We were left [alone] to eat to satisfy our bellies but not because we enjoyed our food. (Susanna, January 2010)

As she suspected, her husband did not return home that night. After her morning chores, Susanna looked for daily work in the marketplace. Finding none, she decided to search for her husband:

> We decided to go and look for my husband in one of the bars around because that's his hide out. We went in and found him dead drunk. He could not recall anything. I carried him on my back. People were just wondering "who is she to carry, her son or her husband?" I showed less concern to what they were saying and focused on my burden.
>
> Eventually we reached home safe and sound. I had to snatch money from his pocket in order to buy the facilities required [for supper]. Besides he is my husband and I have the right to do so since he hasn't been giving me any money. (Susanna, January 2010)

The next morning, Susanna was punished for what her husband maintained was theft. She described the scene:

> I was woken up by slaps and insults from Sam. He was claiming that I stole from him. I tried to explain how I spent the money but he wouldn't listen. All I could receive was a donkey beating. He left me lying unconscious on the bed. I later woked up. My son John was crying and asking me why does his daddy all the time resemble the devil's image. (Susanna, January 2010)

Her husband again left her for the day. She used the money left from the previous night to buy medicine for her son, who was still sick. Together they did the household chores and then took a nap. The rest of the afternoon was tense, as they waited to see whether Susanna's husband would return that night. He did: "In the evening he came with cooked food for John only. He told me my punishment was to sleep hungry. Seems I annoyed [him] that morning. But I wasn't bothered. My happiest dream was to see John eating" (Susanna, January 2010). Although her escape attempt didn't lead her to a *different* violent situation, as did Mary's, it did increase violence at home. Her husband remained contrite only until she agreed to return to their house.

Once home, she was punished for running away and her punishment was ongoing, consisting not only of severe beatings but also of food deprivation. The strategy of *Escape* had propelled her back home but into a more violent home life than the one from which she fled.

The *Escape* strategy had the same consequences for JC, who lived with her boyfriend and her daughter. JC was 20 but her boyfriend, Thomas, was a decade older and was frequently dissatisfied with JC's mothering and housekeeping skills. One of the most frequent triggers for Thomas's rages and flights into name-calling and abuse was when JC left the baby at home alone while she went out to collect water, because she could not simultaneously carry the child and the two-litre jerry cans of water. So when she could not locate a neighbour to babysit, JC would feed the child, put her to sleep on the bed, lock the door, and hurry to the water collection point. Thomas, who did not work but would not, nevertheless, lower himself to help with either water collection or childcare, became infuriated when he discovered the child alone at home. JC estimates that she was beaten for her offence "more than ten times" and that the beatings included kicking her, and punching her in the face and stomach with his fists (JC, February 2014).

One day, Thomas had been drinking early in the day and he arrived home, intoxicated and belligerent, at the same time that JC arrived with her water collection. According to JC, "He hit me so hard before I had even sat down the jerry cans that I blacked out and when I woke, he was kicking me and the water was spilled all over the ground" (JC, February 2014).

Neighbours pulled Thomas off JC and helped her into the house, as Thomas staggered off on his own. When he had not come home that day by five p.m., JC decided to make an attempt at escape. She borrowed a neighbour's cell phone and called a school friend who lived in another area of the slum. This friend seemed like her best hope for shelter and safety. The friend told her to come. JC wrapped the child in a *kanga* (a cotton print fabric wrap, usually rectangular in shape, worn by women across Africa), took a few personal possessions in a basket, and left. Her escape lasted for three days, at which time the friend's husband informed JC that he could no longer feed her and her child. JC returned home that night:

> Thomas was at home and he was drunk. He locked the door and he hit me hard across the face. He told me to take the baby to the neighbour's house and I did. When I came back, he forced me to have sex and then he put his hands around my throat and he said if I ever leave again, he will

> find me and he will kill me and the child. I believe he spoke the truth; I have not tried to leave again as I care more about my child that I do my own safety or happiness. (JC, February 2014)

Another example of *Escape* leading to worse circumstances was described by Catherine. Catherine became dissatisfied with her strategy of enduring frequent survival sex in order to feed herself and her brother. She realized that this strategy came with the risk of not only beatings and violent sex but also pregnancy and HIV infection. Yet jobs such as washing clothes did not bring in enough money to survive, nor were these jobs guaranteed on a regular basis. One day, when she was visiting a friend who also lived in Kibera, they devised a strategy to escape from the need to engage in prostitution:

> She told me there was a friend of hers who had told her that there is a nearby bar and they need bar maids so we agreed that we should go no matter what as long as we get money. So we agreed to meet the next day and accompany each other. I told her that I had no food for our supper and she decided to share equally with me what she had to cook. At least I left for home with something to eat and I called it a day. (Catherine, May 2009)

Catherine eagerly anticipated the possibility of escaping her current lifestyle in favour of a legitimate full-time job:

> The day came up and I had to wake up early so that I may prepare everything for the interview of becoming a bar maid.... I left to call [on] my friend to lead me. We accompanied each other to the bar place. On arrival, I found the manager there. He greeted us and told us welcome. He didn't even move. He told us he will be paying us [one] hundred each day. So it was our turn to start the job.... We stayed there the whole day working and we were sexually abused by most of the clients and whenever you reported to the manager you were told you will lose your job, so you have to give them what they need and the money we were given [by the customers] wasn't ours. It was for the company.... In the evening, we were given our money and [we] left for home everyone completely tired. The only thing which was ringing into my mind was to continue with it or not. I went home and I called it a day. (Catherine, May 2009)

Clearly, Catherine and her friends had not made an escape but had instead gone from the frying pan into the fire. They were now servicing more than one man per day, with the only advantage being that their pay at the end of the day was guaranteed. Certainly, though, it provided no satisfactory alternative to their previous situation. In fact, in many ways, it was worse. Catherine decided not to return, saying, "I didn't go back in the bar because to me it seemed like I was misusing myself and I was not worthy to deserve this" (Catherine, May 2009). Her dream of escape to a real and regular job had vanished in one day. Catherine returned to her previous strategy of submitting to occasional survival sex, which she had to endure, or starve.

Sarah found herself in much the same situation in 2013, when she wrote about an attempted escape from a bad home situation, supplemented by a bad intimate partner relationship. Sarah lived with her mother and siblings but maintained a relationship with a boy in order to pay her way at home and to help out with the children. But late in 2013, she realized that she was both resented at home for the very food she ate and enduring violence at the hands of her boyfriend to procure that food. She felt that she was between two forces that might crush her. She decided to run:

> My mother would very often hit me when I was child and so I know that she is not wanting me here, with the amount I cost her to feed me. I know she was glad when I leave and sorry when I come back. But I have no other roof. My boyfriend is sometimes nice but when he drinks, oooh, then come the blows and the anger from his voice. I hate it when he drinks but the next day, he will be sorry and he will give me money to help at home. Last week he got angry and it never stop, not that night, not next day. I fear him but I think of going again to house of my mother without any amount [of money] to pay my share. So I just walk and walk and walk until finally I am almost to the end of the market and I see a *matatu* [mini-bus taxi] and I get on it. I do not have money for the driver but he says nothing. I ride this as far as I can go until I am in a place in the city that I have not seen and do not know and there are many buses parked there and I think it is the end of the road. So I get off and I set there until dark. And then I sleep there on a bench that is very near a mall on the other side [of the street]. I sleep there till morning. I stay in that mall area and I see that there is

> a woman on the [side of the road] who is selling maize. So I ask her for food and she gives it. I stay there with her for the all day and we talk. It is there that I make a plan. She tells me how she has this business of hers, how she gets maize or other food and cooks and sells on the road. I want to have a business like this for my own. I like her and she made me know that something else is possible. But when the night is coming again, she leaves for home and I do same. When I get back, my mother slaps me for my time away and bringing home completely nothing for food or coins. So I go back to [name of boyfriend] and receive a backhand there too. But now I do truly know that my life will not go forever this way. I will be like the woman on the road. (Sarah, December 2012)

Women in Kibera did not experience exploitation exclusively at the hands of men. Sally, for example, whose parents both died of AIDS in 2004, lived with her aunt, who made and sold illegal liquor. She also used Sally as a servant and prostitute. Sally wrote that her aunt "makes me make love to every man who wants to have me just because she has been given some cash" (Sally, March 2010). Sally lived under constant duress and threat from her aunt:

> Every day she reminds me that if I don't do as she wants me to, she will throw me out of the house and that [is] what I fear most because no one else seems to have any interest in me. I have tried to seek help just to stop living such a miserable lyfe but all is in vain. Everyone I tell about my problems either has her own big problems or can't even take time to think of my problems.... I don't have any other choice but to live with my aunt just to ... get a shelter and daily bread. (Sally, March 2010)

Sally had strong negative feelings, both toward her aunt and toward men in general, but had no recourse against either:

> It hurts me every day, especially when night comes. I just start to think about who will end [up] with me or what will happen.... I don't know what will come today but I pray that today no [man] will show up and I will be able to sleep ... I hate men. First the men who come and take advantage of me and then my aunty who loves money so much ... how can I get out

> of this situation? I am plotting for my time of freedom and I am making a plan. I have tried it already once but came back for lack of shelter. Help me God, AMEN. (Sally, March 2010)

Eliza, too, wrote about an attempted escape from a harsh situation. She lived with a boyfriend because he was her only alternative to street life. After being beaten and forced to have sex with men he brought to the house, she ran away and returned to sleeping in a vacant lot with other street youth. But that, too, was dangerous and she wrote later about not being able to sleep "because I always have one eye open for who will come by and use me or hurt me. And so there is no rest at night and sometimes I wait until the sun is high to sleep" (Eliza, November 2007). Finally, exhausted and hungry, she returned to her boyfriend:

> I went back to his house looking for food and thinking maybe I will be lucky and he is not home. But he was there and he beat me hard for leaving him. I had bruises everywhere and he told me he will kill me if I leave again. There is nowhere else to go where there is not pain and hitting so I did stay. (Eliza, November 2007)

Eliza never managed to escape the violence that surrounded her. Understandably, she often despaired about her life and her existence in Kibera. In fact, in 2007, she wrote:

> Since I was born, I have wondered why did my mother take birth of me? I have a lot of problems and one of them is what am I eating and where am I sleeping? So I am asking, why was I born? (Eliza, December 2007)

Later, she added, "Things don't change. Why have I no place to lie my head..." (Eliza, January 2009). In 2009, her situation improved somewhat when she returned to live with her mother. But, according to Eliza's diary, her mother drank heavily and provided little emotional or economic security. Eliza was often forced to use sex to support them both.

Eliza died in 2010 of complications related to childbirth. She was 25 years old. Her questions remain good and pertinent ones that have no answer. Eliza was born into a world with no social supports, not even a family member who could provide aid or safety. Her life and death urgently speak for the need to create opportunities for girls who stand alone against overwhelming forces.

No Way Out: Long-Term Use of the *Escape* Strategy

Each of these women's accounts provided one example of an escape from a violent situation—from a home of origin, an early marriage, a long-term marriage, and a job. Each attempt was fruitless, leading women into more or similar violence in a *different* setting or continued (sometimes worsened) violence if they retreated to their former position.

Unfortunately, women in Kibera sometimes spend years caught in such escape patterns, in a downward spiral from bad to worse to bad again. Repeated attempts at escape often provided no way out of the abuse.

Such a cycle was evident in the writing of Dee, a participant in the study until 2009. Because Dee attempted many lifestyles during the length of this project, her story was illustrative of how the *Escape* strategy can become a dangerous and debilitating way to cope. In fact, Dee's ongoing inability to find a place of safety after repeated attempts to escape gender-based violence provided a panoramic view of the strategy's ineffectiveness. Ironically, long-term use of the *Escape* strategy only served to tighten the net of gender-based violence in which women such as Dee are caught.

Dee's first escape was from her home of origin. Although her parents were both alive, they lived separately in different parts of Kibera. Dee lived with her mother and four siblings. She ran away from her mother's home, thinking that even the street would be better than the hovel in which she lived. She wrote, "This is the home sweet home that I came from and that made me run away from home to the street—lack of balance food, lack of enough food, can't sleep because of fleas, bed bugs and lack of clean bedding" (Dee, March 2008). On the street, Dee experienced sex at an early age and became pregnant without being married. She wrote, "What comes to my mind is why men were created by God to destroy women's future. My future was bright before I came to know that women were meant for men. I did not understand ... I got my first-born outside the wedlock" (Dee, March 2008).

Soon Dee fell passionately in love with another man and set up housekeeping with him. They immediately had another child, after which the relationship turned violent:

> I have never seen such hatred; he took his time to play with my future. I do remember the first time we met, he was so loving, so kind ... and of course, he is handsome. But for now, he behaves like a killer who is on the pay.... I have gone through a difficult life of being beaten daily without any reason, being beaten till I bleed and there is no pity. (Dee, April 2008)

After living with her abuser for four years, Dee escaped, remarking that she is "lucky to have come out of his house alive" (Dee, April 2008). But she still ran the risk of seeing her former partner on the street:

> Having gone through this kind of life has made me regret how I came to know this man. I even curse the day we met. He promised me a good life but in turn he gave me the worst life I have ever had. Today if I come to meet him on my way I just find a way not to be seen by him. I find somewhere to hide myself here in the slums. There are many streets that I can go through and not be seen. (Dee, April 2008)

But the separation was short lived. Dee began seeing her abuser again, living with him for another month before old patterns once again emerged:

> I still have the love of my kid's dad after he wanted to kill me for the four years we had been together.... Everything was going quite well but in the month of February, things changed.... He was [arrested] and after he got out, he started fights and quarrels most of the time and I spent the night without food. (Dee, April 2008)

Dee wanted to escape again but "by this time, he was supporting me. I used to go to him and get money to maintain Teresa," her second child and his biological child (Dee, April 2008). Soon, though, she became pregnant again and the abuse escalated:

> Little did I know that I will be in a big mess at the month of May—I got pregnant. I kept it to myself but as the tummy became big, I told him and

> [I knew] I was in for a fight. I was beaten up like a dog. He kicked me in the tummy. I think he wanted the baby to die. Since that time, I have never gone to his place again. (Dee, April 2008)

But the punishment wasn't over. She tried to return to her father's house, but when he found out she was pregnant for a third time, he, too, threatened her:

> At six-thirty I was up packing my belongings because I had some conflict with my father after he knew that I was pregnant. I was confused I did not know where to go, the only choice I had was to go to my mother's place. I carried my kid Teresa and we left. (Dee, April 2007)

Dee spent the next few months living anywhere she could, sometimes on the street. She worked odd jobs while she saved money for a house of her own and a mattress. She was particularly proud of her steadfast efforts and paid regular installments on the mattress she imagined would be hers one day. She wrote:

> Since September, I have been paying money for the mattress which I have been paying in installments. I had paid 950 shillings [about $13], so I had a balance of 750 shilling [about $10], which I paid. So then I will pay 250 shillings [about $4] the day I will collect my mattress. The mattress price was 1700 shillings [about $27]. I thank God because I am about to own my own mattress, and I believe a long journey starts with a single step. (Dee, November 2007)

In December 2007, she was finalizing plans to move with her children into a place of her own, believing that "at least now, we will have a little peace" (Dee, December 2007). Unfortunately, neither Dee nor anyone else in Kibera was destined to have peace during the upcoming months.

In December 2007–January 2008, Dee was caught in the political violence that rocked the country. A controversial presidential election was held on December 27 and the process of vote-counting began. The country was tense and poised to erupt at the first sign that the incumbent president, Mwai Kibaki, would retain power. The timing was not good for Dee, who had just made a down payment on her own house, which she hoped to occupy after the first of the year. She was also in her eighth month of pregnancy when the country (and Kibera) exploded in violence. On December 28, Dee wrote:

> I was woken [from a nap] at 6 pm by the neighbours who were running up and down. I woke up and closed the door tightly so that no one can come in. The tension was high as the counting of votes went on and the people were harassing each other because of the tribe they belong [to]. This was the longest day of the week because you couldn't even go to the shop. I don't even remember eating.... People were all sitted with a radio to know how the counting of the votes is going ... we all stayed awake. Nobody slept. (Dee, December 2007)

By December 31, President Kibaki had been declared the winner of the election and violence was rampant in Kibera. Thousands of homes and businesses were burned and looted. Dee assessed the situation and feared that her house would be burned because she is from the Kikuyu tribe but was living in a Luo neighbourhood. She also feared rape, which was going on all around her. She decided to try to escape Kibera before things got any worse:

> I found myself ... wondering what to do next because outside the house people were running not knowing where to go or what to do next, we have being awake all night fearing that my house would be torched down because of the post-election announcement of the Presidential seat, which many say was not fair.... I just felt uncomfortable and disturbed by the ongoing war tribe against tribe. I had nothing to do but take my kid and flee to look for a safer place.... I carried nothing but a shawl and two bottles of medicine and I left. On my way they asked me where I was going and I told them I was taking my kid to the hospital and they gave me way.... I went on journeying until I reached a church at Karonja. I entered the church and they took me in. In the evening, we were about 300 women ... I was tired and I slept on the bench with my kid beside me. I only woke up to find that it was day lite—it was 5 a.m.—and people were still running from side to side. (Dee, December 2007)

Dee looked outside the church and realized that she was still in an area where there was much violence. She decided to go further from the city centre:

> I left the church at six-thirty, carried my kid on my back and as I left some women asked me where I was going but I told them anywhere I can feel peace around me. I cannot sit here listening as the policemen fire tear gas on the air and people are torching homes and stealing from shops.... A young lady with a kid said that I should not leave her behind; she took her kid and we left the church.... On our way we met some policemen who told us if we are seeking refuge we should go to the Nairobi show ground, which was not far from where we were. As we approached the show ground, we saw people who came running. Behind them was a big crowd of people with *pangas* [machetes] and stick[s] and they were beating somebody ... we hurried and now we were at the main road to the gate. I felt pain on my lower abdomen and it forced me to sit down. My kid was crying and saying mum, let's go but I couldn't even stand up and the lady I was with ... called the police. Two policemen came and carried me to the show ground. (Dee, December 2007)

Dee reported being unconscious for two hours and waking up to find a team of doctors around her:

> The doctor in charge said I have walked a long distance carrying the kid on my back with the situation of my pregnancy. Now it was 2 pm and people at the camp were eating and my kid was running around happily to see her mother awake again. I ate lunch and we were given blankets. We looked for a place to sleep in the arena. (Dee, December 2007)

But, although she had reached seeming safety, Dee found that she had once again fled to a place that was worse—this time psychologically—than the place she had begun. She soon realized that she was among the refugee population, which would ultimately be moved to refugee tented encampments where they would be labelled Internally Displaced Persons (IDPs). She wrote:

> I looked at the situation ... I found myself crying. I was a refugee in my own country. It was a bad situation; this was the first week of a new year; I have

> never seen anything like this since I was born. I have heard of refugees but now I am one.... In the evening the well-wishers [Red Cross and NGOs] brought us some clothes to change [into].... I thank Kenyans who give support to people who need it ... [but] I just took my kid and went to my bedding because the reporters came taking photos. I didn't want anybody to take my pictures since I did not appreciate myself as a refugee in my own country.... I felt depressed and found myself awake most of the time at night ... some time I thought I was dreaming and I wanted out of this dream.... I woke up at seven-thirty ... I told myself that this was my last day at the refugee camp. I need to go to my house even if I had nothing to eat. I no longer want to be a refugee. (Dee, December 2007)

On January 4, Dee escaped again, this time fleeing from the refugee camp back to Kibera, where the violence was abating. She went first to her own house and slept with Teresa on the mud floor. For the rest of the month, she alternated living at her unfurnished house and at her sister's home. Unfortunately, though, there were few odd jobs, since the still-sporadic violence kept people mostly indoors and wary. Furthermore, Dee was nearing the ninth month of her pregnancy, making strenuous work difficult. Her lack of earning capacity during this time caused Dee to lose not only her house because she could not pay the rent but also the beloved mattress on which she had been making payments. The mattress and all other personal items in her house were confiscated by the landlord when the rent was not paid on time. During this difficult time, a person whom Dee refused to identify approached her about selling her unborn baby for cash. She refused. On January 25, Dee gave birth to her third child, a boy whom she named Kevin. She began 2008 with no job, no partner, and no home. She had three young children but few prospects for the future. She wrote:

> Now I will start from the roots again. I don't have anything. My bed, my kids' bed, my bedding, my utensils, I can't believe it. I have saved money to buy a nice chair, now I am empty-handed.... Now I have nothing. Oh my, oh my God, in which place do I belong, was I born to go through this kind of pain. I can't even hold my tears. Who am I supposed to go to? (Dee, March 2008)

With few escapes left and only her mother to rely on for partial support, Dee found herself in the world of prostitution. She wrote, "I don't enjoy sex but I enjoy the money because at long last my kids have food to eat and no one will know the kind of business I am up to" (Dee, March 2008). Soon Dee was infected with a sexually transmitted disease (STD) which caused her severe pain in her abdomen and cost valuable money to treat. She reported that she "spent one week in bed, my abdomen was still paining ... I felt deep pain when I washed my private part" (Dee, March 2008). She admitted that prostitution was a "dangerous and dirty business" but she had no option but to continue:

> Being a prostitute is the only option left and yet it is the hardest decision for me to make. I sometimes have no money to feed my kids, they go to bed without food or sometimes spend the day without eating.... I have tasted the money of prostitution. You have everything you want, eat a balance diet and dress properly with the money but [you also may] end up getting infected with HIV/AIDS. (Dee, March 2008)

Seemingly at the bottom of the social world, Dee feared only the impersonal violence of disease and possible death. But her former abuser was still in Kibera, ready and able to inflict very personal blows on her weakened body. He had heard the rumour that Dee was offered the option of selling her baby boy, which was his biological child. Although he declined to support the child, he decided to intervene when he believed she intended to sell the boy for money. One day when she was taking the child to the hospital, her abuser misinterpreted her actions, thinking she was going to the hospital to make a sale:

> When he saw me, he blocked my way. I tried to cross the road to walk away from him because I fear him more than fire. He followed me and pulled me. I was afraid because I knew how he can react. He asked me where are you coming from. I answered "am from the hospital." He said you think I am a fool. I know that you want to sell the kid. Try it and I will kill you before you enjoy the money. I was waiting to see if he will walk away without threatening me but I was wrong. For the first time, he took Kevin and told me to walk away. I pleaded with him to give my child back but I was beaten [with] strong slaps in front of a big crowd. I still begged but the

> more I begged the more I was beaten. This time blood was running down my nose. The only thing I remember is my clothes looking as if they were dipped in blood. (Dee, March 2008)

Dee woke up in the hospital, where she had been taken by the police, who told her that they found her "beaten and left to die" (Dee, March 2008). They asked her who assaulted her and she told them, "It is the man I love most, the father of my kids" (Dee, March 2008). She did not even consider pressing charges, fearing retribution from her abuser. She told the police that she just wanted her son back and was appalled when the police told her they had no knowledge of Kevin's whereabouts. Dee left the hospital and made her way home, where her other children asked her, "Mummy, where is Kevin, have you left him in the hospital" (Dee, March 2008). She appeased the children with bits of food and lay down to nurse her wounds. That evening, there was an unexpected knock at her door:

> It was my boyfriend's mother carrying my son. As she came in, I took my son quickly ... I told her the whole story. She asked if I can have a talk with her, her son, and the father of my boyfriend so that they can understand the problem between us. I refused because I don't want to die before God's good time. (Dee, March 2008)

Dee not only refused the mediation offer but also continued to use side streets and paths through Kibera to avoid further contact with Kevin's father. Again, her escape into prostitution and desperation had brought with it not only its own concomitant suffering—it had also reignited the wrath of her former abuser, adding another level of risk to her already risky life.

Dee's writing during this period of her life provided a multi-episode example of what could happen when a woman in Kibera engaged in a series of consecutive escape attempts from situations of gender-based violence or the threat of it. With each escape, she encountered more or worse violence and also entrenched herself more deeply in a life of cyclical risk.

In 2010, Dee disappeared from Kibera. Repeated attempts to locate her and discover news about her circumstances were unsuccessful. Other study participants who knew Dee reported that they had heard rumours she got married and left Kibera. No one knew whom she purportedly married and no one knew if the rumours were true. Dee's friends have expressed hope that her final escape attempt was truly successful, leading her to a safe and fulfilling life. In one of her final diary entries for the current study, Dee wrote:

> I have a dream that I am walking away from the troubles in my life from being a hopeless mother to a mother with vision, and from poverty to riches, from rags to good and nice clothes and from prostitution to being a politician. I know that with my head high, my dream will one day come to be part of my life. (Dee, November 2009)

Participants in the current study expressed hope that Dee's dream has come true. Unfortunately, in Kibera, the odds are against her.

Analysis of the *Escape* Strategy

The *Escape* strategy was unsuccessful in removing women from situations of gender-based violence. Escapes were often impulsive and, therefore, had little chance of success since the financial, social, and psychological means to support such escapes did not exist. This was not, however, to say that Kiberan women were particularly foolhardy or intrepid. There is an egregious lack of support services for women in Kenya generally, and virtually none in Kibera. Because women knew this, they also knew that an impulsive escape had about the same chance of success as a planned one—that is, virtually no chance. Still, escape was often seen as a preferable strategy to staying put, especially when a woman risked death in her own home.

No Safety Net: Women's Support Systems in Kenya

Women in Kenya lack an effective system for reporting or prosecuting gender-based violence. They also lack temporary protective housing, as well as the societal support to advocate for such services. For example, although passage of the Sexual Offences Act in 2006 made rape a crime, women still lack an effective system through which to report and prosecute it. In order for an investigation or prosecution to begin, a woman must take the initiative by reporting the crime to the police. If she does so, her statement will be recorded in an Occurrence Book, which is held in each police station. However, most police officers are inexperienced and prejudicial in their dealing with gender-based violence, particularly violence between married partners. Many officers are completely untrained, despite a campaign by FIDA-K to provide education through the publication of a police manual on gender-based violence (FIDA-K, 2008). According to Amnesty International (2007):

> Women who seek police intervention are often embarrassed, ridiculed, verbally abused and made to feel as if they are wasting police time. In many interviews carried out by Amnesty International, woman said they were reluctant to approach the police and had only reported their case when the violence had become so extreme that they needed intervention to protect their lives. (p. 7)

Besides the initial reporting, another burden is placed on women who want to begin an investigation or prosecution of violence they have experienced. That is, women must obtain a Medical Examination Report, also known as a P-3 Form. This form must be obtained from a police station before a woman can be examined by a doctor. The procedure is cumbersome and time consuming, requiring the form's first section to be filled out by the police, who subsequently escort a victim to a police-affiliated doctor to be examined. It is not hard to imagine the difficulties inherent in this system, especially for distraught, abused women who are expected to wait in line patiently for forms and official signatures. Furthermore, Amnesty International reported that many women must bribe police in order to procure a P-3 Form in the first place. A common bribe is one hundred shillings, which often amounts to a day's wages in Kibera, decreasing the likelihood that women will spend such valuable cash. Even if a woman has the fortitude to withstand police ridicule and the wherewithal to secure a form, she must still take the P-3 Form to a doctor and submit to an examination. One rape victim described her experience of reporting a rape:

> After I had been taken to a private doctor, he told me not to wash as I would have to report to the police doctor. Since it was 2 a.m., this meant that my report would have to be filed the next day. I could not believe that I would have to sleep with the smell of those men on me.... When I went to report to the police doctor, I found a long line with all sorts of people.

> The nurse assisting him gave me two glass slides and told me to stick my fingers up myself and wipe the semen onto the glass slide. I could not believe what she was saying to me, they were asking me to re-enact the rape. (Amnesty International, 2007)

The difficulties described above are compounded for women in Kibera, for whom police stations and hospitals are likely to be located far from their homes. They would, similarly, be unlikely to be able to pay a bribe to secure a form or to spend time, with children in tow, standing in line in both police and doctors' offices. But even if they persevered in the above instances, they would be unlikely to have the money to take the next step. Bringing a case to court, which means hiring an attorney, is expensive. It must be remembered, too, that victims of *marital* rape do not even have the right to endure the medieval system described above. Marital rape was exempted in the Sexual Offences Act, a compromise necessary to secure passage of the controversial bill. In Kenya, marital rape is not a crime.

In addition to the difficulties women face in reporting or prosecuting gender-based violence, there is also a severe lack of social services for women who need immediate emergency protection. In the general population, a few women's organizations provide counselling or temporary (one or two days) emergency protection but few offer long-term shelter for women who have experienced gender-based violence. There are no shelters of either the short- or long-term variety in Kibera. Furthermore, experts point to an even deeper structural problem:

> The biggest problem observed by organizations that run shelters and women's organizations is that, because of women's economic disempowerment, many victims of abuse still return to their husbands. As the Women's Rights Awareness Program (WRAP) told Amnesty International, "The silence has been broken to a degree. The women come here for refuge but still negotiate to return home." (Amnesty International, 2007)

Given the lack of social services throughout Kenya and the structural disempowerment of women, it is perhaps not surprising that victims of gender-based violence in Kibera, who could not attain even the limited social services of the middle class, often attempted to escape bad situations by impulsively jumping to something worse. After all, change represented hope for something better and many women felt they had nothing to lose. For women in Kibera, though, these gambles didn't usually pay off. In fact, women rarely broke even.

Micro Level

The *Escape* strategy was only effective if a woman was fleeing life-threatening violence and the escape took her to a place where she survived. If the escape was intended to alleviate ongoing gender-based violence, however, it usually provided neither palliative remedy nor long-term cure. On the micro level, the escape strategy was disruptive of familial relationships, often taking the woman to a different location within Kibera, meaning that she lost the social capital she had built in her area, including bonds with her neighbours and her husband's family. Furthermore, her children's bonds with friends and relatives were also disrupted.

Leaving her home would also mean that a woman must relinquish her material possessions, taking with her only what she could carry. In Kibera, losing clothes, bedding, and cooking utensils made it difficult to set up a new living situation. Such items were expensive and difficult to replace. In addition, a woman's stress and anxiety level increased during an escape attempt, adding to her psychological difficulty and sometimes impairing her decision-making power. If she left a relationship but changed her mind—which many women did because of economic dependence on their abusers—she would often suffer punishment and increased violence once she returned home.

Mezzo Level

On the mezzo level, the *Escape* strategy was similarly non-productive. For example, escape from a violent situation often required a change of residence, meaning a change in a woman's community-level contacts. Leaving a violent husband or partner, a woman must seek safety by moving to a different part of Kibera, resulting in the loss of neighbourhood and employment contacts in her former venue. Because a woman often worked (plaiting hair, selling food, washing clothes) in the neighbourhood where she lived, leaving a relationship was often tantamount to leaving a job. Transition to a new neighbourhood might mean not finding work again until she made connections and established trust in the new location. Similarly, if a woman had children, they might have to stop attending school or lose important school time during an escape attempt.

Macro Level

The *Escape* strategy did not benefit the escapee at the macro level, either. While those women who employed *Hoping God Agrees* as a strategy at least appeared to fall under the social dictates of institutionalized gender norms (they tried to be good wives, they fell back on religious faith in times of trouble), escapees' activities often ran counter to the socialized understanding of women's roles and "proper" female behaviour. Leaving a husband, cohabiting with a series of male partners, or reporting violence to the police all run counter to social norms in Kenya.

Amnesty International (2002) reported that women's families and in-laws often pressure them to stay quiet about their experiences of gender-based violence and not to officially report it. Women choosing to go against such social norms by leaving violent relationships or by reporting gender-based violence to authorities often suffer an additional harm—social ostracism and familial condemnation.

Betting against the House

7

The third strategy for coping with gender-based violence was one that expressed a woman's decision to establish only a limited partnership with a man or men in her life. The strategy was utilized by three participants in the current study, making it a unique and provocative—albeit minority—coping strategy among the diarists. The *Betting against the House* strategy was defined as a pragmatic decision to engage in partnerships with men for economic support (with or without love and friendship) but to refrain from both marriage and child-bearing with these male partners. The strategy was described as a long-term one by two diarists. That is, these writers did not speculate about a time when they would not use the strategy. It was described as a short-term strategy by a third diarist, who envisioned a time when she would be able to abandon it.

The purpose of the *Betting against the House* strategy in both the long and short term was to avoid male power and control in a relationship, which often resulted in violence to the female partner. For two diarists, this was the *only* stated purpose of the strategy and these writers did not seem to anticipate a time when they would engage in other kinds of partnerships with men. A third diarist envisioned the strategy only as a short-term way of coping, almost as a delay tactic or stalling device. Unlike the others, she hoped that it would enable her to avoid the entrapment of marriage and children, as well as the violence that came with marriage, until she could secure a modicum of economic independence. In this manner, should she later choose marriage and motherhood, she would have an "out" if the relationship became violent.

The *Betting Against the House* strategy was clearly defined by Elizabeth, whose terse, succinct, even severe journal entries often provided vehemence without detail. Although her journals said little else about the strategy, she clearly articulated its long-term goal:

> I don't always feel good about this beast called men. I call them beast because they ruen my life. I sleep with them and [they] give me money but no one [is allowed] to say I am his woman. When he thinks that you are, he just start having jelousy. When he meets others then he will even start commanding you or even beat you thinking he owns you. That's why I tell every [man] that I have someone [else]. So he will not have any say on [my] self even when they meet together.... They will fear each other. It's another way of surviving here. (Elizabeth, March 2010)

Sarah described in more detail her strategy of engaging in limited partnerships, in which she kept an intentional distance between herself and the men with whom she was involved. She described learning about sex at a very young age from her mother: "My mom is the one who teach me what happen in bed between two people. We always sleep in one room with our mother ... she drinks wine and comes [home] with different men ... and start doing sex even before I get to sleep" (Sarah, March 2010). She described her first sexual experience as taking place one night when her mother locked her out of the house:

> It all started for me one night when I was chased from the house and I went to a guy and was loving him. I stayed there for three days. I always remember the day and the month and the year when I lost my virginity. (Sarah, March 2010)

Sarah soon began sleeping with men for money so that she could buy food for her family and also some personal items such as clothes, underclothes, or sanitary napkins. She discovered, though, that young men would either promise to pay after sex and then *not* pay, or they would provide only a very small sum of money. She wrote:

> I now expect him to give me money first because some, they can't. They will just promise and after giving him what he want, he will chase you or beat you....Young men don't have money to give you ... only a small amount that can't even help. (Sarah, March 2010)

It is at this point—realizing that sleeping with young men, either for money or in the hope of a future relationship, was neither rewarding nor safe—that Sarah formulated a strategy for survival that consisted of forming limited partnerships with certain pre-selected men. She chose men who were, in fact, already married because they were older (that is, more likely to have the funds to pay for her services) and because their marital status would forbid them from making any claims on her. She wrote:

> My [plan] these days is to get with older men who have family at home ... because of their life at home, they have no [ability] to leave [so I find] someone who give me [money], even if he is older.... My mother only get sometimes food for us but it is not inaffe and even it's only one meal every day of *ugali* [corn meal dumplings] and *sukuma wiki* [kale]. But when I get a good man some times [he] gives me 200 shillings ... so for now, my "boyfriend" is not one [person]. I have like three of them. I sometimes buy things for [my siblings] because our mother is someone who lives with *changua* on her mind. (Sarah, March 2010)

Sarah later added, "I never want to marry and become like my mother with many mouths to feed and then deserted by the dad ... rather I will be alone. I just hope I don't get pregnancy" (Sarah, March 2010).

Catherine also articulated the strategy of *Betting against the House.* For Catherine, the strategy was one that evolved from her experiences while she was a participant in the current study. Catherine first experimented with the strategy of *Hoping God Agrees.* She engaged in survival sex with a variety of partners in order to obtain money for food and relied on her faith in God to see her through. Later, she attempted to reject that strategy for a "job" as a bar maid. This escape, however, was worse than her original situation, so she returned to using survival sex, knowing it might entail frequent violence, as well as the risk of pregnancy and/or HIV infection.

During the final phase of the current study, however, Catherine abandoned the use of survival sex, saying:

> There was a time I had given up with my life, such that I had to sleep with men to get money and enable us to survive. But there [came] a day when I settled down and asked myself so many questions. Yes, I went to school up to Form Four. I did all the best I could and got a moderate grade. [Now] here I am with no college to expand my studies, no job, but I made up my mind and said it is better to stop this habit because HIV/AIDS has spread all over and you never know who has it ... so I decided to quit [survival sex] and started washing clothes and at the end of the day, get the small [amount of money] I will get. (Catherine, March 2010)

As Catherine surveyed her options, she evolved a clearly articulated strategy of *Betting against the House,* a strategy that might minimize her risk of violence and maximize her chance of establishing an independent future. Unlike Elizabeth and Sarah, however, she engaged in a relationship with only one man. She openly shared with him her desire not to marry at the present time and not to become pregnant outside of wedlock. Catherine explained her reasons for adopting this strategy:

> Because I see the way my fellow colleagues have been exploited by men. Many girls has dropped out of school due to early pregnancies. Others has died while doing abortions. Others have contracted AIDS and so

> many things. So now I have this guy whom I fall in love with but I always tell him my hopes and dreams. I always hope to get a job or have my own business.... (Catherine, March 2010)

Catherine noted that she would prefer to stay single. She lamented: "If I had a stable job or if I was brought up in a stable family, I could stay single and never get married" (Catherine, March 2010). In fact, she expressed quite a cynical attitude toward marriage in general:

> Because sometimes I see how some women who are married, what they go through in the so-called marriage. You find a lady having five kids. All of them have not gone to school, her husband is jobless, no food, no clothes, fighting every time, in fact, there is no peace and happiness. (Catherine, March 2010)

Catherine did not entirely reject the idea of marriage in her own future but envisioned it as coming *after* she had obtained a steady job, which would help make her partnership one of equality. She wrote: "I always hope to get a job or have my own business so that we [she and her boyfriend] can protect each other for our future if God will allow us to be together and have our own children" (Catherine, March 2010). But she continued to underscore the fact that the time for marriage and children was not now. She said, "What I am up to now is to get a job or have my own business and the rest will follow later" (Catherine, March 2010).

Mary, who worked the bars and discos of Nairobi, usually under the control of a male partner, also came to a new way of looking at how she made a living and how to empower herself within that work. In 2007 and 2008, although she seemed moderately cynical and extremely vocal about her right to use her body in any way she wanted, by 2013, she had become adamant about eliminating the male partner and using the profits of her work for her own interests and concerns. She was clear and focused in that regard. Having established herself with many local establishments and clients and, as she said, "becoming street wise instead of street stupid," she had initiated a plan to work with the owner of an establishment (restaurant, hotel, bar, club), who would connect her with clients. She still found it necessary to provide a fee for that service but the fee was worked out in advance and was predictable. Unlike with the boyfriends she had previously worked with, she did not have to go home with these colleagues, give them more than their share of her earnings, or sleep with them for free. She also had begun working her way out of the sex industry by using her funds to create a small business that she could share with a friend until she could leave the sex work completely in the past. Mary was keen on describing her new project:

> I was before so sure of how I could control the boys. But I have learned several things and they all have to do with power, which is strength power to hit me and hurt me and also street power where the boy I am with will always have the say over what I say or what I want. So slowly I learn from the boys and I watch. And then I see a way to go around these egos and these brutes. In many years of work I have come to know many men who are more powerful than these little street boys I work with. So I go to them and I make my own deals. I know they will be happy to work with me alone because these boys from street only cause trouble in bars like fights and knives. So I make my own plan and arrangements. I then keep more of my money and I say what I do with it because it is all in my ability to do. First I begin by paying rent on my own house so I live with other girls, no boys. Then I save and have almost enough to buy a kiosk where I will sell goods and food. Two other girls who have no jobs they will help do the work and I will still do my nighttime work at least for now. But one time soon I will be without this nighttime work and I will use my kiosk for all my needs and perhaps someday I will build into bigger business. I have a smart mind and I will use it because I have always known that they have more power those boys but I have more brains. (Mary, February 2013)

Lack of Family Planning among Young Women in Kibera

On the surface, the *Betting against the House* strategy appeared smart, savvy, and contemporary. However, a close reading of the diaries revealed that women using this strategy did not seem to combine it with a concomitant birth control regime that was under their personal control. Surprisingly, they resorted to chance (Sarah) or to a partner's willingness to wear a condom (Catherine). Such a flaw in an otherwise thoughtful coping strategy did not appear attributable to lack of knowledge about contraceptives or to their availability. All three diarists describe attending family planning seminars and having knowledge of birth control. Although diarists did not explain their non-use of birth control, it may have been rooted in the inaccessibility of clinics and the procedural difficulty of even a minimal transaction at such a facility.

Contraceptives are readily available throughout Kenya and can be obtained at clinics, even in Kibera. Birth control pills, as well as an injectable birth control (Depo Provera) and Norplant implants are available at very low cost and sometimes, depending on the clinic, they are free of charge. Nevertheless, during the three-year duration of the current study, only two diarists mentioned using birth control pills to prevent unwanted pregnancy. One is an unmarried 18-year-old who participated briefly in this project in 2007. That young woman (JC) described being taken to a clinic by her mother to receive birth control pills and instructions about their usage. Her mother told her that "just because you are illiterate doesn't mean you can't control your own life" (JC, June 2007). The other mention of birth control pills came from Marya (March 2010), who utilized the strategy of *Hoping God Agrees* to cope with gender-based violence. Marya, who already has one child, used pills to avoid another pregnancy while she hoped for someone to marry her.

It was, perhaps, not as surprising that women using *Hoping God Agrees* or *Escape* strategies did not more commonly avail themselves of female-controlled contraceptives. These women, after all, believed in and sought traditional marriage and child-bearing—sometimes believing that finding the "right man" and bearing his children would be their salvation. However, women employing the *Betting against the House* strategy had rejected, at least for the time being, the idea of marriage and children. It is surprising, then, that these women did not avail themselves of birth control methods that would enable them to prevent unwanted pregnancy, with or without partner cooperation. The use of the pill, for example, would seem to raise the odds of economic survival in favour of these women and give them more time to put their strategy into effect. Particularly in the case of Catherine, whose future plans depended on not becoming pregnant, it seemed counter-intuitive not to utilize birth control. However, none of the women who used the *Betting against the House* strategy mentioned using female-controlled family planning methods. One woman (Elizabeth) mentioned nothing about her birth control choices. Another (Sarah) worried about becoming pregnant—a tacit admission that family planning is not under her control. A third diarist (Catherine) mentioned "always" asking her partner to wear a condom, a statement that implied she does not have her own birth control plan.

Because the diarists did not offer reasons for their lack of a safe birth control regimen, my attempts to understand this omission are based on research and observation about clinic location and usage in Kibera, not on diarists' written journals. Clinic inaccessibility has been cited by health experts as a huge problem in Kibera, one that likely affects the diarists. For example, a 2002 study on adolescence in Kibera by the African Population Health and Research Center (APHRC) provides noteworthy statistics. Although the APHRC survey is primarily focused on adolescents' knowledge of HIV infection, it also includes questions on general reproductive health education and choices in Kibera (Erulkar & Matheka, 2007). The survey interviewed 1,675 adolescents aged 10–19, asking them, among other things, about their knowledge and use of birth control. A total of 921 young women took part in the survey, of which 16% were already married. Of those not married, 36% were sexually active. The study reported that 56.4% of married or sexually active young women had used a family planning method and, of those, most had used the male condom (37.4%). Although 41.5% knew about injectable contraceptives and 46.1% knew about birth control pills, only 19% had ever used injectables and only 16.7% had ever used birth control pills. A staggering 1 in 10 young women depended on "safe days" to avoid pregnancy. Like the diarists, then, these adolescents know about female-controlled contraceptive options but still do not use them. Such statistics may imply that it is not education that is lacking in Kibera but the ability to put that education into practice.

Clinic Accessibility

Part of the problem may lie in the inaccessibility of clinics and health centres in Kibera. There are currently no public (government subsidized) clinics in the slum. Clinics that do operate in Kibera are operated by private NGOs, such as CARE, UNICEF, and AMREF, as well as a variety of churches and faith-based groups. Although there is no accurate estimate of the number of health clinics in Kibera (some are extremely small and many are ephemeral), the Global Alliance for Africa (GAA, 2010) estimates that "there are four viable health clinics in Kibera" and that "these clinics are being overwhelmed by the demand for services from the ever-growing population." The Global Alliance is currently constructing a clinic in the Kibera village of Kianda, where they estimate that there is "only one other proper medical facility serving a population of 350,000" (GAA, 2010). According to the GAA, many people do not attempt to utilize these clinics "due to the long distance of the nearest clinic or lack of finances" (GAA, 2010). Indeed, travel to/from clinics, plus long on-site waits, may result in loss of a day's wages. In addition, there may be a cost for care. Private clinics vary in their policies about consultation fees and payment for medicines or drugs such as birth control pills. One clinic that is currently operating in conjunction with CARE International waives the 30-shilling consultation fee for its poorest patients but does charge for medications dispensed (GAA, 2010). Other clinics may choose an opposite strategy, providing pills or injectables for free but asking for a consultation or "visiting" fee from the patient. Consequently, for a woman seeking birth control pills, the "cost" to her may be a long walk to a clinic, a long wait, and then, finally, an undefined expense that her budget may not be able to absorb. Thus, women in Kibera may not have time or money to invest in the long (and repetitive) process of obtaining birth control. Ironically, short-term dependence on subsistence daily labour may stand in the way of long-term reproductive independence.

Analysis of the *Betting against the House* Strategy

Micro Level

Nevertheless, if pregnancy was avoided, the *Betting against the House* strategy was moderately and temporarily successful at the micro level of diarists' lives. That is, engaging in *Betting against the House* provided women with a degree of economic security at the same time that it limited the male partner's ability to exercise control over them or abuse them. However, the strategy was successful only if the women who employed it remained childless. If women did become pregnant, there was little likelihood that the fathers would marry them or continue to support them. Many men distanced themselves from women with whom they had fathered children, even if they knew that woman did not seek marriage, because they would not or could not pay to support a child (Catherine, March 2010; Cathy M., March 2010). If a diarist bore a child, the *Betting against the House* strategy was no longer effective for them. Having children rendered mothers more economically dependent on men than childless women were, making it less likely that mothers could control what kind of partnerships they engaged in with men (Kimuna & Djamba, 2008). Indeed, women with children often had to accept whatever partners they could get and on whatever terms.

Thus, *Betting against the House* was actually a risky strategy and one with high stakes. The strategy was viable only if combined with a female-controlled family planning regime. Unfortunately, diarists in the current study appeared not to be using reliable birth control. For Elizabeth, Sarah, and Catherine, then, the *Betting against the House* strategy was more like a ticking time bomb than a sustainable solution to gender-based violence.

Mezzo Level

On the mezzo level, the strategy was only semi-successful because it was out of sync with patriarchal social norms. Having relationships with multiple partners (Elizabeth) or married partners (Sarah) might not stand women in good stead among neighbours and peers in Kibera, who would likely consider that these women were simply prostitutes. Even Catherine would not find social favour for long. Although her relationship with her current boyfriend was monogamous (on her part), it still did not comply with patriarchal standards for female behaviour, which dictate that women should prioritize marriage and motherhood, not careers (Amnesty International, 2007). Indeed, since there were few opportunities for viable women-owned/operated businesses in Kibera, a woman like Catherine would need either incredible luck or outside help, perhaps in the form of a microloan, to make her strategy work. In order to secure such a loan, even in Kibera, a woman must have some kind of social capital, perhaps a relationship with a local NGO, such as UNICEF or AMREF. Lacking special connections or the confidence to achieve them, women using this strategy were racing against time. As they spent their days doing laundry, for example, they lost touch with other employment skills. As their years out of school *increased*, their marketable skills *decreased*. Indeed, the longer they were delayed in establishing careers, the less likely it was that they would establish them at all.

Macro Level

Structural change is coming to Kenya. Advocates for women's rights and for equality in women's employment are increasing. Among the mainstream population, the average monthly wage of a working woman is still only two-thirds that of a male doing the same job. Nevertheless, in 2007, the Kenyan government pledged to set aside one-third of existing civil service positions for women (US Department of State, 2010) and although this pledge has not yet been implemented, the promulgation of the new Kenyan constitution pushed it further toward fruition (Constitution of Kenya, 2010). The constitution, adopted in August 2010, includes language on women's rights in both community and home environments and may enable progressive legislation on women's issues within the next several years. Nevertheless, women in Kibera like Catherine, Sarah, and Elizabeth are aging and do not have much time to wait for structural changes on the macro level to trickle down to them. Unless women's opportunities increase in Kibera, the *Betting against the House* strategy may time itself out, leaving them no choice but to marry or to struggle through their middle years in a downward spiral of subsistence-level poverty.

Gender and Political Violence in Kibera 8

Although the purpose of the current study is to describe and analyze coping strategies used by young women dealing with violence from their intimate partners, it would be inappropriate to omit the diarists' descriptions of gender-based aspects of the political violence they endured during December 2007–January 2008. Previous discussion included an account of Dee's attempt to escape the Kibera inferno; however, she was not specifically escaping gender-based violence but trying to flee to a place where members of her tribe would be safe. But many diarists wrote about gender-based aspects of the post-election violence, which clearly targeted women regardless of ethnic affiliation. In some instances, political violence was an excuse for a free-for-all on women that included kidnapping, rape, gang rape, and murder.

During the political upheaval in December 2007, Kibera writhed and burned. The violence was mainly a war between the Kikuyu and Luo ethnicities. Many of the diarists described the mayhem and murder they saw—mobs hacking people to death with machetes, chopping off heads, burning down homes with families still inside. Diarists described fear, horror, hiding in alleys, and sneaking out of the slum under the cover of darkness. These experiences were common to both women *and* men. However, some experiences were common *only* to women and happened not because there was an ethnic conflict but because the tribal war gave men (of either ethnicity) an excuse to make war on women. Women sought to survive by any means possible. Many of the descriptions below were written in March 2010, when the promulgation of the new constitution, a new voter registration drive, and a visit to Kenya by Kofi Annan brought back memories of the 2007–2008 turmoil and caused diarists to reflect on their experiences during that turbulent time.

Diarists in the current study frequently wrote about their perception that rape was generalized beyond ethnic boundaries and that women were sexually targeted. For example, Jane wrote:

> It was a very long night.... It was like day because of the fire everywhere. Next day, we and other girls were helping each other to remove their belongings [from their houses]. People were passing by being cut, bleeding, going to the hospital. It went on till the end of the day. A lot of women were being cut only because they were women. Also they say they were raped. (Jane, March 2010)

Jane also commented on the sexual free-for-all, in which young men and boys raped any woman they could find, regardless of age: "Other boys were raping women who were older than their mother" (Jane, March 2010).

Sometimes women trusted men of their own ethnicity to aid them during the riots, only to find that trust misplaced. These women experienced first-hand the reality that sharing an ethnic affiliation did not necessarily protect them from being raped by men or gangs of men who were empowered by the chaos. For example, Betta described her experience when she trusted some young men of her tribe to help her search for her younger sister, who had become lost during the riots:

> My mother came and told me she can't see our smallest sister. I panic and started crying. My friend came and told me to stop crying. We can go and look for her. It was around 9:30 at night and on the road, we found some guys we knew. They told us they will help us to find my sister. But after that, they were drinking. They locked us in a house and they were having sex with us every time they wanted and forcing us to do whatever they want, telling us if we try to run, they will kill us. Till now, I haven't stopped thinking about that.... I also see these criminals around. Nothing I can do to them. (Betta, March 2010)

Although the main "war" was between the Kikuyu and Luo tribes, no women were safe. Women who belonged to an ethnicity other than Kikuyu or Luo were also fair game when it came to rape. Catherine, who belonged to the Kamba ethnicity, found that being a non-party to the conflict did not protect her. She managed to prevent her own rape by a quick and effective lie. Her neighbour women were not so adroit or so lucky. Catherine described her family's calculations of whether they should try to walk out of Kibera and risk exposure on the streets or stay home and risk attack:

> By this time, my mum had communicated with my uncle who lives in a rural area [and decided] to bring us there. But me, I wasn't going to go ... because at this time [even] policemen had taken advantage wherever they know there is a pretty lady. They were storming houses and raping them. So I didn't want any of them to see me during the day because, if they do, I had to face the consequences. So I told my mum to leave me behind and leave with my young sister and brother because they are young and nobody would probably take advantage of them when they see them.... So they talked with one of the policemen and he agreed to accompany them to the nearest bus station.... So they left and here I was with my dad and some few neighbours, not knowing what to do and with nothing to call food. But at least we were from the same tribe [Kamba] as our neighbours, so we have trust. (Catherine, March 2010)

Later that night, Catherine regretted that she had not gone with her mother to a rural area. She wrote:

> Little did I know that it was our turn that night. I should have gone with my mum. The night came and no one could sleep because of the fear of being attacked. We closed tightly our door, although the doors are so bad such that, if one kick it, it's down, so we just stayed calm.... Suddenly I heard people storming our gate. I trembled and within one second, I was under the bed. From there, I could hear my neighbours screaming one second and the next minute, they keep quiet, meaning they were dead. I knew this was the end of us.... In a few seconds, they stormed our door, gangs of boys entered. I found myself screaming, forgetting I was hiding. They attack my father and ask what tribe he was. When my dad told them, they cooled a bit.... By this time, I was pleading with them not to kill us but one of them said, "Let's rape her." I screamed and suddenly something ran into my mind. I told them that I was HIV positive and thank god, this saved me. They left me. They took everything valuable they could find and left us.... I went back under the bed, thinking they might change their mind and come back. There I cried the whole night. (Catherine, March 2010)

The next morning, Catherine found that her neighbours had been killed and the women raped, despite the fact that they were Kamba:

> In the morning when I opened the door, I was trembling but when I saw stains of blood starting from our door step, I knew [the neighbours] were dead ... two of our neighbours were dead and the woman was raped.... Later she was taken to the hospital because she had so many injuries. I could imagine how she felt after all those more than seven men going through her. It was just by the grace of God that I did not go through the same. (Catherine, March 2010)

Conclusions

Participants in the current study were shocked and horrified by the political violence of December 2007–January 2008. It is likely that many of them are still suffering from post-traumatic stress disorder (PTSD). Diarists described not only the trauma—"until the day I kiss the grave, I will never forget" (Catherine,

March 2010)—but also the frustration of seeing the men who raped them walking around the community unpunished when the riots were over. It is possible that the gender-based violence women experienced during the political turmoil enabled them to see their daily violence in a different light and that it may have prompted them to see their "private troubles" as a version of the hegemonic patriarchy and the devaluation of poor women. No diarist made any political comments in her journals, nor indicated she believed she was qualified to make such remarks *before* the post-election violence. *After* the violence, however, women wrote the first diary entries in which they speculated about their nation's political future and questioned the roots of the violence. Dee, for example, wrote:

> Since the election, being a Kenyan is not something to be proud of. Many people lost their lives, while others lost their beloved ones; a lot of blood was shed down.... I dream of a Kenya of different tribes [but] one people. We should love one another ... and not let our economy favour the rich ... because for now the rich are benefiting while for the poor, everything is at a high price. (Dee, February 2008)

Similarly, Catherine, in an uncharacteristic entry about the roots of political violence, wrote:

> Nairobi, especially Kibera slum, is among the most physically and psychologically violent places on earth. Not only is crime and violence a feature of everyday life, but slum dwellers are emotionally assaulted daily by greedy politicians who don't care about their living conditions, by opportunistic landlords who think nothing of charging rent for a mud hovel with no toilet, by employers who pay them a pittance and by a government that spends millions on politicians and then claims to have no money for public service. For most of us slum residents, the grind of getting through the day is fraught with hazards. Most mothers ... give their kids alcohol to stop them from pleading for food. Most of the girls are raped by their drunkard fathers or by men in the street and there is no one to help them. The slum is being neglected by policymakers who think that, in our poverty, we are the ones to blame for what we do. (Catherine, March 2010)

No conclusion can be drawn from the current study about the relationship between the post-election riots of 2007 and the growth of Kiberan women's political and social concern. However, future research might attempt to discover whether the gender-based aspects of the 2007–2008 political violence are related to women's understanding of and concern about the larger national patriarchal context in which gender-based violence is situated.

Part Three

The Implications

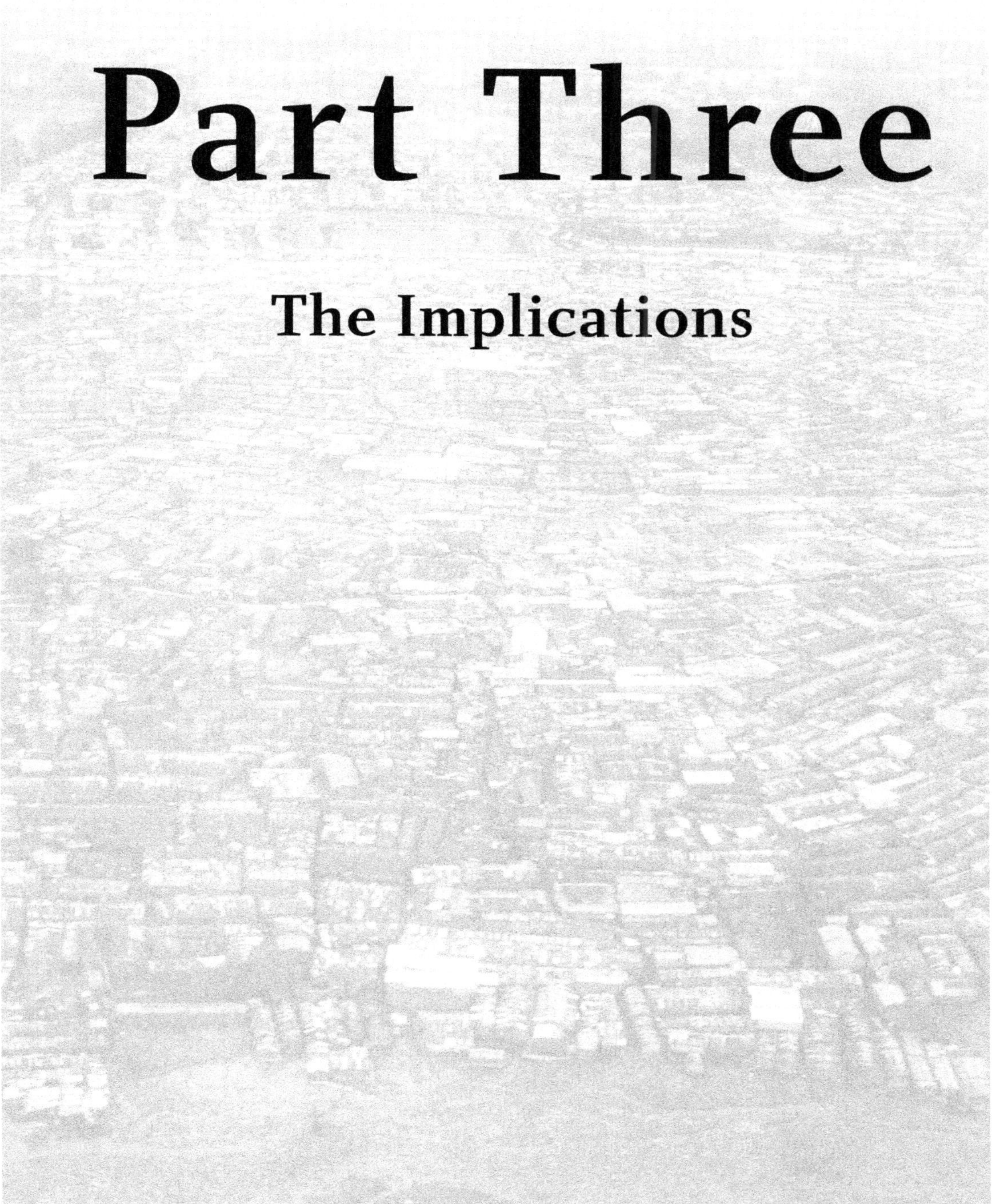

9 Learning from the Diary Data

In order to really hear and respond to the voices of the diarists, it is important to listen not just to what they say but to why they say it. What are their choices? Why do they make them? And how are these choices embedded in the structural problems that are manifest in Kibera? Most importantly, how do these women use their choices not only to survive but to create opportunity for change?

Prevalence and Efficacy of Coping Strategies

The current study shed important light on what kinds of strategies women used to cope with intimate partner violence and, in fact, which strategies were the most effective in keeping women safe. How many women used what strategy and why?

More participants in the current study (12) chose the *Hoping God Agrees* coping strategy than either *Escape* (5) or *Betting against the House* (3). One participant changed strategies, experimenting with all three strategies during the course of the study.

Hoping God Agrees appeared to be the strategy that had the greatest possibility of keeping women alive. That is, women using this strategy appeared to consolidate the benefits of their current situation (home, food, stable neighbourhood relations), while minimizing the risks that would come with leaving those things. Unlike women who chose the *Escape* strategy, they appeared to be adept at playing gender roles to mitigate the need to escape. And, unlike women who chose *Betting against the House*, they appeared to prefer staying within the bounds of social approval, maximizing the social capital that came with community approval. If social services existed in Kibera, the strategies of *Escape* or *Betting against the House* would likely hold greater potential for helping women eliminate violence from their lives. But since there was no safety net for women who tried to escape violence—and since material necessities that are needed to underpin alternative strategies were difficult to access—the *Hoping God Agrees* strategy appeared to provide the best option for women trying to protect themselves and their children from male abuse.

But, although *Hoping God Agrees* was the most widely used and possibly the most effective in keeping women alive, diarists did *not* appear to choose this strategy out of passive acceptance or a belief that they deserved abuse. In fact, they expressed anger and unhappiness about their abuse and resistance toward their abusers. The fact that their strategy choice appeared to be out of sync with their attitudes toward the violence seems to indicate that their strategies were chosen out of necessity, not preference. If Kiberan women had access to social services or economic empowerment, their strategy choices would likely change. If conditions existed to give them what one diarist called "a hand up" (Sally, March 2010), they would likely take it and not look back. Unfortunately, at the time of this writing, the city of Nairobi has no plans to offer social services to Kibera residents and NGOs' limited budgets are outstripped by Kibera's burgeoning population.

Redefining Agency

Global feminist theory encourages us to inspect the webs of domination that affect women and to analyze the intersections of various types of oppression.

Applying such a theoretical construct to results from the qualitative component of this study provides a unique way of understanding the choices of coping strategy made by various women.

All of the diarists experienced the intersection of intimate partner violence and the structural conditions of extreme poverty, as well as the oppressions of class, age, and ethnicity. The web of oppression was difficult to circumvent, given that there are few social services in Kibera and that patriarchal norms govern the macro, mezzo, and micro levels of their lives. There are, indeed, few chinks in the armour of domination. Yet women made choices, exhibited agency, and lived their lives within these constraints. I suggest that they did so by consciously "doing" gender in the way they saw as most self-serving and self-protective. Thus, each of their strategies was an interaction ritual—a way of "doing gender" that women hoped would work to their advantage.

Women who chose *Hoping God Agrees*, for example, tried to side-step gender-based violence by playing the role of the good and patient woman—a preferred role for women in Kenyan society—while ironically, stepping outside those bounds when necessary for survival. They espoused social norms while defying them. In such a way, they "did" gender to ameliorate intimate partner violence by performing the appropriate socially acceptable woman's role, calling only on God for help and support when the need came to openly defy those roles. Such a choice provided them with familial support (from both their own and their partner's family); with support from a church or faith-based community; and with sympathy, a kind of social capital emanating from the community's understanding that women are fighting against overwhelming odds.

Women who chose *Escape* as a strategy, on the other hand, attempted to find an opening in the web of oppression and to use it, although often to their own disadvantage. It appeared that women who used *Escape* as a strategy had more access—or paid closer attention—to media sources such as television, radio, and newspapers. There was a distinctly higher reportage in their diaries of reacting to news events or spending lengths of time reading or listening to news broadcasts. Dee mentioned magazines, books, or radio eleven times in her diaries; Susanna mentioned listening to the radio four times in her writing; and Catherine mentioned reading novels and watching both movies and television five times. No other project participant mentions any interaction with news media more than twice. Dee's mentions of media were the most extensive and she appeared to use the media as a point of departure for her own writing. Sometimes she commented on articles she read in newspapers. Other times, she described a reverie brought on by a particular song. For example, she wrote:

> I stayed awake for a long time and read the magazine until I was tired. The only thing left to do was listen to music. I wondered why I was the only one feeling lonely and having no one to share my love with. For some months now, I have not seen my daughter's father, who is the only man I want to spend my future with. But things fall apart.... In my life, I have been inspired by Whitney [Houston] and this song: "I will live my life the way I like, no matter what, I'm gonna keep it real. And it's time for me to do it on my own." I can't tell at what time I fell asleep but I remember waking up at night to find the radio still on. [I] put it off and went back to sleep. (Dee, November 2007)

It is possible that the global media was influential in providing role models for women who chose the *Escape* strategy and that it affected what they perceived as appropriate or available choices. However, such choices may only have been appropriate in mainstream society, where greater economic opportunity and social services, such as emergency shelters for battered women, were in place. Such a possibility underlines the importance of creating those needed and expected social services in Kibera—more clinics, more reporting venues where women are believed and respected, and more safe houses or routes of escape to shelters in other parts of the city. It is a tall order but one that must be fulfilled.

Women who chose *Betting against the House* as a strategy chose to "do gender" in a subversive manner, by co-opting the institutions that held them down (e.g., marriage, motherhood as defined in Kibera). They were determined not to marry or bear children, at least not until they had created a base of personal economic empowerment. They hoped not to fall into the trap, so aptly described by Catherine, of the battered "lady" with no education and an increasing number of children every year. However, because this seemingly intelligent and forward-thinking strategy was not supported by necessary material advantages—such as birth control choices that were under women's control—it actually was nothing more than *Hoping God Agrees* under a more progressive guise.

Indeed, each diarist chose a strategy for "doing gender" that was congruent with her perceived options and opportunities. In this way, women negotiated the web of domination by constructing gendered interaction rituals that enabled them to traverse the complicated terrains of their daily lives. As they were "doing gender" they were also exercising agency by actively choosing to live, to endure, and to work to create new coping strategies that worked better and produced better long-term results.

Narrative Style and Coping Strategy

The qualitative component of the current study also revealed an intriguing overlap between coping strategy and narrative style. Schegloff (1997) has remarked that narrative data occupy a space at the "intersection" of language and action. This intersectionality of language and action had particular implications for the current study because the diaries described coping strategies (actions) through the use of particular narrative styles (language). Furthermore, diary narrative was necessarily "retrospective meaning-making" (Chase, 2005). The narrative style of a diarist indicated how she chose to interpret her past experience and how she portrayed herself in the activity of coping with intimate partner violence. In other words, writers described what had happened—what violence they had experienced and how they dealt with it—from the standpoint of looking back upon the violence and its after-effects. Each diarist had, therefore, two kinds of strategy—a *coping* strategy and a *narrative* strategy, through which she described how she coped.

Analysis of diary data revealed three narrative strategies most commonly used by writers: *generalized reportorial*, *dramatic storytelling*, and *future-oriented reportorial*. Perhaps not surprisingly, these narrative styles corresponded closely to diarists' coping styles. Not all diarists who employed a particular coping strategy used the same narrative style in all of their writing. Some writers, most notably Catherine, used varying and inconsistent narrative styles. Nevertheless, it is important to note that coping strategy and narrative style did correspond in enough cases that future research is warranted to determine their relationship.

The first narrative strategy, generalized reportorial, was the narrative style most often used by women who chose *Hoping God Agrees* as a way to cope. This narrative style was consistently used by seven of the eleven women who employed this strategy. The narrative style was characterized by short, succinct sentences or phrases that depicted a situation as stationary and unchanging. For example, Marya wrote, "My father, he comes at night drunk. He always drinks every day because of the life and stress ... every day to wake up and find the situation the same. We eat the same meal every day" (Marya, March 2010). When she described experiencing intimate partner violence, she described it in generalized terms. For example, "When I told my boyfriend I have [become] pregnant, he rejected [me] and say I am prostitute and beat me" (Marya, March 2010). Jane, who similarly used the *Hoping God Agrees* coping strategy, spoke in the same short, generalized style. She wrote, "Sometimes I feel that I can go somewhere far and die there. When I think how life is treating us. Sometimes our house is closed. My father being told to pay the months [of rent] he has not paid" (Jane, February 2010). She also wrote, "Kibera is a place called bad names by rich people.... It is not our wish to be here. I was born here, also my parents. My father can't afford anything. We lead very bad life" (Jane, February 2010). When she described the intimate partner violence she experienced from her boyfriend, she did so in declarative and generalized terms: "Sometimes he beat me when he smoke bangi ... but men is just men" (Jane, February 2010).

A second narrative strategy—dramatic storytelling—was distinctly different from the generalized reporting style. Dramatic storytelling was characterized by the presentation of information in a literary manner, with many descriptive details, metaphors, and dialogue. This narrative style was most commonly used by writers who chose *Escape* as their coping strategy. In fact, four of the six writers who employed *Escape* as their coping strategy also used a dramatic storytelling narrative style. For example, Dee wrote about the first time her son stole money:

> My plan is to prove that being a street girl is not a challenge to being a good mother. This is my strongest principle and I work hard to achieve it. My son had gone once to the street. He stole money from my mum's pocket and he ran away from home. The amount was 900 [shillings]. For an eight-year-old, stealing 900 is a lot of money. I looked everywhere

> for him. I found him around 9:30 pm. He had used 400 shillings. The balance was 500 but I added my own money on top and lied to my mum that Rodney didn't take the money. I just found the money in the house. Mum believed and I told Rodney to lie because if the truth came out, he could be chased out of my mum's house and be back in the street for good. (Dee, May 2009)

When she described her experience of intimate partner violence, it was similarly in the form of a dramatic story, with herself at the centre. The following excerpt is from a much longer description of an incident in which she was beaten by a former partner and woke up in a local hospital:

> I opened my eyes. I was shocked to see doctors around me. I sensed danger. Around the bed were two policemen and a doctor and a nurse. They asked me my name and where I am from. I told them and asked them where was my son? They were shocked, they looked at each other. And the doctor asked me, "You mean you have a child?" I answered I don't only have one child, there are three. I asked them who brought me here. The police guard said we are the ones who found you beaten up and left to die. (Dee, May 2009)

Clearly, Dee's storytelling style was very different from the reportorial style of women who simply recounted that "he beat me."

Similarly, Susanna, who also chose the *Escape* strategy for coping with gender-based violence, used a dramatic storytelling style in her diary. For example, she described the beginning of a day: "It was raining cats and dogs. I woke early. I didn't want to be late for the second day of my new work. I had to rush like the wind to get ready" (Susanna, March 2010). Similarly, she described each of her many instances of intimate partner violence in dramatic mode. For example:

> Oh, no, another fight again. This time he claimed that why is his breakfast not on the table. I tried to explain that I had not yet set his table because he hadn't finished dressing. He really makes little conflicts to turn up and seem big. It came to the point that he even left without having taken breakfast. I kept telling myself that it was nothing I could be blamed for. I completed

> my chores in due time. Later I took a nap. As the sun was about to settle in the west, supper was ready. Since my husband had not arrived home yet [I] ate with John [her son]. I woke up around midnight and found Sam [her husband] was not home yet. I came to find a note at the door which was saying he would never come home again. (Susanna, January 2010)

Recounting her experiences in story form, with visual cues about the weather and the sunset, denoted a very different narrative strategy from the generalized reportorial style used by women employing *Hoping God Agrees* as a coping strategy. Susanna's long and detail-laden description of being deserted by her intimate partner was told in dramatic, dialogic fashion. Although she and Jane were describing the same kind of incident, Susanna's account was very different in style and content from Jane's blunt statement "he rejected me."

Finally, a third strategy, future-oriented reportorial, was used by all three women who chose *Betting against the House* as their strategy of coping with intimate partner violence. This narrative style was similar to the generalized reportorial style. It too, consisted of short, declarative sentences and spoke more often in generalities than in specifics. However, there was one distinct difference in the two styles, in that the future-oriented style spoke of things that could be, of plans that might occur at a later date. Elizabeth spoke of a plan in which her strategy would cause men to compete for her and not exert control over her. She says, "They will fear each other ... that's another way to survive here" (Elizabeth, March 2010). Similarly, Catherine recounted: "I have this guy that I fall in love with but I always tell him my hopes and dreams. I always hope to get a job or to have my own business so that we can protect each other for the future if God will allow us to be together and have our own children" (Catherine, March 2010).

When describing her strategy, Catherine said, "What I am up to now is to get a job or have my own business and the rest will follow later" (Catherine, March 2010). Unfortunately, her diaries indicated no clear plan about how the "rest" would follow. In fact, all three women who utilized the *Betting against the House* strategy lacked realistic underpinnings to make their coping strategies successful. Similarly, their narrative styles were devoid of detail, metaphor, and adjectival description. They speculated about their futures but did not portray themselves as active agents in the evolving dramas of their lives.

The Efficacy of Storytelling

The close correspondence between coping strategy and narrative style brings up many questions that cannot be definitively answered through the current study. For example, the writers in the current study who employed the *Escape* strategy also most often employed a dramatic storytelling narrative style. This parallel in strategy and style raises provocative questions. Is there a relationship between the ability of a diarist to present herself as an active agent in her own drama and her ability to resist or escape abuse? Do her attempts to escape abuse *create* the narrative style, or does the narrative style contribute to the resistance? Unfortunately, since few safety nets exist in Kibera, most women who used *Escape* as a strategy were not rewarded for it. But, if social services *did* exist, it is likely that the women who attempted to escape abuse would be more likely to actually *accomplish* that escape. More research is needed on the relationship between the ability of a woman to dramatically construct her own subjective story and her real-life ability to exert personal agency in her life. It is possible that diary projects such as this one, in which women have the opportunity to "star" in their own life story, may aid in the learning or *honing* of women's capacity for agency, resistance, and social change. But such projects, although important, take a back seat to the structural change that will provide opportunities for women in Kibera to actually realize agentic capacity. Clearly, Kiberan women are ready to use their agency in creative, intricate, and stubborn ways. However, they lack the stage upon which to enact this performance.

The diary project has been an effective way to learn about the personal stories of women and their diversity. In the future, women's writing may be combined with theatre and other art projects to further give voice to women's reality in Kibera. Through such subjective means of expression, women externalize not only their personal strengths and stories but also gaps in social needs and important social problems that have not been uniformly articulated or added to policy agendas.

10
Learning from the Survey Data

The results of the two-hundred-woman survey administered in conjunction with the diary project provided context for the thematic diary data, as well as an illuminating backdrop for the personal stories revealed in the diaries. It also provided a means by which to better understand diarists' experience of gender-based violence in relation to that of their peers.

Survey respondents were asked to specify their age, birthplace, living arrangement, number of children, and source of income (see table 3).

The mean age of survey participants was 24.2 years, with a minimum age of 18 years and a maximum age of 36 years. Women born in Kibera made up 40.5% of survey respondents, with other women hailing from a wide range of provinces. Nyanza Province and Rift Valley Province were the most widely represented

TABLE 3: Demographics of Survey Population (N=200)

	Mean	SD	Min	Max	Percent	Number
Age	24.2	4.1	18	36		
Years in Kibera (if not native)	8.6	4.7	1	20		
Number of biological children	1.4	1.2	0	5		
Children living w/you	3.6	2.9	0	9		
Marital Status						
Single					31.8	62
Married					49.2	96
Divorced					5.6	11
Separated					7.7	15
Widowed					5.7	11
Living Arrangement						
Alone					14.5	29
With husband					46.5	93
With boyfriend					6.0	12
With children only					11.5	23
With relatives					21.0	42
With roommates					0.5	1
Something else					0.0	0
Source of Income						
Work					30.3	60
Supported by male					44.9	89
Supported by relative					24.2	48
Something else					0.5	1

provinces of origin for those not born in Kibera. Non-native respondents reported a mean time of 8.6 years living in the slum, with a minimum of 1 year and a maximum of 20 years of residency in Kibera.

Almost half (49.2%) of the survey respondents reported being currently *married*, while 31.8% reported being *single* and 5.7% *widowed*. Another 5.6% said they were *divorced*, while 7.7% referred to themselves as *separated* from an intimate partner. The mean number of biological children reported by respondents was 1.4, with a minimum of no children and a maximum of 5 children. However, when asked how many children currently *lived* with them, the mean was 3.6, with a minimum of 0 and a maximum of 9, indicating that women may sometimes house and/or support children who are not their biological offspring.

When asked about their current living arrangement, 46.5% of respondents reported living with a *husband*; 21% said they lived with *relatives*; 14.5% said they lived *alone*; and 11.5% reported living with *children only*. Only 6% reported living with a *boyfriend* and only one respondent reported living with a *roommate*. Women's source of income was primarily from a male partner, with 44.9% of respondents reporting being supported by a husband or boyfriend. Others indicated that they worked (30.3%) or were supported by relatives (24.2%).

Survey results showed that 84.5% of women had experienced some form of gender-based violence in their lifetime. Survey respondents were also asked to report their lifetime experience with 11 different *types* of gender-based violence from an intimate partner (see table 4).

TABLE 4: Experience of Gender-Based Violence (N=200)

	Perpetrator			Frequency		
Experience	**Yes**	**Husband**	**Boyfriend**	**1-5**	**6-10**	**11+**
Said something to humiliate	61.9	69.9	29.2	38.0	8.0	8.0
Threatened you or someone close to you	35.9	70.2	29.8	19.5	5.0	4.5
Pushed, shaken, thrown something at you	35.1	71.0	29.0	64.3	16.1	19.6
Slapped or twisted arm	35.6	74.2	25.8	62.7	15.3	22.0
Punched with fist or other object	26.8	65.9	34.1	52.6	23.7	21.1
Kicked or dragged you	27.3	69.5	30.5	46.2	28.2	23.1
Tried to strangle or burn	20.4	79.2	20.8	54.5	27.3	18.2
Threatened with knife, gun, or weapon	15.5	71.4	25.0	56.5	26.1	17.4
Attacked with knife, gun, or weapon	13.0	76.2	19.0	52.9	29.4	17.6
Physically forced you to have sex	36.1	71.2	27.1	69.4	16.3	14.3
Forced you to perform other sexual acts	30.9	57.4	40.7	65.7	8.6	25.7

The most frequently reported type of gender-based violence was being *humiliated* in front of others, with 61.9% indicating that they had experienced this type of abuse. The second-most frequently reported type of violence was the physical *forcing of unwanted sex*, with 36.1% of women reporting that they had been forced by an intimate partner to have sexual intercourse when they did not want to. Other types of violence included being threatened or having someone close to them threatened (35.9%); being slapped or having arms twisted (35.6%); being pushed, shaken, or having something thrown at them (35.1%); being forced to perform unwanted sexual acts other than intercourse (30.9%); being kicked or dragged (27.3%); being punched with a fist or another object (26.8%); being strangled or burned (20.4%); being threatened with a knife, gun, or (other) weapon (15.5%); and actually being attacked with a knife, gun, or (other) weapon (13%).

In each of these categories, for women reporting that they had experienced a particular type of violence, a husband, rather than a boyfriend, was the most frequent perpetrator of the violence. Percentages of husband-initiated violence ranged from 79.2% (tried to strangle or burn) to 57.4% (forced woman to perform unwanted sexual acts other than intercourse). Respondents who had experienced abuse in a particular category were also asked to report how many times they had experienced that abuse. They were provided with three frequency rates: 1–5 times; 6–10 times; or 11 or more times. In each of the 11 categories, most respondents indicated that they had experienced the lowest frequency rate (1–5 times). Interestingly, in most categories, respondents indicated that the rate of frequency was slightly lower for each step *up* the frequency scale. Three categories differ from this pattern. For these categories—*forcible sex acts other than intercourse, slapping/twisting arms*, and *pushing/shaking/throwing an object*—more women had experienced that type of violence 11 or more times than had experienced it 6–10 times. For example, 22% of women had experienced being slapped or having their arms twisted 11 or more times, while 15.3% had experienced that type of violence 6–10 times. Similarly, 19.6% of women had been pushed or shaken 11 or more times, while 16.1% had experienced that violence 6–10 times. The greatest discrepancy between the middle-frequency rate (6–10 times) and the highest frequency rate (11 or more times) occurs in the category of forcible sex acts other than intercourse, where 8.6% of respondents reported experiencing that type of violence 6–10 times, while 25.7% indicated experiencing it 11 or more times. This gap may indicate that, for this type of gender-based violence, when it happens at all, it happens frequently. This is also the category where boyfriend-initiated violence (40.7%) is the highest, perhaps indicating that both husbands and boyfriends perpetrate this type of violence on female intimate partners, with boyfriend-perpetration accounting for the increase in reported frequency.

Women's Help-Seeking and Coping Strategies

Survey participants were also asked whether they talked about their abuse with anyone (see table 5). Women who talked to family (39.1%) represented the largest category of respondents who said they discussed the violence they experienced. A smaller percentage (22.8%) reported discussing their abuse with friends, while 20.7% said they talked to no one. Some women discussed their abuse with a counsellor (14.7%); with the abuser himself (15.2%); or with their children (4.3%).

TABLE 5: Women Who Reported Talking to Someone about Their Abuse (N=200)

	Percent Yes	Number
Talked to Family	39.1	72
Talked to Friends	22.8	42
Talked to No One	20.7	38
Talked to Husband/Boyfriend	15.2	28
Talked to Counselor	14.7	27
Talked to Minister/Priest	7.7	14
Talked to Children	4.3	8

Note: Women could check all answers that applied.

Survey participants were also asked what was most helpful in enabling them to cope with the violence they experienced (see table 6). A full 39.1% of participants said that having faith in God was the thing that helped them most. Another 22.8% reported that they sought professional counselling; 20.7% said they ended the relationship; 15.2% said they got their partner to change; 14.7% said they became better wives/partners themselves; and 7.7% indicated that their most helpful strategy was something other than any of the above-presented options. Only 25.7% of participants indicated they had ever sought medical attention for the abuse they received.

TABLE 6: Factors Most Helpful In Coping with Gender-Based Violence (N=200)		
	Percent Yes	**Number**
Had Faith in God	39.1	72
Professional Counseling	22.8	42
Ended Relationship	20.7	38
Got Husband to Change	15.2	28
Became a Better Wife	14.7	27
Something Else	7.7	14

Note: Women could check all answers that applied.

Finally, survey participants were asked to define their subjective feelings about the violence they experienced (see table 7). Forty percent (40.1%) said they felt angry; 20.2% said they felt that they did not deserve the abuse; 17.1% said they felt very upset about the violence they experienced; 16% reported feeling sad about the abuse; and 3.7% said they felt that they did deserve the abuse they received from their partners. An additional 9.6% used a write-in option to indicate that they felt something other than the above options presented to them. Those write-in descriptions ranged from feelings of suicide to feelings of not wanting to have future relationships with men. Three women wrote that the category did not apply to them because they had never experienced violence from an intimate partner.

TABLE 7: Subjective Feelings Related to Experience of Abuse (N=200)		
	Percent Yes	**Number**
Feel angry	40.1	75
Feel I did not deserve it	20.2	38
Feel very upset	17.1	32
Feel sad	16.0	30
Something else	9.6	18
Feel I did deserve it	3.7	7

Note: Women could check all answers that applied.

Women's Attitudes toward Gender-Based Violence

In addition to asking about experiences with victimization, the survey asked respondents to reply to four questions indicating their attitude toward gender-based violence, and under what circumstances, if any, that violence might be justified. Three of the four questions had between four and five subparts, eliciting gradations of opinion on one particular subject. For example, respondents were asked if a husband or boyfriend would be justified in hitting or beating his partner in five particular situations: *going out without telling him; neglecting the children; arguing with him; refusing sex;* and *burning the food.* Results showed that there was no category in which more than 28% of women thought beating might be justified. A solid 70% or more of participants replied that beating was *not* justified in *any* of the categories presented to them. The category "refusing to have sex" received the highest percentage of "not justified" responses, with 87.1% of respondents saying that a man was not justified in beating a wife or girlfriend for denying him sex. Burning food received the second-highest level of "not justified" responses, with 86.5% of respondents indicating a man was not justified in beating his partner for burning dinner. Participants indicated that men were not justified in beating partners for arguing (78.4%); going out without telling him (74.2%); and neglecting the children (70.2%).

Another category of questions sought information on women's attitudes about their right to refuse sexual participation with an intimate partner (see table 8). Participants were asked whether they believed they were justified in refusing to have sex in four very different situations. Women responded that they believed they were justified in refusing sex if they knew a partner had a sexually transmitted disease (84.8%); if they had recently given birth (83.7%); if they were tired and not in the mood (81.1%); and if they knew he saw other women (79.5%). Respondents were also asked if they believed they were justified in asking a partner to wear a condom if they knew he had a sexually transmitted disease (see table 9), to which 92.9% responded that they thought they *were* justified in asking for condom use.

TABLE 8: Is a Woman Justified in Refusing Sex Under Certain Conditions? (N=200)

Condition	Percent Yes	Number
If she knows partner has STD	84.8	162
If she knows partner has sex with other women	79.5	151
If she has recently given birth	83.7	159
If she is tired and not in the mood	81.1	154

TABLE 9: Is a Female Partner Justified to Ask for Condom Use When She Knows Her Male Partner Has an STD? (N=200)

	Percent Yes	**Number**
Justified in asking for condom use	92.9	183

Another series of questions asked respondents whether they thought their husbands or boyfriends had a right to engage in certain punishing actions if they refused to have sex with them (see table 10). Eighty-four percent of participants said that husbands or boyfriends did *not* have a right to use force if a woman refused to have sex; 83% said they did *not* have the right to see other women; 80.3% said they did *not* have the right to refuse to give the woman household money; and 71.9% said the partner did *not* have the right to get angry.

TABLE 10: Does a Male Partner Have the Right to Engage in Punishment If a Woman Refuses Sex? (N=200)

	Percent No	**Number**
Right to get angry	71.9	138
Right to refuse woman money for household expenses	80.3	151
Right to use force to have sex	84.0	158
Right to have sex with someone else	83.0	156

Women's Agency in Relation to Intimate Partner Violence

Survey respondents were asked to reply to a series of questions designed to gauge their sense of agency or control over the violence they experienced (see table 11). Only 29.3% indicated that they had *no* control over the violence, while 48.4% indicated they had *some* control, in that they did not accept the violence and were considering options to handle it. Eighteen percent of participants indicated they accepted the partner's violence as something that was important and valuable; 13.2% indicated they accepted the partner's violence because doing so conformed to social norms; and 8.5% indicated they accepted the violence because someone else insisted that they do so and non-conformity would cause "trouble" in their daily lives.

TABLE 11: Factors Related to Women's Agency among Survey Participants (N=200)

Statement	Not at all true	Not very true	Somewhat true	Completely true
	Percent			
I do not have any control over whether my partner is violent with me.	53.4	12.6	4.4	29.3
Someone else insists I comply with my partner's commands.	71.4	13.8	6.3	8.5
I accept my partner's violence so people will approve of me and respect me.	64.0	20.6	2.1	13.2
I accept my partner's violence because I believe it is valuable and important.	57.7	17.5	6.9	18.0
I do not accept my partner's violence and have considered options for how to handle it.	35.1	9.6	6.9	48.4

The series of agency questions was based on an adaptation of the Ryan-Deci scale (Pillay, Rishi, & Kulkarni, 2004; Pillai & Alkire, 2007), which was designed to elicit much more nuanced information than reported here. For example, when responses are aggregated into a weighted index, the scale provides a Relative Autonomy Index, which illuminates the multiple ways that agency may be socially constructed by more than one social factor at a time. It enables a respondent to indicate that "several or even all possible reasons" for exercising agency (or not) might "be present to varying extents" at the same time (Centre for Development Studies, 2007). For example, a woman may indicate she has some agency in a certain situation but that she also modifies that agency to please her father-in-law, without which family life would be difficult, and that she also feels somewhat coerced by social norms and what the neighbours think. A questionnaire based on the Ryan-Deci framework has recently been "developed, piloted, and revised" to make it "appropriate for inclusion in a survey ... addressing women who are destitute or below the poverty line" (Centre for Development Studies, 2007, 2013) in Kerala, India. Although an in-depth analysis of agency using the Ryan-Deci framework is beyond the scope of this study, the series of questions included in the current study may provide fertile ground for future research, particularly since the scale has recently been used among a similar slum population. Comparisons between the Kerala population and the Kibera population may provide a seed for future research projects.

Summary of Survey Results

Results of the current study's survey component yielded demographic characteristics of participants and provided information about the type, prevalence, and attitude toward the gender-based violence they had experienced. Most survey participants were in their early to mid-20s. About half of them were married and indicated they were living with their husbands. Women's sources of income were primarily from their male partners.

Survey respondents indicated that being publicly humiliated was the most frequent type of violence experienced (61.9%). The physical forcing of unwanted sex was the second-most often reported experience of violence (36.1%), followed closely by being threatened or having someone close to them threatened (35.9%) and being slapped (35.6%).

Questions about women's attitudes toward gender-based violence indicated that most survey respondents did *not* agree that men had a right to behave violently toward their female partners in order to punish them or educate them. Seventy percent did *not* agree with the idea that a man had a right to beat his wife in *any* of the posited situations, from burning dinner to refusing to have sexual intercourse. The category "refusing to have sex" received the most "not justified" responses, while "neglecting the children" received the lowest percentage of "not justified" responses.

When asked if a woman had a right to refuse to have sex with her partner in certain posited situations, 79.5% or more of women indicated that a woman *did* have the right to refuse sex in each of the posited categories. Ninety-three percent of women also replied that they thought they had a right to ask their partners to wear condoms if they knew those partners had sexually transmitted diseases. Further, a full 84% of participants indicated that a man did not have a right to use force if a woman refused to have sex.

When they were asked to define their subjective feelings about gender-based violence, women's responses were in line with their attitudinal preferences. Forty percent said they felt angry about the abuse; 20% said they did not deserve it; 17% said they felt very upset about it; and 16% said they felt sad. Fewer than 4% said they believed they deserved the abuse or found it constructive or educational.

Although these above responses appear to indicate that many women reject patriarchal norms and ideas, participants' responses to a series of questions about help-seeking seem to indicate women had no effective channels through which to seek economic or emotional support. Only 39% of women talked to family and only 23% talked to friends; 21% of women said they talked to no one about their abuse and 39.1% indicated that having faith in God was their chosen coping strategy.

Comparison of Diary and Survey Findings

A comparison of demographic results of the survey to the qualitative diary data showed more similarities than differences. For example, a large percentage of women participating in both qualitative and quantitative components of the study had been born in Kibera. Approximately 40% of the survey participants were native Kiberans, while half of the diarists had been born in the slum.

Most women in both study components indicated the *importance* of male economic support to their ongoing survival. Forty-five percent of women surveyed indicated they were supported by male partners, while 30.3% indicated that they were working, and 24.2% said they were being supported by relatives. Diarists repeatedly wrote that they could not survive economically without some sort of male support from a boyfriend, husband, or father, and that this support had to be combined with another job to meet basic economic needs. Such reports from the diarists indicate that the survey question—asking participants to choose one answer to the question of how they supported themselves—was not nuanced enough to provide realistic data. In hindsight, it is now patently obvious that Kiberan women support themselves through *multiple* means at the same time—not working *or* being supported by a male but working *and* being supported by a male. All but two of the diarists indicated their source of income as a combination of male economic support and their own work. The other two writers reported a combination of all three sources of income. The clarity and nuance provided by the diarists' accounts may help refine and reshape survey questions about income that are posed in future surveys of this population.

The survey sample showed a higher number of married participants (49.2%) than was found among the diarists, among whom only two were currently married during the course of the study. One diarist was officially divorced. Among survey participants, 5.6% said they were divorced and 7.7% indicated they were separated from former intimate partners.

Experience and Frequency of Violence

A total of 84.5% of survey participants indicated they had experienced some type of violence from an intimate partner during their lifetime. Among the diarists, 95% (all but one) reported having experienced violence from a recent or current intimate partner. The three most highly reported types of violence among survey participants were verbal humiliation (61.9%), forced sex (36.1%), and being threatened (35.9%) (or having someone close to you threatened). The first and last categories closely paralleled diarists' accounts. Among the diarists, all but one made at least one mention of verbal humiliation or public "put down" by an intimate partner; half reported being threatened or made to feel fear by an intimate partner.

In relation to forced sex, the percent of diarists reporting it was much higher than women participating in the survey, with 75% (15 out of 20) indicating they had been forced to have sex when they did not want to. It should be noted, however, that diarists did *not* provide enough detail to determine how much of this unwanted sex was reluctant acquiescence to a male partner's demands and how much was forcible rape. Sentences like "he makes me have sex, even when I am on my period," did not differentiate between coercion and force. In addition, 30.9% of survey participants reported that they were forced to perform sexual acts other than intercourse. Four diarists (25%) alluded to other sexual acts ("things I cannot explain," or "things you would not believe") but did not specify what the acts were.

Women's Attitudes

Most diarists did not describe their abstract ideas about gender-based violence in the highly specific contexts delineated in the survey, especially if they had not personally experienced those contexts. Consequently, it was not possible to construct a direct correlation between the specific survey questions ("Is a man justified in beating his wife if she burns the food?") and the diarists' daily accounts of their intimate partner experiences. However, it *was* possible to construct a general comparison between the survey responses to the question "How do you feel about the violence you experienced?" and diarists' personal accounts of their emotional responses to intimate partner violence. For example, among survey participants, if the categories for *anger, not deserving abuse, feeling upset,* and *feeling sad* were combined, they indicated that 93.4% of survey respondents had experienced some or all of those feelings. Similarly, among diarists, all but one expressed some or all of those feelings during the course of the study. Although 3.7% of the survey participants said they believed they *did* deserve the violence, this sentiment was not echoed among any of the diarists.

Women's Agency

A cursory comparison of agency between survey participants and diarists was all that could be provided by the current study. Nevertheless, it was interesting to note that 40% of diarists exhibited an unconventional coping strategy in regard to gender-based violence (either *Escape* or *Betting against the House*). This figure is very close to the percentage of survey participants (48.4%) who said that they "did not accept" the violence they experienced and were "considering options to handle it."

Women's Coping Strategies

Thirty-nine percent of the survey participants reported talking to family about gender-based violence. Only four diarists reported talking to family about their abuse. Instead, about half of the diarists reported talking to friends, while only about 20% of survey participants reported "girl talk." Among the survey participants, 20.7% indicated that they talked to no one, while among diarists, only 10% talked to no one about their abuse.

When asked what helped most to cope with gender-based violence, 39.1% of survey participants indicated that having faith in God was their best source of support. This may correspond to the *Hoping God Agrees* category among diarists (55%), in which they experienced domestic abuse, sought solace in prayer and religious faith, and struggled to reconcile the violence with gender norms. Although 22.8% of the survey sample said they sought professional counselling, such a strategy was not widely represented among diarists, of whom only 10% reported seeking counselling. Fifteen percent (15.2%) of survey participants said they got their partner to change (no diarists reflected this response) and

14.7% said they became better partners (no diarists reflected this response). The 20.7% of survey participants who cited ending the relationship as the thing that helped most to cope with intimate partner abuse may correspond to diarists who reported the coping strategy of *Escape* (25%), a usually unplanned and hasty exit from a situation of abuse. Among survey participants, 7.7% of participants indicated that something other than the options offered by the survey instrument was a coping method. Unfortunately, the survey instrument did not provide women with the option of writing in what this "something else" was. It would be fascinating to know if any of these responses corresponded to the limited partnership category among diarists (15%). Future surveys may refine this category and yield more nuanced information.

Summary

There were few but, nevertheless, interesting differences between survey participants and diarists. Survey participants were more frequently married than were the diarists. Survey participants more frequently talked with family about their abuse, while diarists talked more frequently to friends. Survey participants also showed a greater tendency to seek professional counselling to cope with gender-based violence (22.8%) while very few diarists mention counselling as a coping strategy. These differences may be attributable to the fact that more of them were single, perhaps encouraging "girlfriends" to talk among one another in a way married women would not. It is also possible that the higher percentage of survey participants who sought professional counselling indicated that survey respondents were more educated than diarists, among whom only two had achieved any education above the primary level.

Similarities between the survey population and the diarists, however, far outweighed differences. Although the lifetime experience of gender-based violence was slightly higher among the diarists (95%) than among survey participants (84.5%), both percentages reflect an extremely high level of abuse, and a level of abuse considerably higher than that of the general population (44%) as reported in the KDHS (2014). Similarly, the emotional response to violence among survey participants and diarists was very similar, with virtually *all* women indicating they felt angry, upset, sad, and that they did not deserve the abuse. Another significant similarity was found in the area of coping strategy, with survey participants indicating that *religious faith* helped most to cope with violence and diarists indicating *Hoping God Agrees* as their most frequently chosen coping strategy.

Moving Forward 11

Limitations of the Study

The study was limited by its small sample size—20 diarists, supplemented by a survey of 200 women in the same age range. Such a small sample does not enable the generalization of results beyond the parameters of the particular Kiberan women participating in the research. The survey participants were drawn from three Kiberan villages (Laini Saba, Mashimoni, and Soweta East). However, I hope that some of the many limitations may be outweighed by the ability of these data to provide a rich and detailed insiders' perspective into the unique culture of Kiberan women.

Implications for Micro Policy

Since 2000, a bill to criminalize domestic violence has been stalled in a committee of the Kenyan Parliament. National and well-organized feminist advocacy to the contrary, the bill has not been able to pass onto the floor of Parliament for a vote. The Kenyan Federation of Women Lawyers (FIDA-K) has provided parliamentary committees with testimony, statistics, and legal precedents to support the bill's passage. But advocates have, nevertheless, been unable to surmount the weight of cultural tradition and institutionalized patriarchal power in the country. It is my hope that the current study will provide articulate personal descriptions of abstract social issues, making these issues at the same time more pertinent and less easy to dismiss. A case in point is the sometimes disputed connection between gender violence and the spread of HIV/AIDS. While quantitative studies in the larger population (Zulu, Dodoo, & Ezeh, 2002; Kimuna & Djamba, 2008) continue to bring forth mixed results about this link, diary accounts discussed in the current study provide vivid descriptions of how the threat of violence and the desperate need for money leads to unprotected sex, which, in turn, may lead to HIV infection. It is my hope that such personal stories will bring life to abstract issues, thereby turning advocacy into policy. Indeed, if the results of this study help to create laws that protect victims and hold perpetrators accountable in Kenya, the project will have empowered women not only in Kibera, but in the country as a whole.

Implications for Macro Policy

The current study gives credence to the recent report by UN Women (2016) which proposes an agenda for public action to transform economies so that they might progress toward substantive equality for women and girls. According to the report:

> Progress towards a substantive equality should be measured against how inclusive it is of the rights of all women and girls, especially those from marginalized groups. When the most disadvantaged are able to share both paid and unpaid work with men and boys in their families and communities and enjoy an adequate standard of living; when they can live a life that is free from stereotyping, stigma, and violence; and when they are

> able to participate meaningfully in the decisions that affect their lives, then it is possible to speak of lasting transformation toward substantive equality. (p. 235)

The report sets 10 policy priorities that can be deliberated and fine-tuned according to the setting, and each would necessarily involve the active participation of civil society organizations that represent the interests of women and girls. Each of these policy priorities is desperately needed in Kibera and the diaries of the women testify to the urgency of their implementation. The priorities are to create more and better jobs for women; reduce occupational segregation and gender pay gaps; strengthen income security throughout the life cycle; recognize, reduce, and redistribute unpaid care and domestic work; invest in gender-responsive social services; maximize resources for the achievement of substantive equality; support women's organizations to claim rights and shape policy agendas at all levels; create an enabling government for the realization of women's rights; use human rights standards to shape policies and catalyze change; and generate evidence to assess progress on women's economic and social rights. Calls for some of their actions have already been made in previous chapters of this text (e.g., the need for more data and the assessment of interventions). And, although this list is admittedly one the achievement of which will be of long duration, it is nevertheless a challenge to international social workers, NGOs, and international policy makers to prioritize and proceed with these priorities in Kibera. Because these priorities stem from a rights-based economic policy agenda (UN Women, 2016), each of them is adaptable to Kibera and each will strengthen women's agency and opportunity.

Implications for Future Research

It would be both useful and fascinating to obtain a larger picture of young women's lives in Kibera by expanding both the qualitative and quantitative components of the current study to a larger population within Kibera. Such an expansion of the boundaries of the study would enable us to understand whether variables such as ethnic affiliation and geographic location *within* Kibera change the demographics and experience of intimate partner violence. It would also be instructive to expand the age range of participants to include women in their 30s and 40s. Previous studies have indicated that these women may be more isolated and less likely to seek help than younger women are (Kimuna & Djamba, 2008). An expansion of the current study would enable a comparison of help-seeking behaviours among women in different age-group cohorts and could recommend services specific to women in specific age ranges, such as safe houses, support groups, and shelters.

Future studies that compare intimate partner violence in Kibera with that of the general population are urgently needed. As the current study has done on a limited basis, such studies might attempt to replicate the KDHS Domestic Violence Module, but among a larger population in Kibera, thus enabling important comparisons between the slum population and the general population. If such studies corroborate this study's finding of a much higher rate of intimate partner violence in the slum, it will also be important to find out *why* such a huge discrepancy in violence rates exists. Variables that should be considered include social norms in the slum that stigmatize the female child; education in the slum; and living conditions, such as overcrowding, noise, pollution, and extreme poverty.

Future research is also needed that will compare intimate partner violence in Kibera with that in other mega-slums in the developing world. Because mega-slum populations continue to increase, it is urgent that issues relating to intimate partner violence in these communities be addressed in slum-specific terms. That is, solutions to the problem of gender-based violence in slums and informal settlements are likely to be strategically different from those that are effective in general populations. Slum solutions will likely be linked to alleviating situations of structural violence, such as overcrowding and subsistence-level poverty and to elevating the status of female children.

Implications for Practice

Results of the current study indicate that use of the *Escape* strategy as a way to cope with gender-based violence may be linked to the availability of media sources, which help educate women and orient them to lifestyles outside the slum. All forms of media—including social networking capabilities—are now penetrating Kibera, indicating that more women may be exposed to media sources in the next decade. If media availability and participation are, indeed, linked to women's attempts to escape, then it is urgent that a safety net of social services be promulgated in Kibera. International social workers and human rights activists have several options. They can educate international NGOs with offices in Kibera about the results of studies such as this one. These NGOs may, in turn, originate or expand services for women who are survivors of intimate partner violence. Social workers and advocates can also share research results and cooperate with Kenyan women's rights organizations, such as FIDA and CLICK. Such partnerships may help provide data to be used in on-the-ground advocacy for women's legal rights in the area of gender-based violence. Workers might also accompany women to police centres to report violence; accompany women to court and offer legal advice to prosecute violence; and locate safe house facilities or medical help for survivors.

The current study indicates that writing and journaling projects may help empower women, if they have the time and the safety to participate in them. Therefore, more writing projects should be instituted in the slum, along with street theatre, poetry, painting, and other forms of creativity. These not only help externalize oppressions like intimate partner violence for the survivor but also provide public education for the community. Women may gain self-esteem and self-actualization, while the proliferation of such projects would also provide the necessary data to test how and in what ways they improve women's lives.

Study results also indicated that women's coping strategies that are not accompanied by economic empowerment are inadequate to escape intimate partner violence. Although some microloan opportunities exist in Kibera, the study revealed that there are not enough of these to assist all women and girls in need of support or to leverage women into a central place in the national marketplace. Participants in the current study have indicated that job training seminars would be helpful in aiding women to find jobs outside the slum, especially for Kibera girls who have not attended secondary school. Their lack of education decreases their employment opportunities and increases their dependence on men and, thus, their susceptibility to intimate partner violence. Job training seminars may be one means of helping women gain the economic support needed to put their knowledge and business acumen into practice.

Finally, the study has led to a unique "decolonization" effort that may serve as a useful example for future researchers. Others, of course, have preceded it. Cram

(2009) pointed out two key examples. In Australia and New Zealand, non-Maori researchers have been instructed about how to share their skills with their Maori collaborators and "many funding agencies have instigated training and scholarship opportunities for Maori interested in research careers" (Cram, 2009, p. 312). Similarly, in Hawaii, efforts are underway to build a Native Hawaiian research capacity (Braun, Tsark, Santos, et al., 2006). The World Health Organization (WHO, 1997) has remarked that

> the increasing numbers of indigenous peoples who have slowly taken the initiative in their own research ... have turned the bogeyman of "otherness" on its head. They now seek to determine the agenda of research about themselves, what to study, how, and who will do the research. (WHO, 1997, p. 10; UN Women, 2016)

Such agenda-setting must happen in Kibera and is currently in progress in regard to this study. Kiberan women are taking over not only the data collection for a writers' project of their own but also determining the aims and purposes of that activity. International researchers, ethnographers, and social workers have the opportunity to encourage indigenous research and the obligation to discontinue the imposition of Global North methods and goals on Global South projects. If the current study has done nothing else, it has undergirded the idea that local, on-the-ground populations should be setting their own research agendas. Indeed, any Western-imposed agendas will be off the mark unless they incorporate local methodologies and knowledge into research projects. Only by incorporating indigenous methods, aims, and goals can micro projects be transformed into macro social change.

The current study is one of the first to analyze both long-term qualitative and quantitative data from Kibera. For that reason, the study's quantitative findings will be strategic in the ongoing effort to determine the general demographics of intimate partner violence in the slum. At the same time, the qualitative dimensions of the study make it the very first of its kind to put a personal "face" on gender violence. Therefore, it is my hope that the study will be a unique and compelling voice in the ongoing societal debate about intimate partner violence in marginalized communities. The Kibera diarists are helping to close the gender inequality gap in their community and to normalize the indigenous voice in academic research. They are creating opportunity where there was none and they are opening the door for future generations of women to do the same.

Epilogue

Readers may want to know about some strategic events in individual diarists' lives, which supplement the foregoing text and comment in important ways on how women can exert agency to create opportunity. Lives that have dramatically changed since the diary project ended include the following:

Susanna

In 2015, Susanna left Sam and moved in with two female friends. They live in another of Nairobi's informal settlements but the distance from Kibera, although not great, seems sufficient to prevent frequent contact between Susanna and Sam. Her two female friends, who also have children, share childcare with Susanna and they all work at odd jobs. They have made this arrangement work for almost one year and Susanna reports that she feels confident she will never return to her abusive husband.

Terry

In 2015, Terry married a man 10 years her senior and moved out of the house of her parents. She reports that there is no violence in the relationship so far. The couple have started a small business selling *sukuma wiki* (kale) in the slum, as well as other vegetables. Terry says she is content for the first time in her life.

Cathy M.

In 2013, Cathy M. bartered childcare services to a neighbour in exchange for being taught hairstyling techniques, including braiding and plaiting. She then opened her own small kiosk, offering these services to Kiberan women. By 2015, she had saved enough money to move out of her brother-in-law's home and into a roommate situation with a female friend. She is currently making plans to expand her business.

Judy

Judy and her husband, whose daughter is now school-age, have moved out of Kibera to live with her husband's father in a neighbourhood where their daughter can access free public primary school. Judy says she has to work harder than ever to compensate for their use of the father-in-law's facilities and resources but that nothing is more important to her than her daughter's education. She still reports that her marriage is completely without violence.

JC

JC got a day job working with an environmental clean-up service in Kibera. She lives alone in a "very small house" on what she earns but she says that for the first time in her life she is "content and left at peace."

Sarah

Sarah has managed to complete her plan of being "like the lady on the road." Sarah approached the woman whose small business she admired. Sarah asked if she could work for or with her and the woman agreed. Sarah now helps distribute food from the woman's kiosk to other streets and neighbourhoods. She has acquired a bicycle, which enables her to reach more customers. She and the woman-by-the-road have become business partners and Sarah has moved out of Kibera.

Cara

Cara's mother died in 2014. Cara has moved into a house with two other single women in Laini Saba. They share childcare and Cara cooks food to sell at the market. Cara hopes to be instrumental in moving the Women Writers Project to the next stage of development and is the group's coordinator.

Catherine

Catherine, who gained confidence through her small typing business, attracted the attention of others through her business acumen. In 2013, she received a university scholarship and will graduate in 2017.

Appendix

The following websites and films have been chosen to provide sources of further information and insight into four areas of particular concern in this book. Below are resources for learning more about (1) being a global citizen, (2) understanding extreme poverty, (3) making informed choices in the global marketplace, and (4) standing up for women and girls. Each connection you make below will lead you to another and another, creating a network of intersections for action and questions for further contemplation.

Making Global Connections Websites

- Common Dreams (www.commondreams.org) provides progressive news, resources, and commentary, including information about resistance to the "alt-right" political agenda in the US.
- Global Citizen (www.globalcitizen.org/en) is an international organization supporting sustainable development and campaigning against extreme poverty.
- Global Exchange (www.globalexchange.org) is an international human rights organization that sponsors "reality tours" with a progressive perspective to countries in the Global North and South.
- Grameen Bank (www.grameen-info.org) is a microfinance lending organization that turned banking upside down by pioneering microfinance in Bangladesh and expanding the concept around the globe.
- Inequality.org (www.inequality.org) is maintained by the Institute for Policy Studies and contains data on inequality within the United States and around the world.
- Kenya Vision 2030 (www.vision2030.go.ke) is a source of information on Kenya's plans to incorporate the UN Sustainable Development Goals (2030).
- The Movement for Black Lives (m4bl.org) provides resources about social programs relating to Black freedom, justice, and human rights in the US and internationally.
- United Nations Development Program (www.undp.org) is a great source of international information on development, inequality, and the Sustainable Development Goals (2030).

Films

- *Beasts of No Nation* (2015): A film directed by Cary Joji Fukunaga about child soldiers in West Africa.
- *Inequality for All* (2013): Narrated by former Secretary of Labor Robert Reich, this documentary exposes the growing inequality gap in America and its threat to democracy.
- *Life and Debt* (2003): Using Jamaica as her focus, filmmaker Stephanie Black presents an in-depth examination of the impact of the International

Monetary Fund's structural adjustment policies on the developing world.

- *No Logo: Brands, Globalization and Resistance* (2003): Based on the best-selling book by Canadian journalist and activist Naomi Klein, this documentary discusses the backlash against the increasing economic and cultural reach of multinational companies.
- *The Corporation* (2003): This documentary traces the history of the modern corporation and its rise to multinational global dominance.
- *The Story of Stuff* (2007): This 20-minute animated film by garbage-activist Annie Leonard engages us in a conversation about the cultural costs of consumption.

Extreme Poverty Websites

- Living on One (livingonone.org) is a production and social impact studio that creates films and educational videos to raise awareness and inspire action around pressing global issues, such as living on a dollar a day.
- ONE (www.one.org/international) is an international organization fighting extreme poverty, with special emphasis on women and girls.
- Shining Hope for Communities (SHOFCO, www.shofco.org) combats gender inequality and extreme poverty in urban slums by linking tuition-free schools for girls to holistic social services for all.
- The Hunger Project (www.hungerproject.org) is a global, non-profit, strategic organization committed to the sustainable end of world hunger. In Africa, Asia, and Latin America, the Hunger Project seeks to end hunger and poverty by empowering people (especially women) to lead lives of self-reliance.
- The Hunger Site (www.hungersite.org) focuses the power of the Internet on a specific humanitarian need: the eradication of world hunger. It is a leader in online activism, helping to feed the world's hungry and food insecure.

Films

- *13th* (2016): A documentary by Ava DuVernay about race in the US and how slavery is perpetuated through mass incarceration.
- *A Dollar a Day* (2008): This six-part series of 50-minute films explores what it is like to live on a dollar a day and what opportunities are needed to

transform lives. The programs revolve around the theme of access—capital, basic needs, markets, jobs, health care, and good governance.

- *A Path Appears: Transforming Lives, Creating Opportunity* (2014): Based on their book of the same name, in this film, journalists Nick Kristof and Sheryl WuDunn identify successful local and global initiatives and share stories from the front lines of social activism. We see the compelling, inspiring truth of how real people have changed the world, upending the idea that one person can't make a difference.
- *End of Poverty* (2010): This provocative film explores the possibility that poverty is not an accident but instead the result of colonization, land seizure, forced labour, and other forms of exploitation of the "have-nots" by the "haves."
- *Kibera Kid* (2006): This documentary follows the life of a young boy growing up in the poverty and violence of Africa's largest slum.
- *Through a Child's Eyes: Views of Global Poverty* (2010): This documentary focuses on the plight of underprivileged nine-year-olds across the world—revealing their hardships and challenges as well as the resilience with which they often meet their circumstances.

Consumer Power in the Marketplace Websites

- Fair Trade Federation (www.fairtradefederation.org) helps create opportunities for economically marginalized creators of goods from coffee to crafts to textiles.
- International Labour Organization (www.ilo.org/global/about-the-ilo/lang--en) supports workers' human rights internationally, working with employees, employers, and governments to create international policy.
- KIVA (www.kiva.org) puts microfinance in the hands of the people. For as little as $25, you can make a loan to an entrepreneur in the developing world.
- Ten Thousand Villages (www.tenthousandvillages.com) is a non-profit fair-trade retailer that markets handcrafted goods made by disadvantaged artisans in more than 35 nations.
- United Students against Sweatshops (usas.org) campaigns against sweatshops in the United States and around the globe. It has chapters on over 150 campuses across the United States.

Films

- *Blood Coltan* (2007): Our cell phones cannot work without a mineral called coltan, which is mined in the eastern Congo. This documentary examines the exploitation of the Congolese for this mineral that has become essential to our digital lives.
- *Blue Gold: World Water Wars* (2009): Creators of this documentary posit the idea that wars of the future will be fought over water as they are over oil today. As water enters the global marketplace and political arena, corporate giants and private investors are rushing to acquire and control the world's supply.
- *Buyer Be Fair* (2006): This video documentary looks at two major trade goods—timber and coffee—to find out how fair trade certification works and whether it helps the world's poor and their lands.
- *The World According to Monsanto* (2008): This documentary is based on a three-year investigation into the corporate practices of United States multinational corporation Monsanto, and the devastating effects these activities have on indigenous communities, agriculture, and the environment.
- *Wal-Mart: The High Cost of Low Price* (2005): This controversial documentary investigates the negative effects of this giant corporation's policies related to such issues as workers' rights, unions, health care, and small business.

Standing Up for Women Websites

- Campaign for Female Education (CAMFED, www.camfed.org) advocates for girls' education and empowerment in Africa.
- Equality Now (www.equalitynow.org) campaigns and lobbies against the sex trade around the globe.
- International Center for Research on Women (www.icrw.org) works to promote the importance of gender in sustainable development.
- MADRE (www.madre.org) is an international women's human rights organization that uses human rights to advance social justice.
- One Billion Rising (OneBillionRising.org). An international activist organization, founded by Eve Ensler, whose aim is to eradicate global violence against women. OBR and its sister organization, V-Day, have helped create the City of Joy in the Democratic Republic of Congo.

- Shining Hope for Communities (SHOFCO, www.shofco.org) combats gender inequality and extreme poverty in urban slums by linking tuition-free schools for girls to holistic social services for all. The first free school for girls in Kibera was established by this organization and is thriving.
- The Girl Fund (www.thegirlfund.org), part of the UN Foundation, promotes health care and education for women and girls, particularly in the developing world.
- UN Women (www.unwomen.org), known formally as the United Nations Entity for Gender Equality and the Empowerment of Women, works for the empowerment of women around the globe.
- Women for Women International (www.womenforwomen.org) connects women sponsors with women in need around the globe.
- Women Thrive Worldwide (www.womenthrive.org) is dedicated to international advocacy for women living in poverty.
- Women's World Banking (www.womensworldbanking.org) promotes microfinance organizations that assist women in obtaining small loans to create their own businesses.

Films

- *A Path Appears: Transforming Lives, Creating Opportunity* (2014): This film features the inspiring stories collected by Nicholas Kristof and Sheryl WuDunn in the book of the same name, which show how creating opportunity for women creates macro social change.
- *Awakening: Empowering Women through Microfinance* (2007): Showing how small loans empower women in Afghanistan and India to overcome enormous cultural and economic barriers, this film provides a first-hand look at the impact of microfinance on poverty and gender equality in the developing world.
- *Born into Brothels* (2005): This winner of the Academy Award for best documentary 2005 chronicles the lives of prostitutes in a Calcutta slum and of their children, who are given cameras to document their own lives.
- *City of Joy* (2016): A documentary which tells the story of a remarkable center for women and girls who have experienced horrific gender-based violence in DR Congo. The center provides classes, counseling, medical

attention, and community and is empowered by and through the women who utilize its services.

- *First They Killed My Father: A Daughter of Cambodia Remembers* (2017): A documentary directed by Angelina Jolie about human activist Loung Ung and the terror she experienced under the Khmer Rouge.
- *Girl Rising* (2013): This film tells the stories of nine girls from developing countries, showing how they overcome great obstacles to obtain an education and change their fates.
- *Half the Sky: Turning Oppression into Opportunity for Women Worldwide* (2009): The film, based on the book by Pulitzer Prize–winning journalists Nick Kristof and Sheryl WuDunn, shows how unleashing the power of women and girls can create sustainable change in the developing world.
- *In Plain Sight* (2014): Filmmaker Erica Jordan follows renowned photographer Lisa Kristine on an unforgettable journey into the front lines of modern-day slavery.
- *Maquilapolis* (2006): This is a gritty and uncompromising film showing how women workers in sweatshops along Mexico's northern border struggle against violence, poverty, and injustice.
- *Maya Angelou: And Still I Rise* (2016): This is the first documentary about poet, writer, and civil rights activist Maya Angelou, directed by Rita Coburn Whack and Hercules.
- *Mo'Ne Davis: I Throw Like a Girl* (2015): This film by director Spike Lee features 13-year-old Mo'Ne Davis, who challenges gender stereotypes in sports and throws a 70 mph fastball.
- *Moolaade* (2004): A powerful film about female genital mutilation (FGM) set in Burkina Faso and directed by Ousmane Sembene.
- *No Woman, No Cry* (2011): This searing documentary investigates the dangers related to pregnancy and childbirth in the Global South.
- *Seasons of a Life* (2008): In this fictional film from Malawi, a young housemaid is sexually abused by her employer. She must overcome great odds to achieve an education and reclaim her child.
- *The Girl in the River* (2016): The winner of the 2016 Academy Award for Best Documentary, this film by director Sharmeen Obaid-Chinoy reveals

the stark horror of honour killings in Pakistan. Because of this film, laws in Pakistan are being changed in an effort to eliminate honour killings.

- *To Catch a Dollar: Muhammed Yunus Banks on America* (2010): For 30 years, microfinance pioneer Muhammad Yunus helped more than seven million Bangladeshi—mostly women—move out of poverty. In this documentary, he collaborates with women in Queens, New York, to create opportunities and achieve their dreams.
- *The Uncondemned* (2016): Directed by Nick Louvel and Michele Mitchell, this documentary describes the first-ever International Criminal Court trial to define rape as a war crime.
- *Women, War and Peace* (2011): This PBS mini-series documents the complex and devastating effects of war on women and confronts the urgent need for more women to become policy decision-makers.

Maps

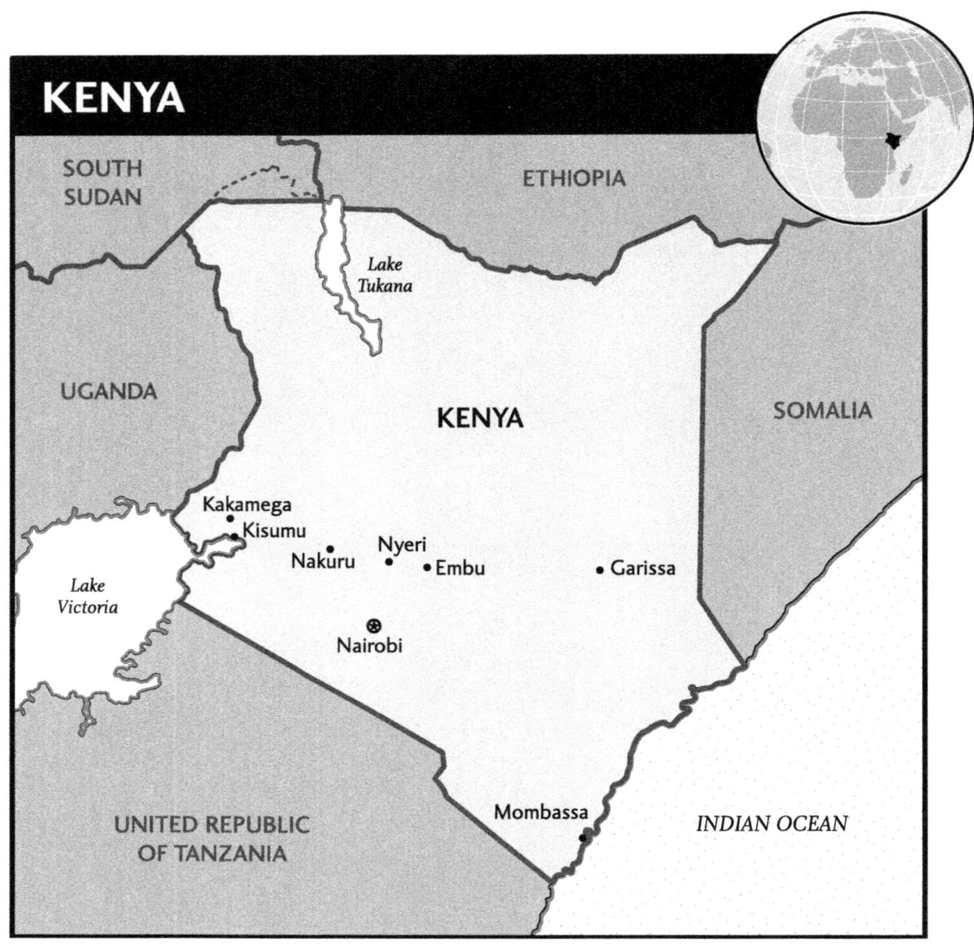

MAP 1: Nairobi, Kenya

Source: UN Office for the Coordination of Humanitarian Affairs (OCHA)

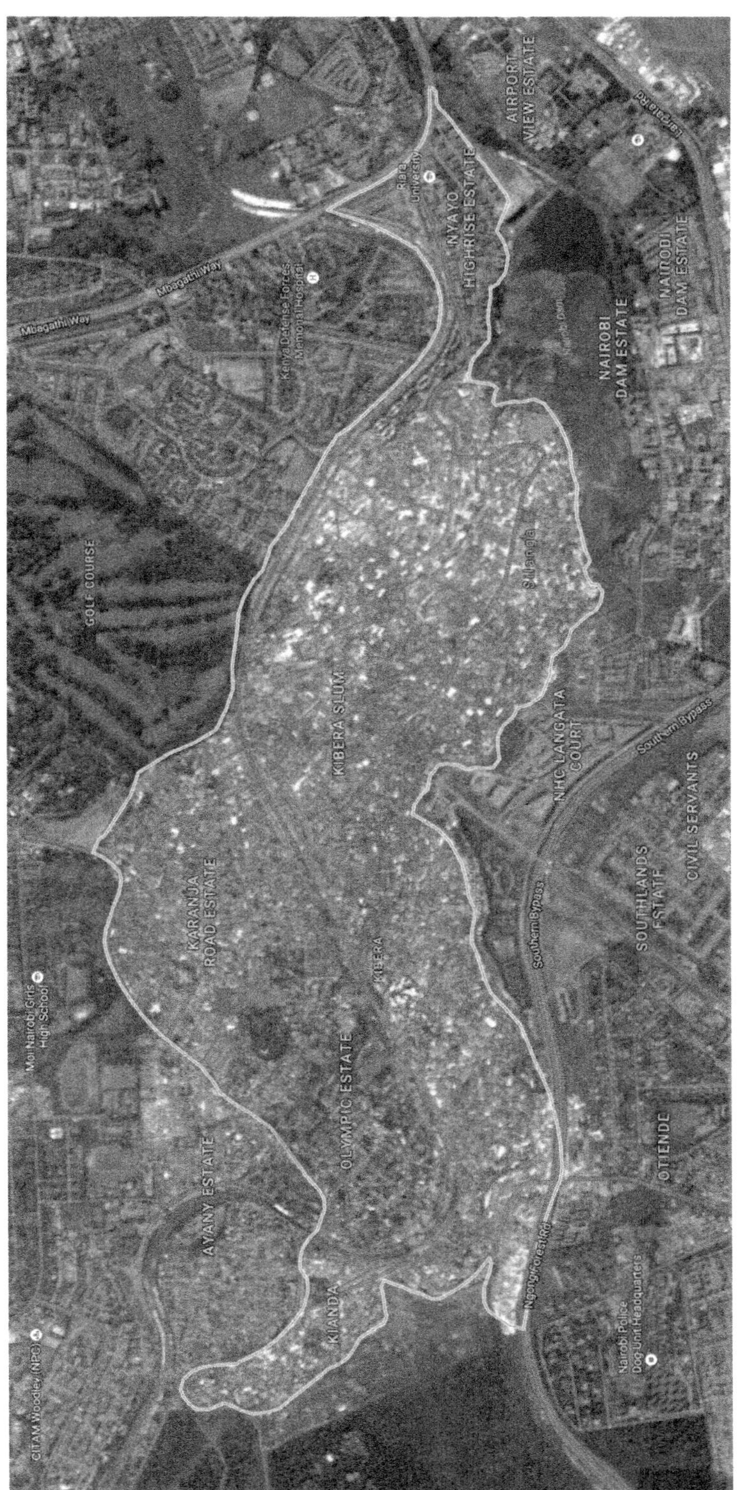

MAP 2: Satellite Image of Kibera

Source: Image ©2016 CNES / Astrium, DigitalGlobe; Map data ©2016 Google

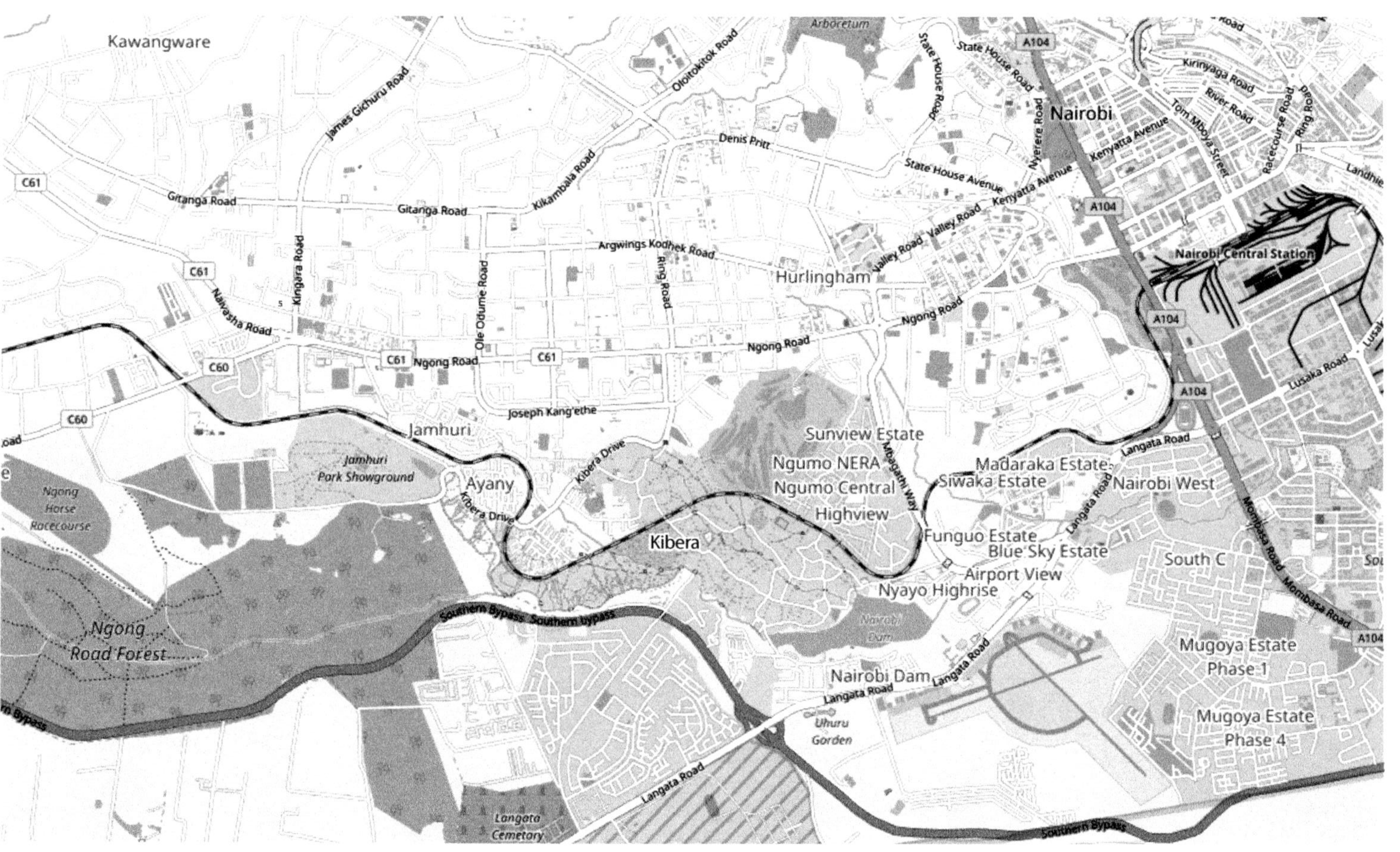

MAP 3: Kibera in Relation to the City of Nairobi

Source: Open Street Map

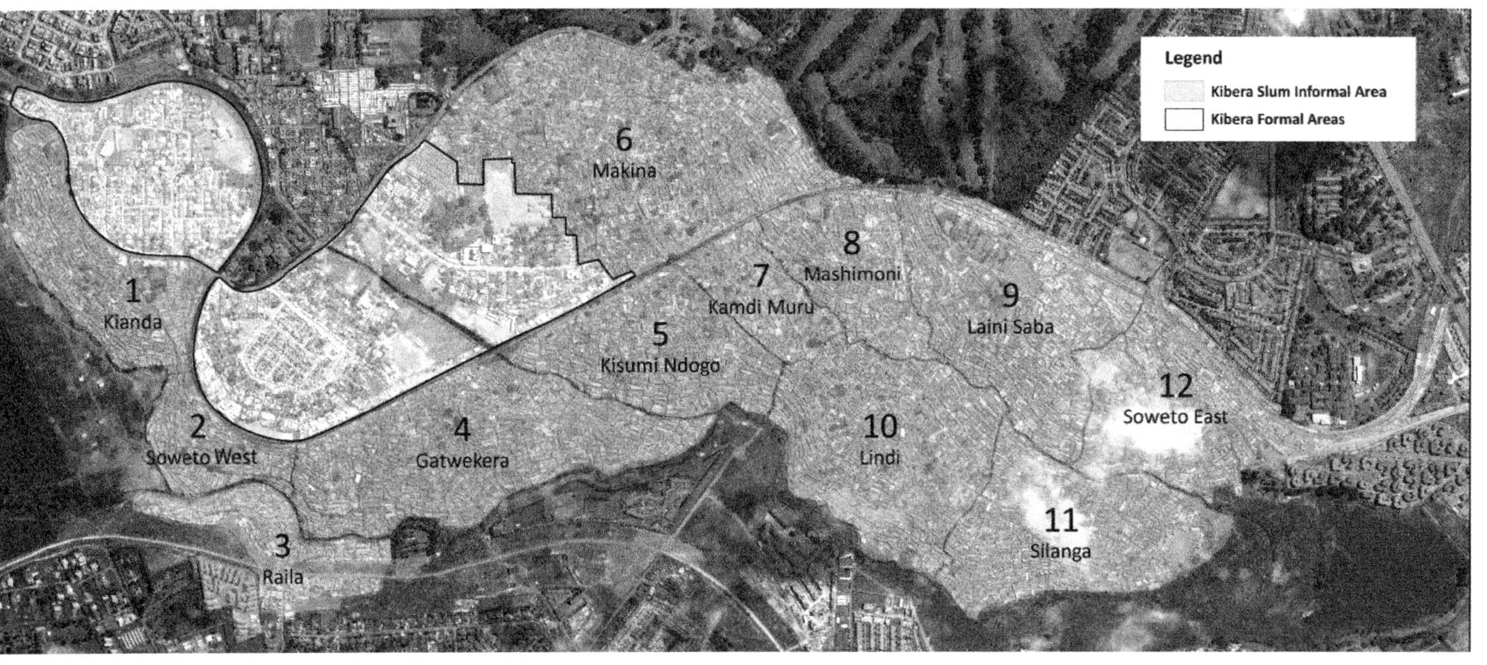

MAP 4: Kibera and Its Villages

Source: Research Centre of the Slovenian Academy of Sciences and Arts

References

Abebe, J. O., Jepkiyeny, A., & Angaga, A. (2012). *A survey of sexual and gender-based violence in Kibera, Kenya.* New York: LAP Lambert Academic Publishing.

Africa Online News Service (AFROL). (2008). Kenya: Gender profiles. Retrieved October 28, 2008 from www.afrol.com/Categories/Women/profiles/kenya

African Population and Health Research Center (APHRC). (2002). *Health and livelihood needs of residents of informal settlements in Nairobi City.* Nairobi: APHRC.

Alder, G. (1995). Tackling poverty in Nairobi's informal settlements: Developing an institutional strategy. *Environment and Urbanization, 7*(2), 85–107.

Ali, N. (2008). The costs of marital rape in Southern Africa. *The Independent,* August 18, 2008.

Amis, P. (1984). Squatters or tenants: The commercialization of unauthorized housing in Nairobi. *World Development, 12*(1), 87–96.

Amis, P. (1988). Commercialized rent housing in Nairobi, Kenya. In C. V. Patton (Ed.), *Spontaneous shelter: International perspectives and prospects* (pp. 235–357). Philadelphia: Temple University Press.

Amnesty International. (2002). *Rape: The invisible crime.* New York: Amnesty International.

Amnesty International. (2007). *Rape in Kenya.* New York: Amnesty International.

Amnesty International. (2010). *Insecurity and indignity: Women's experiences in the slums of Nairobi, Kenya.* New York: Amnesty International.

Amnesty International. (2016). Kenya submission to the United Nations Committee on Economic, Social and Cultural Rights. Retrieved July 11, 2016 from www.amnesty.org/en/documents/afr32/3413/2016/en/

Babb, J., & Taylor, P. E. (1981). *Border healing woman: The story of Jewel Babb.* Austin: University of Texas Press.

Baca Zinn, M., & Dill, B. T. (1996). Theorizing difference from multi-racial feminism. *Feminist Studies, 22*, 23–29.

Bailey, A. (2000). Locating traitorous identities: Toward a view of privilege-cognizant white character. In U. Narayan & S. Harding (Eds.), *Decentering the center: Philosophy for a multi-cultural, post-colonial and feminist world* (pp. 283–298). Bloomington: Indiana University Press.

BBC Online News. (2009, October 7). Kenyans re-arming for 2012 poll. Retrieved October 10, 2010 from www.bbc.co.uk/news/

Belsky, J. (1980). Child maltreatment: An ecological integration. *American Psychologist, 35*(1), 320–335.

Bettie, J. (2003). *Women without class: Girls, race, and identity.* Berkeley: University of California Press.

Boserup, E. (1989/2011). *Women's role in economic development.* New York: Earthscan Publishers.

Braun, K. L., Tsark, J. U., Santos, L. A., Aitaoto, N., & Chong, C. (2006). Building Native Hawaiian capacity in cancer research and programming. *Cancer, 107*(8), 2082–2090.

Butler, J. (1990). *Gender trouble: Feminism and the subversion of identity.* New York: Routledge.

Butler, J. (2011). *Bodies that matter: On the discursive limits of sex.* New York: Routledge.

Central Intelligence Agency. (2009/2011). Kenya: The world factbook. Retrieved March 1, 2011 from www.cia.gov/library/publications/the-world-factbook/goes/ke.html

Centre for Development Studies. (2007). *Measuring individual agency or empowerment: A study in Kerala.* Kerala, India: CDS.

Centre for Development Studies. (2013). Gender and development. Kerala, India: CDS. Retrieved October 10, 2013 from www.cds.edu/research/research-themes/gender-and-development-ged/

Charmaz, K. (2003). Grounded theory: Objectivist and constructivist methods. In N. K. Denzin and Y. S. Lincoln (Eds.), *Strategies of qualitative inquiry* (pp. 249–291). Thousand Oaks, CA: Sage.

Chase, S. E. (2005). Narrative inquiry: Multiple lenses, approaches, voices. In N. K. Denzin & Y. S. Lincoln (Eds.), *The Sage handbook of qualitative research* (pp. 651–679). Thousand Oaks, CA: Sage.

Clark, D. (1972). *Kibera: Social dynamics of a low income neighborhood in Nairobi.* Makerere: Makerere University Press.

Collins, P. H. (2000). *Black feminist thought: Knowledge, consciousness, and the politics of empowerment.* New York: Routledge.

Community structures supporting gender-based violence in Kibera, Kenya. (2008). Retrieved October 1, 2010 from paa2008.princeton.edu/download.aspx?submissionId=81442

Connell, R. W. (2002). *Gender.* Malden, MA: Polity Press.

Constitution of Kenya (2010). Retrieved May 15, 2016 from www.kenya-information-guide.com/kenya-constitution.html

Convention on the Elimination of All Forms of Discrimination against Women (CEDAW) (1979). *CEDAW preamble and convention.* New York: United Nations.

Cram, F. (2009). Maintaining indigenous voices. In D. Mertens and P. Ginsburg (Eds.), *The handbook of social research ethics* (pp. 308–321). Thousand Oaks, CA: Sage.

Crawley, S. L., Foley, L. J., and Shehan, C. L. (2008). *Gendering bodies.* New York: Rowman & Littlefield.

Culley, M. (1986). *A day at a time: The diary literature of American women from 1764 to the present.* New York: Feminist Press.

Davis, M. (2006). *Planet of slums.* New York: Verso Books.

de Smedt, J. (2009). Kill me quick: A history of Nubian gin in Kibera. *International Journal of African Historical Studies, 42*(2), 201–220.

Desgroppes, A., & Taupin, S. (2012). Kibera: The biggest slum in Africa? *Les Cahiers de l'Afrique de l'Est, 44*, 23–34.

Deutsch, F. (2007). Undoing gender. *Gender and society, 21*(1), 106–127.

Dodoo, F., Zulu, E., & Ezeh, A. C. (2007). Urban-rural differences in the socio-economic deprivation-sexual behavior link in Kenya. *Social Science and Medicine, 64*, 1019–1031.

Doyle, A. (2006, December 14). Half of humanity set to become urban. *Daily Nation*, pp. A1–2.

East African (2010). Another delay halts housing plan. July 15, 2010, p. 5.

Ekdale, B. (2010). Kibera's history. Retrieved June 30, 2016 from www.brianekdale.com

Erulkar, A., & Matheka, J. (2007). *Adolescence in the Kibera slum of Nairobi, Kenya.* Nairobi: Population Council.

Ferraro, G. P. (1978/1979). Nairobi: Overview of an East African city. *African Urban Studies, 3*(Winter), 1–14.

Ferraro, K. (2014). Sexual violence in the Kenyan slums. Global Health at Northwestern University (blog post). Retrieved on September 2, 2015 from blog.globalhealthportal.northwestern.edu/2014/02/sexual-violence-in-kenyan-slums/

FIDA-K. (1997). *Sauti ya akina dada (Women's voices): Women's rights monitoring and report writing programme.* Nairobi: Federation of Women Lawyers, Kenya.

FIDA-K. (1998–2008). *FIDA Kenya annual reports.* Nairobi: Federation of Women Lawyers, Kenya.

FIDA-K. (2007). *A shadow report to the 5th and 6th combined report of the government of the Republic of Kenya on the International Convention on the Elimination of All Forms of Discrimination against Women (CEDAW).* Nairobi: Federation of Women Lawyers, Kenya.

FIDA-K. (2008). *Step by step: Forward or backward?* Nairobi: Federation of Women Lawyers, Kenya.

FIDA-K. (2015). *Key gains and challenges: A gender audit of Kenya's 2013 election process.* Nairobi: Federation of Women Lawyers, Kenya.

FIDA-K. (2016). Publications. Nairobi: Federation of Women Lawyers, Kenya. Retrieved June 10, 2016 from fidakenya.org/dr7/?q=publications

Fontana, A., & Frey, J. H. (2005). The interview: From neutral stance to political involvement. In N. K. Denzin and Y. S. Lincoln (Eds.), *Sage handbook of qualitative research* (pp. 695–727). Thousand Oaks, CA: Sage.

Gallup Poll. (2009). Gallup religiosity index. Retrieved December 10, 2010 from www.worldview.gallup.com

Geertz, C. (1973). *The interpretation of cultures.* New York: Basic Books.

Giddens, A. (1990). *The consequences of modernity.* Cambridge: Polity Press.

Harding, S. (1991). *Whose science, whose knowledge: Thinking from women's lives.* Ithaca, NY: Cornell University Press.

Harding, S. (2006). *Science and social inequality: Feminist and post-colonial issues.* Chicago: University of Illinois Press.

Harraway, D. (1988). Situated knowledges: The science question in feminism and the privilege of partial perspective. *Feminist Studies, 14,* 575–600.

Harrison, F. V. (1991). Women in Jamaica's urban informal economy: Insights from a Kingston slum. In C. Mohanty, A. Russo, & L. Torres (Eds.), *Third world women and the politics of feminism* (pp. 173–196). Bloomington: Indiana University Press.

Heifer International (2015). Retrieved August 4, 2015 from www.heifer.org/endinghunger/index.html

Heise, L. (1993). Violence against women: The missing agenda. In M. Koblinsky, J. Timyan, & J. Gay (Eds.), *The health of women: A global perspective* (pp. 171–195). Boulder, CO: Westview Press.

Huchzermeyer, M. (2008). Slum upgrading in Nairobi within the housing and basic services market: A housing rights concern. *Journal of Asian and African Studies, 43*(1), 19–39.

Human Rights Watch. (2003). Double standards: Women's property rights violations in Kenya. *Human Rights Watch, 15*(5), 1–3.

Hunt, A. M., & Winegarten, R. (1983). *I am Annie Mac: An extraordinary black Texas woman in her own words.* Austin: University of Texas Press.

Hunter, M. L. (2005). *Race, gender, and the politics of skin tone.* New York: Routledge.

Institute for Education in Democracy (IED). (2015). *Towards sustainable gender responsiveness in Kenya: Dissecting the two-thirds gender debate.* Nairobi: IED.

Institute of Economic Affairs (IEA Kenya). (2007). *Annual report.* Nairobi: IEA.

Institute of Economic Affairs (IEA Kenya). (2015). *Implementing the constitutional two-thirds gender principle: The cost of representation.* Nairobi: The National Women's Steering Committee in partnership with IEA.

Inter-Press Service. (2015). Dispatch from Kibera, East Africa's largest slum. Retrieved September 3, 2015 from www.heifer.org/

IRIN. (2007). *Kenya: Sexual and domestic violence prevalent.* Humanitarian News and Analysis: UN Office for the Coordination of Humanitarian Affairs.

IRIN. (2009). Slum-dwellers priced into hunger. Retrieved August 2, 2015 from www.irinnews.org/report/84577/kenya-slum-dwellers-priced-into-hunger

IRIN. (2010). *Wilbroda Wandera: We won't sleep hungry when I have 40 shillings.* Humanitarian News and Analysis: UN Office for the Coordination of Humanitarian Affairs.

Jacobs, R. H. (1979). *Life after youth: Female, forty—What next?* Boston: Beacon.

K'Akumu, O. A., & Olima, W. H. A. (2007). The dynamics and implications of residential segregation in Nairobi. *Habitat International, 31*(1), 87–99.

Kanyago, N. (2001). *Beyond the door: The challenges ahead. FIDA Kenya annual report 2001.* Nairobi: Federation of Women Lawyers, Kenya.

Kennedy, E. L., & Beins, A. (2005). *Women's studies for the future: Foundations, interrogations, politics.* New Brunswick, NJ: Rutgers University Press.

Kenya. 21 July 2006. The sexual offences act *2006*. Retrieved October 10, 2010 from www.sexualoffencesbill.co.ke/documents/sexual_offences_act.pdf

Kenya Demographic and Health Survey. (2003). *CBS, MOH, & ORC Macro.* Calverton, MD: Central Bureau of Statistics.

Kenya Demographic and Health Survey. (2008). *CBS, MOH, & ORC Macro.* Calverton, MD: Central Bureau of Statistics.

Kenya Demographic and Health Survey. (2014). *CBS, MOH, & ORC Macro.* Calverton, MD: Central Bureau of Statistics.

Kenya moves 1,500 slum residents to new homes. (2009, September 16). *The Standard*, p. 16.

Kenya Vision 2030. (2016). Retrieved July 5, 2016 from www.vision2030.go.ke/

Kenyan Parliament (2003, 2006). *Parliamentary proceedings.* Nairobi: Government of Kenya.

Kibera Law Centre (2015). Facts. Retrieved March 1, 2015 from kiberalawcentre.org

Kibera upgrade plan. (2008, September 4). *The Standard*, p. 10.

Kibera upgrade progress slow. (2009, June 12). *The Standard*, p. 7.

Kimuna, S., & Djamba, Y. (2008). Gender-based violence: Correlates of physical and sexual wife abuse in Kenya. *Journal of Family Violence, 23*, 333–342.

Kinyanjui, M. N. (2014). *Women and the informal economy in urban Africa.* London: Zed Books.

Kristof, N., & WuDunn, S. (2009). *Half the sky: Turning oppression into opportunity for women worldwide.* New York: Vintage.

Kristof, N., & WuDunn, S. (2014). *A path appears: Transforming lives, creating opportunities.* New York: Knopf.

Lawoko, S. (2008). Predictors of attitudes toward intimate partner violence: A comparative study of men in Zambia and Kenya. *Journal of Interpersonal Violence, 23*(8), 1056–1074.

Legal action derails Kibera upgrading. (2010, July 19–25). *The East African*, p. 16.

Lockhart, L., & Danis, F. S. (2010). *Domestic violence intersectionality and culturally competent practice.* New York: Columbia University Press.

Lorde, A. (2000). *The collected poems of Audre Lorde.* New York: Norton.

Lucal, B. (1999). What it means to be gendered me: Life on the boundaries of a dichotomous gender system. *Gender and Society, 13*(6), 781–797.

Lugones, M. (1987). Playfulness, "world"-traveling and loving perception. *Hypatia, 2*(2), 3–21.

Map Kibera. (2016). Making the invisible visible. Retrieved July 11, 2016 from www.mapkibera.org/

Martin, P. Y. (2003). Said and done versus saying and doing: Gendering practices, practicing gender at work. *Gender and Society, 17*(3), 342–366.

McIntosh, P. (1989). *White privilege: Unpacking the invisible knapsack.* Berkeley: University of California Press.

Mendez, M. (2008). *Experiences, attitudes, and beliefs about interpersonal violence: A study of Costa Rican adolescents.* Orlando: University of Central Florida.

Miller, J. (2008). *Getting played: African American girls, urban inequality, and gendered violence.* New York: New York University Press.

Mohanty, C. T. (2003). *Feminism without borders: Decolonizing theory, practicing solidarity.* Durham, NC: Duke University Press.

Mohanty, C. T. (2013). Transnational feminist crossings: On neo-liberalism and radical critique. *Signs, 38*(4), 967–991.

Mohanty, C. T., Russo, A., & Torres, L. (1991). *Third world women and the politics of feminism.* Bloomington: Indiana University Press.

Muchomba, F. M. (2014). Colonial policies and the rise of transactional sex in Kenya. *Journal of International Women's Studies, 15*(2), 80–93.

Mugisha, F., & Zulu, E. (2004). The influence of alcohol, drugs and substance abuse on sexual relationships and perception of risk to HIV infection among adolescents in the informal settlements of Nairobi. *Journal of Youth Studies 7*(3), 279–293.

Mutisya, E., & Yarime, M. (2011). Understanding the grassroots dynamics of slums in Nairobi: The dilemma of Kibera informal settlements. *International*

Transaction Journal of Engineering, Management, and Applied Sciences and Technologies, 2(2), 197–213.

Mwereru, J. I. (2013). Effects of gender based violence on girls and women in Kibera informal settlement, Nairobi County. Retrieved January 2015 from ir-library.ku.ac.ke/handle/123456789/7571

Narayan, U. (1997). *Dislocating cultures: Identities, traditions, and Third World feminism.* New York: Routledge.

Narayan, U., & Harding, S. (2000). *Decentering the center: Philosophy for a multicultural postcolonial and feminist world.* Bloomington: Indiana University Press.

Ndung'u, N. (2006). *The Sexual Offences Act.* Nairobi: FIDA-K.

Parsons, T. (1997). Kibra is our blood: The Sudanese military legacy of Nairobi's Kibera location, 1902–1968. *The International Journal of African Historical Studies, 30*(1), 87–122.

Penn, M. L., & Nardos, R. (2003). *Overcoming violence against women and girls: The international campaign to eradicate a worldwide problem.* New York: Rowman & Littlefield.

Personal Narratives Group. (Eds.). (1989). *Interpreting women's lives: Feminist theory and personal narratives.* Bloomington: Indiana University Press.

Pflanz, M. (2010, August 14). In Kenya slums, women risk rape daily to get to a bathroom. *Christian Science Monitor,* p. 7.

Pillai, V., & Alkire, S. (2007). *Measuring individual agency or empowerment: A study in Kerala.* Kerala, India: Centre for Development Studies.

Pillay, R., Rishi, M., & Kulkarni, K. G. (2004). *Social justice and the agency of women: The Kerala story.* Draft paper presented at the 2004 Annual Allied Social Sciences Associations (ASSA) Meeting, San Diego, CA.

Population Council. (2015). Adolescent girls initiative—Kenya. Retrieved August 3, 2015 from www.popcouncil.org/research/kenya

Ridgeway, C. L. (2009). Framed before we know it: How gender shapes social relations. *Gender and Society, 23,* 145–160.

Riverbend. (2005). *Baghdad burning: Girl blog from Iraq.* New York: Feminist Press at CUNY.

Ruddick, S., & Daniels, P. (Eds.). (1977). *Working it out: 23 women writers, artists, scientists, and scholars talk about their lives and work.* New York: Pantheon.

Sandoval, C. (2000). *Methodology of the oppressed.* Minneapolis: University of Minnesota Press.

Sartori, G., Nembrini, G., & Stauffer, F. (2002). *Monitoring of urban growth of informal settlements and population estimation from aerial photography and satellite imaging: Occasional paper #6*. Geneva: Geneva Foundation.

Saukko, P. (2000). Between voice and discourse. *Qualitative Inquiry, 6*, 299–317.

Schegloff, E. (1997). Narrative analysis thirty years later. *Journal of Narrative and Life History, 7*, 97–106.

Schiwy, M. (1994). Taking things personally: Women, journal writing, and self-creation. *Journal of the National Women's Studies Association, 6*, 234–254.

Searle, J. R. (1969). *Speech acts: An essay in the philosophy of language*. Cambridge: Cambridge University Press.

Sernau, S. (2014). *Social inequality in a global age*. Thousand Oaks: Sage.

Sexual Offences Act (2006). *Act No. 3 of 2006*. Retrieved November 23, 2016 from www.chr.up.ac.za/undp/domestic/docs/legislation_40.pdf

SHOFCO. (2015). Retrieved August 15, 2015 from www.shofco.org/

Shohat, E. (2001). *Talking visions: Multicultural feminism in a transnational age*. New York: MIT Press.

Silva, J. M. (2008). A new generation of women: How female ROTC candidates negotiate the tension between masculine culture and traditional femininity. *Social Forces, 87*(2), 937–960.

Smith, D. (1989). *The everyday world as problematic: A feminist sociology*. Boston: Northeastern University Press.

Smith, D. (1991). *The conceptual practice of power: A feminist sociology of knowledge*. Boston: Northeastern University Press.

Smith, L. T. (2012). *Decolonizing methodologies: Research and indigenous peoples*. New York: Zed Books.

Steger, M. B. (2013). *Globalization: A very short introduction*. Oxford: Oxford University Press.

Stewart, M. W. (2003). Gender. In L. T. Reynolds & N. J. Herman-Kinney (Eds.), *Handbook of symbolic interactionism* (pp. 761–850). Lanham, MD: Rowman & Littlefield.

Stiglitz, J. E. (2003). *Globalization and its discontents*. New York: W.W. Norton and Company.

Strauss, A., & Corbin, J. (1998). *Basics of qualitative research: Techniques and procedures for developing grounded theory*. Thousand Oaks, CA: Sage.

Sullivan, S. (2006). *Revealing whiteness: The unconscious habits of racial privilege*. Bloomington: Indiana University Press.

Swart, E. (2008). Words are a place to stand: Journals by young women in Kibera, Kenya. *Affilia: Journal of Women and Social Work, 24*(1), 1–12.

Swart, E. (2012). Gender-based violence in a Kenyan slum: Creating local woman-centered interventions. *Journal of Social Service Research, 38*(4), 427–438.

Syagga, P. M., & Kiamba, J. M. (1992). Housing the urban poor: A case study of Pumwani, Kibera, and Dandora estates. *African Urban Quarterly, 7*(1 & 2), 79–88.

Temple, N. W. (1974). *Housing preferences and policy in Kibera, Nairobi.* Nairobi: University of Nairobi Institute for Development Studies.

Thomas, W. I., & Znaniecki, F. (1918/1927). *The Polish peasant in Europe and America* (Vol. 2). New York: Alfred A. Knopf.

Thorne, B. (1993). *Gender play: Girls and boys in schools.* New Brunswick, NJ: Rutgers University Press.

Tjaden, P., & Thoennes, N. (2000). Prevalence and consequences of male-to-female and female-to-male intimate partner violence as measured by the National Violence against Women Survey. *Violence Against Women, 6*(2), 142–161.

Train derails, kills several. (2009, May 5). *Daily Nation*, p. 2.

Underhill, W. (2010, July 26). Map Kibera. *The Design Observer*, pp. 2–3.

UN-AIDS. (2006). *Violence against women and girls in the era of HIV and AIDS.* Nairobi: UN-AIDS Kenya.

UN-HABITAT. (2003). *The challenge of slums: Global report on human settlements 2003.* London: United Nations.

UN-HABITAT (2015). *The role of ICT in the proposed urban sustainable development goal and the new urban agenda.* New York: United Nations.

UN-High Commissioner for Human Rights. (2008). *Report from OHCHR fact-finding mission to Kenya, February 6–28, 2008.* New York: United Nations.

UNICEF. (2015a). Education statistics: Kenya. Retrieved August 3, 2015 from www.childinfo.org/files/ESAR_Kenya.pdf

UNICEF. (2015b). *Communication for development (C4D) regional strategic framework 2015–2017.* New York: United Nations.

UNIFEM. (2006). *HIV/AIDS: A gender-equality and human rights issue.* New York: United Nations.

UN Women (2016). *Progress of the world's women 2015–2016: Transforming economies, realizing rights.* New York: UN Women.

US Department of State. (2010). Human rights report: Kenya. Retrieved October 10, 2010 from www.state.gov/g/drl/rls/hrrpt/2008/af/119007.htm

Van Putten, S. (2011). Economic empowerment and HIV prevention among young women and girls in Kenya: Lessons from the study of economic empowerment programs. *Independent Study Projects (ISP) Collection*. Paper 1201.

Van Zwanenberg, R. (1972). History and theory of urban poverty in Nairobi: The problem of slum development. *Journal of East African Research and Development, 2*(2), 163–205.

Voice of Kibera. (2010). Retrieved November 1, 2010, from www.voiceofkibera.org

Wangui, E. E., & Darkoh, M. B. K. (1992). A geographical study of Kibera as an example of an uncontrolled settlement. *Journal of East African Research and Development, 22*, 75–91.

West, C., & Zimmerman, D. H. (1987). Doing gender. *Gender and Society, 1*(2), 125–151.

Williams, S. L. (2002). Trying on gender: Gender regimes, and the process of becoming women. *Gender and Society, 16*(1), 29–52.

World Bank. (2015). Extreme poverty rates continue to fall. Retrieved September 3, 2015 from data.worldbank.org/news/extreme-poverty-rates-continue-to-fall

World Health Organization. (1997). *World report on violence and health*. Geneva: WHO.

World Health Organization. (2002). *World report on violence and health*. Geneva: WHO.

World Health Organization. (2004). *Violence against women and HIV/AIDS: Critical intersections between intimate partner violence and HIV/AIDS*. Geneva: WHO.

World Health Organization. (2005). *WHO multi-country study on women's health and domestic violence against women*. Geneva: WHO.

Zulu, E. M., Dodoo, F., & Ezeh, A. C. (2002). Sexual risk-taking in the slums of Nairobi, Kenya, 1993–1998. *Population Studies, 56*(3), 311–323.

Index

A

advocacy for GBV
- and CEDAW, 58–59
- by FIDA-K, 59–60, 61, 155, 206
- laws in Kenya, 59–61

African Population and Health Research Center (APHRC), 61, 62, 63–64, 166

agency by women
- and gender, 28–29, 31
- redefinition, 180–183
- in survey and diaries, 196–197, 201

Alder, G., 68, 69

Amnesty International
- on police threat, 88, 155
- violence against women and girls, 85–86, 87–88, 120–121, 158

author
- data analysis issues, 19–20
- directive to diarists, 15
- idea of diaries and survey, 13–15
- in Kibera, 12–13, 15–16
- social work experience, 15–16
- uncomfortable situations and immersion, 18–19, 98
- whiteness and privilege, 15–19, 96–97

axial coding technique, 44, 49–51

B

Baca Zinn, M., 24

Bailey, Alison, 95–96

Betta, 37, 74, 87, 126–127, 172–173

Bettie, Julie, 19, 20, 119

Betting against the House strategy
- analysis of, 167–169
- birth control and contraceptives, 164–166, 168
- and childlessness, 167–168
- description, 4, 159
- "doing gender" use, 182–183
- examples in diaries, 160–164
- narrative style in, 186
- prevalence and efficacy, 180
- purpose in short and long term, 159–160
- success and risks of, 167–169, 186

birth control and contraceptives, 164–166, 167, 168
- *See also* condoms

blogs, use by women, 112

blog Voice of Kibera, 89–90
Blumer, Herbert, 27
Boserup, Ester, 7
boyfriends, as survival strategy, 125–126, 127–129, 131–132
businesses, by women, 56
Butler, Judith, 29, 31

C

Cara
- on continuation of project, 104–105, 106, 107
- description as participant, 37–38
- in informal economy, 68, 70
- on injustices, 106
- length of diary entries, 116
- post-project changes, 215
- silences in diary, 116–117
- writing style, 117

Catherine
- birth control, 166
- description as participant, 38
- escape from prostitution, 142–143
- example of diary, 45
- *Hoping God Agrees* strategy, 122–125
- limited partnerships, 162–163, 168
- on marriage, 163
- and media, 182
- narrative style, 186
- on political violence, 175
- in post-election violence, 173–175
- post-project changes, 215
- prayer as strategy, 122–123
- survival sex use, 123, 124–125, 142, 143, 162
- underlines in diaries, 117–118
- writing style, 117

Cathy M.
- on continuation of project, 105, 107
- description as participant, 38
- *Hoping God Agrees* strategy, 127–128
- post-project changes, 214
- survival sex use, 71, 128

Centre for Legislative Information Concerning Kenya (CLICK), 59
changaa, for income, 9
childlessness, in strategies, 167–168
chronemic communication, 115–116
cities, population of, 1–2
clinics in Kibera, 166–167
Collins, Patricia Hill, 24
colonialism in Kenya, 17, 79–80
colour (skin colour), 21–22
community level. *See* mezzo level
Community Structures study, 121–122
condoms, 86–87, 132, 195–196
- *See also* birth control and contraceptives

Connell, R. W., 28
consent for study, 34, 36, 37
Constitution of Kenya (2010), 57, 74–75, 169
contraceptives. *See* birth control and contraceptives
control by women. *See* agency by women
Convention on the Elimination of All Forms of Discrimination against Women (CEDAW), 58–60, 61
coping strategies against IPV
- description and role, 4
- diarists on, 4, 50–51, 103, 201–202
- as dual strategies, 119–120
- and economic empowerment, 209
- as goal of study, 98
- as indigenous project, 98–99
- in Kibera, 3–4
- and narrative style, 183–186, 187
- prevalence and efficacy, 179–180
- and social norms, 121
- in survey, 4, 193–194, 201–202
- survey questions, 35
- work as strategy, 209
- *See also Betting against the House; Escape; Hoping God Agrees*

Corbin, J., 49–50
Cram, F., 15, 209–210
Crawley, S. L., and colleagues, 29
credit, access to by women, 56
Crenshaw, Kimberle, 30, 31
Culley, M., 112
culture, 26–27, 98

D

data analysis of diaries and survey, 19–20, 44, 51
Davis, Mike, 2, 12, 78–79, 84
decolonization, 102–105, 209–210

Dee
- coping strategies in diaries, 50–51
- description as participant, 38–39
- diary writing, 115
- disappearance, 153–154
- escapes and outcomes of, 146–154
- example of diary, 46
- and media, 182, 183
- narrative style, 184–185
- on political violence, 175
- in post-election violence, 148–151
- prostitution, 152
- writing style, 117

Desgroppes, A., 83
Deutsch, F., 29
diaries
- analysis of, 44, 47–51
- authors of (*See* diarists / diary writers)
- and chronemic communication, 115–116
- coding techniques and results, 44, 49–51
- and context, 113
- data analysis and interpretation, 19–20, 44
- as data for research, 111–113, 211
- description of project, 32, 33–34
- efficacy of, 187
- as empowerment tool, 209
- examples (scans), 45–46
- idea of author, 13–14
- as indigenous research project, 103
- and kinesic communication, 117
- methodology, 32–34, 36
- and paralinguistic communications, 117–118
- as physical documents, 112
- and proxemic communication, 114–115
- silences in, 116–117
- *vs.* survey results, 199–203
- as text as drama, 113–114
- theoretical framework (*See* theoretical framework)
- transcription, 35, 44
- unwritten cues in, 113–114, 118
- use by women, 111–112

diarists/diary writers

age and lifestyles of, 21, 33
attitudes toward GBV, 200–201
condoms use, 86–87, 132
consent of, 34, 36
continuation of diary project, 103–108, 210–211
coping strategies against IPV, 4, 50–51, 103, 201–202 (*See also* specific strategies)
critique of project, 102–108
description and list of, 33, 37–43
directive from author, 15
diversity in, 20
"doing gender" use, 120, 181–183
double duty, 73
economic dependence, 73–74
education, 43, 92
experience and frequency of violence, 200
and future research, 207–208, 210
gender performance, 29–32, 129–130
gender views of, 20
in global feminist theory, 180–183
inclusion criteria, 34
income sources, 199
in informal economy, 8, 68, 70
on IPV, 4, 97–98
language of, 17, 43–44
length and pacing of entries, 115–116
limitation in sample, 205
male economic support, 199
media role, 182–183
narrative styles used, 183–186
political concerns, 175–176
post-project changes, 213–215
potential issues with research, 14–15
and privilege, 22, 96–97
prostitution, 9, 126–127, 136, 142–143, 152, 161, 163–164
protection of, 36–37
pseudonyms and names for, 36
racism and colour, 21–22
as representation of lives of women, 51–52
as research partners, 14, 15
social services and support, 180, 187
survival sex use, 9, 71, 123, 124–125, 128–129, 142, 143, 162
survival strategies use, 120, 123–125
themes and topics in diaries, 14–15, 44, 47–50
and time and space, 115
in 2007–08 post-election violence, 11, 148–151, 171–176
volume, pitch, quality of voice, 117–118
work of, 8
writing style, 117
See also specific participants; specific strategies

Dill, B. T., 24
discrimination against women, 58–60
Djamba, Y., 63, 64
do-good by whites, 15, 16–17
"doing gender"
as strategy, 120, 181–183
theory on, 27–29, 32
domestic violence, 59–60, 61, 62–64, 206
Domestic Violence (Family Protection) Act (2000), 59–60, 61, 206
double duty, 73
dramatic storytelling, 183, 184–186, 187
dwellings, in Kibera, 2, 81, 90–92

E

ecological model
global feminist theory in, 24–27, 32
for IPV, 22–24, 32
symbolic interactionist perspective, 27–28, 32
as theoretical framework, 22–24
economic dependence, 73–74, 199, 209
economic need, in diaries, 49
economy, informal. *See* informal economy
education
free tuition for girls, 92–93
and gender, 55, 72–74, 92
in Kibera, 72, 92–93
and poverty, 72
and rape, 93
use of media in, 208–209
Education in Democracy (IED), 76
election of 2007. *See* post-election violence of 2007–08
elections, and gender, 56–57
Eliza, 43, 145–146
Elizabeth, 39, 160, 166, 186
Emma, 39, 118, 129
English language use by diarists, 17, 43–44
environmental degradation in Kibera, 84
equality for women and girls, 206–207
Escape strategy
analysis of, 154–158
description, 4, 135
examples in diaries, 136–146, 147–154
factors in Kibera, 23
long-term use example, 146–154
and media, 182–183
narrative style in, 184–186, 187
outcomes, 135–136, 141, 142, 146, 153–154, 156–158
prevalence and efficacy, 180
and social norms, 158
ethics in project, 36–37
ethnicity
in Kibera, 83, 99–100
in violence of 2007–08, 172–173
extreme poverty in Kibera, 65

F

faith. *See* religion
family planning in Kibera, 164–166
Federation of Women Lawyers (FIDA-K)
advocacy efforts, 59–60, 61, 155, 206
on CEDAW, 59, 60
gender equality in politics, 57
publications by, 61
rape reporting, 64
writing stories of IPV, 106
feminism, 111–112
See also global feminist theory
Ferraro, K., 71
films and filmmakers in Kibera, 12
finance, access to by women, 56
Fontana, A., 114

food and food prices, 65–66, 68, 70
Frey, J. H., 114
future-oriented reportorial, 183, 186

G

garbage in Kibera, 84
Gemma, 39–40, 130
gender
  agency by women, 28–29, 31
  and division of labour, 69–70
  "doing gender" theory, 27–29, 32
  and education, 55, 72–74, 92
  illiteracy, 72
  and informal economy, 67–70
  intersectionality theory, 30
  laws and conventions, 58–61
  and performance, 29–32, 129–130
  and politics, 56–57, 74–76
  and property ownership, 56
  and rent payment, 106–107
  social norms in work, 69
  views of diarists, 20
  and work, 7, 30, 31, 67–70
Gender and Human Rights (FIDA-K), 60
gender-based violence (GBV)
  advocacy (*See* advocacy for GBV)
  attitudes of women toward, 194–196, 200–201
  in diaries, 49–50, 202–203
  domestic violence, 59–60, 61, 62–64, 206
  ecological model, 22–24, 32
  experience and frequency, 200
  feelings about, 194
  gender as performance, 31
  and globalization, 10
  implications of study, 206–211
  in Kibera, 3–4, 10–11
  laws and legislation in Kenya, 59–61
  media for education, 208–209
  police training, 61, 155
  policy (*See* policy for GBV)
  and political concerns, 175–176
  and poverty, 119–120
  prevalence in Kenya, 11, 120–121
  and religion, 122
  shelters in Kenya, 156
  and social norms, 121, 158
  survey questions and results, 34–35, 191–193, 202–203
  and survival strategies, 120–121
  tolerance of, 121–122
  types of violence, 191
  women support systems, 154–157, 180
  work as coping strategy, 209
  See also intimate partner violence (IPV)
generalized reportorial, 183, 184
Giddens, Anthony, 4–5
Global Alliance for Africa (GAA), 167
global feminist theory
  in ecological model, 24–27, 32
  and strategies of diarists, 180–183
globalization
  definition and process, 4–5
  and GBV, 10
  and inequalities, 4–6
  and racism, 21–22
  and work, 6–7
Global South, 2, 5
"gold mine" metaphor, 17–18
"good white people", 15, 16–17

H

Harding, Sandra, 95, 99
hawking, 67–69, 70
health care and clinics in Kibera, 86, 166–167
Heise, L., 22
Heise ecological model, 22–23
help-seeking strategies, 193
HIV/AIDS, 62, 64, 206
Hope for Communities (SHOFCO), 92
Hoping God Agrees strategy
  analysis of, 131–133
  description, 4, 120
  "doing gender" use, 181
  examples in diaries, 122–131
  irony within, 133
  as main strategy, 4, 120
  narrative style in, 184
  prayer and religion, 120, 122–123, 126, 201
  prevalence and efficacy, 180
  short *vs.* long term, 131
  and social norms, 133
housing, in Kibera, 2, 81, 90–92
Humans of Kibera, 90
Hunter, M. L., 21–22

I

illiteracy in Kibera, 72
implications of study, 206–211
Ina, 43, 72–73, 118
income, 8–9, 62, 169 199
India, dowry murders, 26
indigenous research
  continuation of diary project by diarists, 103–108, 210–211
  goals of projects, 100–102, 104–105
  imperatives of, 99–100
  methodology and methods, 99, 210
  potential for, 98–99, 209–210
inductive coding techniques, 44
inequalities, 4–6, 55–56, 72
informal economy, 7–8, 67–70
informal retailing, 67–69, 70
informed consent for study, 34, 36, 37
Institute for Economic Affairs (IEA), 74–76
Institutional Review Board (IRB), 34, 36
International Monetary Fund (IMF), 5, 6
intersectionality theory, 30
Intervening project, 101, 105–106
"interviewing the text" technique, 114
interviews, 112–113, 114, 119
intimate partner violence (IPV)
  agency by women, 196–197, 201
  attitudes of women toward, 194–196, 200–201
  continuation of project by diarists, 103–106
  coping strategies (*See* coping strategies against IPV; specific strategies)
  cultural norms, 26–27
  description, 11
  diarists on, 4, 97–98
  ecological model, 22–24, 32
  experience and frequency, 200
  feelings about, 194
  gender as performance, 31–32
  idea of writing stories, 106
  in Kibera, 3–4, 11, 85
  research on, 64, 208, 210–211
  self-defence, 105–106

as social norm, 133
speaking about, 97–98
survey questions and results, 4, 34–35, 191–193
types of violence, 191

J

Jane
description as participant, 40
Hoping God Agrees strategy, 127, 128
narrative style, 184
police violence, 88
on post-election violence, 172
Janet, 40–41, 136
JC, 40, 116, 141–142, 165, 214
jua kali jobs, 67, 68–69
Judy
condoms use, 86
on continuation of project, 104
description as participant, 41
on double duty, 73
Hoping God Agrees strategy, 130–131
post-project changes, 214
writing style, 117
Jumpstart International, 89

K

Kenya
census, 62
colonialism in, 17, 79–80
demography of women, 11
independence, 80–81
map, 226
market liberalization, 6
religion in, 122
urbanization, 6
women support systems, 154–157, 180
See also specific topics
Kenya Demographic and Health Survey (KDHS), 11, 35, 62, 64
Kenya Food Security Steering Group, 66
Kenya Slum Upgrading Programme (KENSUP), 90–92
Kenyatta, Uhuru, and government, 75
Kibaki, Mwai, 148–149
Kibera
author in, 12–13, 18–19
dangers to women and girls, 85–88
description today, 82–83
diarists (*See* diarists / diary writers)
environmental degradation, 84
equality for women and girls, 207
future research, 207–208, 210
geography, 82–83, 89
history, 79–82
life as survival, 97
living conditions, 2–3
mapping project, 89–90
maps, 227–229
as mega-slum, 79
population of, 2, 81, 83
villages in, 2, 82–83, 229
Westerners in, 12–13
women's lives in, 3–4
Kibera Highrise, 90
Kibera School for Girls, 93
Kibera Women Writers Project, 107–108
Kimuna, S., 63, 64
kinesic communication, 117
King's African Rifles (KAR), 80
Kinyanjui, Mary Njeri, 7
Kristof, Nicholas, 92–93

L

labour. *See* work
landlords, and rent payment, 106–107
language
of diarists, 17, 43–44
self-critique by author, 15, 17–18
latrines in Kibera, 84, 87–88
laundry work, 8
Lawoko, S., 64
laws and legislation
discrimination against women, 59
domestic violence, 59–60, 61, 62, 206
GBV, 59–61
gender quota in politics, 76
See also specific legislation
Lia (friend of Susanna), 137–138
life histories, as data for research, 111–113
living on a dollar a day, 65, 66–70
Lorde, Audre, 51
Lucal, B., 29
Lugones, Maria, 98

M

macro level
in ecological model, 22–24
implications of study, 206–207
in strategies, 132–133, 158, 169
male economic support, 74, 199
Maori people and research, 104, 210
Map Kibera project, 89–90
marital rape, 61, 156
market liberalization, 6
marriage, 56, 73–74, 136–137, 163
Martin, Patricia Yancey, 28–29
Mary, 43, 100, 136, 163–164
Marya
birth control, 165
on continuation of project, 107
coping strategies against IPV, 103
description as participant, 41
Hoping God Agrees strategy, 125–126, 129
on mud, 107
narrative style, 184
self-defence classes, 105
work and social norms, 69
McDonald, Alun, 65, 66
media, 21–22, 182–183, 208–209
medical examination, for rape report, 155–156
Medical Examination Report (P-3 Form), 155–156
mega-cities, 78
Menezes, Gabrielle, 66
metaphor, self-critique by author, 15, 17–18
methodology
consent and inclusion criteria, 34
in diary project, 32–34, 336
and indigenous research, 99, 210
vs. method, 99
in survey, 34–35, 36–37
method *vs.* methodology, 99
mezzo level
in ecological model, 22–24
in strategies, 131–132, 157, 168–169
micro level
in ecological model, 22–24
implications of study, 206
in strategies, 131, 157, 167–168
Miller, J., 34

Mohanty, Chandra, 25–26
mud, and naming, 107
Mugisha, F., 63–64
Mwereru, J. I., 11

N

Nairobi, description, 77
Naming project, 102, 105–107
Narayan, Uma, 26
narrative
  and coping strategies, 183–186, 187
  personal narrative for research, 111–113
National Gender and Equality Commission (NGEC), 57
Ndung'u, Njoki, 60
NGOs, work in Kibera, 12
Nubian soldiers, 78–79

O

Odede, Kennedy, 92, 93
Ojiema, Joyce, 36
omissions in diaries, 116–117
open coding technique, 44, 47–48
oral interviews, 112–113, 114, 119
otherness and othering, 26–27

P

paralinguistic communications, 117–118
participants in study
  core themes in diaries, 44, 47–50
  description and list of, 33, 37–43
  open coding results, 47–48
  See also specific participants
partnership ethic, 14, 15
patriarchy, in Kenya, 11
personal level. *See* micro level
personal narrative, as data for research, 111–113
P-3 Form (Medical Examination Report), 155–156
the pill, 165
police, 61, 64, 88, 154–155
policy for GBV
  conventions and CEDAW, 58–59, 61
  data for, 60–61
  implementation and formulation, 61–62
  post-implementation, 64
  research for, 63–64
  and UN-AIDS survey, 62–63
political violence. *See* post-election violence of 2007–08
politics and power, and gender, 56–57, 74–76
post-election violence of 2007–08
  in Dee's escape attempt, 148–151
  description, 172
  diarists on, 11, 148–151, 171–176
  and political concerns, 175–176
  trauma of, 174–175
poverty
  and daily survival, 9–10
  and domestic violence, 62
  and education, 72
  and GBV, 119–120
  in Kibera, 65
  living on a dollar a day, 65, 66–70
prayer, 120, 122–123, 126, 201
pregnancies, 86, 132, 164–166
primary education, 9, 55, 72, 92
privilege
  author's experience in Kibera, 96–97
  critical rejection, 95–96
  and diarists, 22, 96–97
  See also whiteness and privilege
property ownership, and gender, 56
prostitution
  description, 9, 71
  escape from, 142–143
  in Kibera, 9
  as survival strategy, 132
  use by diarists, 9, 126–127, 136, 142–143, 152, 161, 163–164
proxemic communication, 114–115

Q

quantitative survey. *See* survey

R

racism, 21–22
rape
  and education, 93
  in Kibera, 85, 88
  laws in Kenya, 60–61
  in post-election violence, 172–175
  reporting and prosecution of, 64, 154–156
  research and data, 64
  in toilet visits, 87, 88
refusal to have sex, 195–196, 198
religion
  as coping strategy, 120, 122–123, 126, 201
  in GBV in Kenya, 122
  as survival strategy, 126
rent payment, 106–107
Rich, Adrienne, 17–18
Ryan-Deci framework, 197

S

safe sex, 86–87, 132, 195–196
Sally, 41–42, 144–145
sanitation in Kibera, 34, 87–88
Sarah
  birth control, 166
  on continuation of project, 107
  description as participant, 42
  escape from home, 143–144
  limited partnerships, 160–162
  post-project changes, 215
  prostitution, 161
Schegloff, E., 183
Schiwy, M., 112
secondary education, 55, 72
self-defence, 105–106
sex industry. *See* prostitution
Sexual Offences Act (2006)
  awareness of, 122
  description and implementation, 60–61, 62, 63
  medical examination in, 155–156
  post-implementation, 64
  report and prosecution of offences, 154–156
sexual violence. *See* gender-based violence (GBV); intimate partner violence (IPV)
shelters in Kenya, 155
Shining Hope School, 92–93
silences in diaries, 116–117
Silva, J. M., 29
single women, education and work, 74
slums, 1, 78–79, 208
Smith, Linda Tuhiwai, 99, 100–102, 104
social mobility, 7
social norms, 69, 121, 133, 158
social services, 89, 154–157, 180, 187
societal level. *See* macro level
space, and diary writing, 115
space-taking, self-critique by author, 15, 18–19

SPSS (v 16) for data analysis, 51
Stewart, M. W., 31
Stiglitz, Joseph, 5, 6
storytelling, 26, 183, 184–186, 187
strategies for coping. *See* coping strategies against IPV
Strauss, A., 49–50
structural adjustment programs, 5–6
sub-Saharan Africa, urbanization, 6
subsistence poverty in Kibera, 65
support systems for women, 154–157, 180
Supreme Court of Kenya, 76
survey
- administration of, 36–37
- and agency by women, 196–197, 201
- attitudes of women toward GBV, 194–196, 200–201
- consent for, 37
- coping strategies against IPV, 4, 193–194, 201–202
- data analysis, 51
- demographic results, 189–191
- description, 34–35
- *vs.* diary findings, 199–203
- experience and frequency of violence, 200
- and future research, 207–208, 210
- GBV results, 191–193, 202–203
- help-seeking strategies, 193
- idea of author, 14
- limitation in sample, 205
- male economic support, 199
- methodology, 34–35, 36–37
- participants, 34, 205
- questions in, 34–35
- refusal to have sex, 195–196, 198
- role of, 190
- summary of results, 198–199

survival sex
- description as strategy, 9, 71
- by diarists, 9, 71, 123, 124–125, 128–129, 142, 143, 162
- exchanged items, 71

survival strategies
- boyfriends as, 125–126, 127–129, 131–132
- to cope with GBV, 120–121
- prostitution as, 132
- religion as, 126
- short *vs.* long term, 131
- use by diarists, 120, 123–125

Susanna
- condoms use, 86
- on continuation of project, 105, 106
- on coping strategies against IPV, 103
- description as participant, 42
- escape attempts and return home, 136–141
- and media, 182
- narrative style, 185–186
- post-project changes, 213–214
- on rent payment, 106
- on self-defence, 106
- toilets and rape, 88

Swahili language, 17, 43
Swart, Elizabeth. *See* author
symbolic interactionist perspective, 27–28, 32

T

talking about abuse, 194, 201
Taupin, S., 83
Terry, 42–43, 126, 214
text, as drama, 113–114
theoretical framework
- "doing gender" theory, 27–29, 32
- ecological model, 22–24, 32
- gender as performance, 29–32
- global feminist theory, 24–27, 32, 180–183
- intersectionality theory, 30
- symbolic interactionist perspective, 27–28, 32

Thomas, W. I., 111
Thorne, B., 27–28
time, and diary writing, 115
toilets and latrines in Kibera, 84, 87–88

U

Uganda Railroad, 82
UN-AIDS survey, 62–63
uncomfortable situations and immersion, 18–19, 98
unemployment in Kibera, 2–3
UN-HABITAT, 91
UNICEF, 72
United Nations, IPV survey, 62
United States, IPV and guns, 26
university education, 55
UN Office of Humanitarian Affairs, 8
UN Office on Women (UN Women), 10, 206
UN World Food Program (UNWFP), 65
unwritten cues in diaries, 113–114, 118
urbanization and urban growth, 1–2, 6, 78–79

V

violence, for women and girls in Kibera, 85–88
- *See also* gender-based violence (GBV); intimate partner violence (IPV)

Violence to Women and Girls in the Era of HIV and AIDS: A Situation and Response Analysis in Kenya (UN-AIDS), 62
Vision 2030, 75
Vizenor, Gerald, 100
Voice of Kibera blog, 89–90

W

Wandera, Wilbroda, 69–70
water in Kibera, 65–66
West, C., 27
Westerners in Kibera, 12–13
whiteness and privilege
- data analysis issues, 19–20
- and global racism, 21–22
- self-critique by author, 15–19
- *See also* privilege

Williams, S. L., 29
work
- creativity for, 70
- of diarists, 8
- and division of labour, 69–70
- double duty, 73
- to escape GBV and IPV, 209
- and gender, 7, 30, 31, 67–70
- and globalization, 6–7
- in informal economy, 66–68
- in Kibera and Kenya, 2–3, 7–9, 169
- and social norms, 69

World Bank, 5
World Health Organization (WHO), 210
World Trade Organization (WTO), 5
writing style of diarists, 117
written data, *vs.* interviews, 112–113
WuDunn, Sheryl, 92–93

Z

Zimmerman, D. H., 27
Znaniecki, F., 111
Zulu, E., 63–64

CPSIA information can be obtained
at www.ICGtesting.com
Printed in the USA
BVOW07s1447170118
505283BV00060B/890/P